BERNARD SHAW

MUSIC IN LONDON
1890–94
CRITICISMS CONTRIBUTED WEEK BY WEEK
TO THE WORLD

IN THREE VOLUMES

VOLUME I

NEW YORK
VIENNA HOUSE
1973

There are people who will read about music and nothing else. To them dead prima donnas are more interesting than saints, and extinct tenors than mighty conquerors. They are presumably the only people who will dream of reading these three volumes. If my wisdom is to be of any use to them it must come to them in this form. And so I let it go to them for what it is worth.

SOMETHING had better be done about this Royal Italian Opera. I have heard Gounod's Faust not less than ninety times within the last ten or fifteen years; and I have had enough of it. Here is Tristan und Isolde, which we can no longer afford to do without, now that all the errand boys in New York can whistle it from end to end: yet to hear it I have to go to Germany—to cross that unquiet North Sea, the very thought of which sets my entrails aquake. Tristan is more than thirty years old; and as the composer died in 1883, at the age of seventy, I am sanguine as to the possibility of driving Mr Harris to produce it presently as "Wagner's new opera." It pays to pitch into a man like Mr Harris: the stirrings of the new time have got into him: there is enterprise in his profile: only hit him hard enough, and you will fetch him out of the Donizettian dark ages as you never could have fetched Gye or Mapleson, whose benightedness left him with half-a-century of leeway to make up. (I know that this metaphor is mixed, and I dont care: it is as well to come to an early understanding on these points.) Mind, I do not say that Gounod's Faust, etc., is not to be kept on the stage. The rights of the younger generation include access, and frequent access, to Faust; but I protest against the inhumanity of selecting it to introduce new prima donnas, since on such occasions the critics have to attend; and what critic has not long ago exhausted the interest of Jean de Reszke's Faust, Madame Scalchi's Siebel, Brother Edouard's Mephistopheles, and the soldiers' chorus as performed by the Augustan Household troops, horse and foot, from Drury Lane? However, the thing is done now; and I have sat Faust out again. The house was in a bad temper, Brother Edouard having cried off on account of sudden indisposition, and his place being taken by M. Orme Darvall. If this unfortunate gentleman had sung like an angel, the gallery would have borne him a grudge for supplanting their beloved *basso cantante*; but as he entered into his part to the extent of singing quite in the contrary manner, pressing every note hard on the grindstone, and trying to make Dio dell' or go by sheer violence, with the natural result that he was inhumanly hissed, and did not recover his voice for an act and a half afterwards; as, furthermore, he went out by the wrong doors, and got into difficulties with his sword, which came off just before he wanted it in the Kermesse scene; as, by way of climax, he finished the church scene in an attitude under the curtain, to an improvised choral episode of "Look out, there!" "Mind your head, sir!" etc., from the flies, I am afraid it would be useless to pretend that M. Darvall was not a failure.

Before reproaching him for having thus thrown away an enviable chance, mainly by subordinating his common sense to his artistic ambition, I must confess with a blush that the critics are much to blame in the matter. If we had not set a silly fashion years ago—in Faure's day—of writing up Barbier and Carré's stage fiend as an acting part of all but unfathomable profundity, we should not now be plagued with the puerile inanities of baritones with impossible eyebrows, who spend the evening in a red limelight and an ecstasy of sardonic smiling.

Mlle Nuovina, the newest Margaret, did not promise well at first. To begin with, she wore her own black hair. There was no suggestion of naïveté in her manner: her very self-possession jarred with our notions of Gretchen. Besides, her voice, for Covent Garden, lacks amplitude: in the broader concerted passages she was shrill and unsteady. Nevertheless, she ended by conquering a safe position for herself. Artists are always indignant if you call them useful; otherwise I should congratulate her on having established herself in the front rank of thoroughly useful dramatic sopranos. Her voice, instead of having, as usual, no middle and a few screams at the top, is sound and pure, if a little thin, all over; whilst her vocal touch is light, and managed with intelligence and discretion. She has dramatic intelligence, too,

2

and is never for a moment out of her part, or at a loss for appropriate business. For love of a heavenly piece of music she sang the last trio right through without sparing herself according to custom by shirking the full repetition in B natural. Finally, she shews none of the operatic bumptiousness of our modern American and cornstalk prima donnas.

Brother Jean's voice is better than it was last year. He sang Salve dimora very finely indeed; and when the audience, foolishly disappointed at his not taking the high C from his chest, hesitated a moment at the end, he gave them to understand, gracefully but firmly, that he had done his duty, and now expected them to do theirs. Whereupon, abashed, they gave him a salvo of prolonged and reverent applause. Brother Jean is still vaguely romantic rather than intelligent in his acting. The only part in Faust I ever saw him act reasonably was Valentine; but that, of course, was in his baritone days. D'Andrade falls very short of him in the part. In an opera company, D'Andrade passes for a good actor because he always makes it plain that he knows what the opera is about; but when this intellectual triumph becomes a little more common, he will find his place hard to hold. Would any really fine actor sing Dio possente—that tremblingly earnest prayer of a simple-minded young soldier—with the air of a man obstreperously confident that no difficulty could be made over any application from a baritone hall-marked with the unreticent throatiness familiar to the patrons of the Paris Opéra?

Valero, the new tenor from Madrid, made his first appearance on Tuesday in Carmen with Miss de Lussan. As he is a finished exponent of the Gayarré style of singing, which I maintain to be nothing but bleating invested with artistic merit (though I admit the right of anybody to prefer it to the round pure tone and unforced production without which no singing is beautiful to my ears), I should probably have had nothing good to say of him had he not disarmed me by acting throughout with unexpected willingness, vivacity, and actually with a sense of humor. My heart re-

3

tained the hardness set up by his vocal method until Carmen
began singing the *seguidilla* at him, when he licked the
finger and thumb with which he was putting on his glove (to
shew his indifference to the siren, poor wretch!), and gave a
little toss of his head and knock of his knee that there was no
resisting. A man who makes me laugh by a legitimate stroke
of art charms all the criticism out of me; and I confess to
having enjoyed Valero's Don José as well as any that I have
seen, although he is too transparently amiable and social to
seriously impersonate Mérimée's morbidly jealous and diffident dragoon.

Miss de Lussan shews remarkable cleverness as Carmen; but Carmen is degenerating into a male Mephistopheles. Every respectable young American lady longs to
put on the Spanish jacket and play at being an abandoned
person, just as the harmless basso craves to mount the scarlet cock's feather and say to himself, like Barnaby Rudge's
raven, "I'm a devil, I'm a devil, I'm a devil!" Miss de Lussan is no more like Carmen than her natty stockings are like
those "with more than one hole in them" described by
Mérimée. Perhaps, as Charles Lamb's ghost may think,
stage Carmens are only delightful when and because everybody can see that they are pure make-believe. But I am not a
Lambite in this matter. I miss the tragic background of un-
governable passion and superstitious fatalism to the levity
and insolent waywardness which Miss de Lussan makes so
much of. The truth is, she cannot act the tavern scene, nor
sing the prophetic episode in the fortune-telling trio, to anything near conviction point.

The loan collection of portable wind instruments at the
Military Exhibition is worth a visit, though it is exasperating to have to study them as a professor of harmony studies
classical music—with one's eyes. It is all very well to hang a
facsimile of a veritable buccina (found in Pompeii) on the
wall for my inspection; but I had as soon inspect a gaspipe—
what I want is to hear it. Richter, for whose entertainment
the original was blown at Brussels, declares that it sounds

like four trombones rolled into one. Such a description makes my ears water; for I love an apocalyptic trumpet blast. From the buccina up to the sarrussophone and the latest brass counterbassoon of Mahillon, nothing, as far as I can recollect, is wanting. Those who have pestered me of late with the question, "What on earth is a corno di bassetto?" I can now refer to this loan collection, where there are plenty to be seen. The giant bassoon made for Handel is only one of several curious monsters in the collection. Distin's amazing tenor saxhorn would make a capital electrolier if an incandescent light were placed in each of its seven bells.

The old *flauti d' amore* and *oboi di caccia* will interest Bach students; but I do not want to hear the big *flûtes-à-bec*. I have heard them already, and can certify that their tone, though quaint, is abjectly feeble, whilst their intonation I must really be allowed to describe as damnable. The new instruments are wonderful; but where are the performers to come from? At the concerts of the Royal College of Music, the wind instruments have to be taken for the most part by professional players; and even in the profession the state of things is such that, by simple assassinating less than a dozen men, I could leave London without a single orchestral wind instrument player of the first rank. I was studying the woodwind during those delicate *entr'actes* in Carmen the other night; and with the exception of an occasional touch from Mr John Radcliffe, I did not hear a single phrase that surpassed in elegance or individuality the playing that Mr Maskelyne gets from his automata. Imagine a city with five million inhabitants and only one satisfactory bassoon player!

I was not able to get to the Grosvenor Club on the ladies' night in time to hear Sapellnikoff play; and there is nothing fresh to be said about the *salon* performances of Johannes Wolff and Hollmann. The worst of it is that the extreme smartness of these functions leaves the audience entirely preoccupied with their consciousness of being immensely in it; so that the artists, hampered and distraught by the incessant chattering and rustling, do not settle down to any

5

sort of serious work. One irascible virtuoso was driven to astonish an incorrigible group of talkers by a fierce "Sh-sh-sh-h-h-h-h!" in the middle of his piece and of their conversation.

Paderewski, like the Philharmonic, must excuse me until next week, when I shall have a legion of pianists to deal with.

4 June 1890

LAST week I mildly suggested that the usual combination of a new prima donna with an old opera was a little hard on the critics. The words were still wet from the pen when I received a stall for Madame Tetrazzini's first appearance as Leonora in Il Trovatore. Now a subscription night Trovatore is a dreadful thing. This is not an explosion of Wagnerian prejudice. I know my Trovatore thoroughly, from the first drum-roll to the final chord of E flat minor, and can assert that it is a heroic work, capable of producing a tremendous effect if heroically performed. But anything short of this means vulgarity, triviality, tediousness, and failure; for there is nothing unheroic to fall back on—no comedy, no spectacle, no symphonic instrumental commentary, no relief to the painful flood of feeling surging up repeatedly to the most furious intensity of passion; nothing but love—elemental love of cub for dam and male for female—with hate, jealousy, terror, and the shadow of death throughout. The artists must have immense vital energy, and a good deal of Salvini's skill in leading up to and producing a convincing illusion of terrible violence and impetuosity, without wrecking themselves or becoming ridiculous. At no point can the stage-manager come to the rescue if the artists fail. Mr Harris has secured the success of Les Huguenots, Faust, Die Meistersinger, and William Tell by drill and equipment, costume and scenery; but for Il Trovatore he can do nothing but pay band, conductor, and principals; let them loose on the work in his theatre, and sit looking at them, helpless. Unless, indeed, he were to go

down next day and read out the unfavorable press notices
to them, emphasizing the criticism with the homely eloquence of which he is a master.

On Saturday week Trovatore was bâtoned by Bevignani,
concerning whom some of my fresher colleagues came out
last winter (in dealing with the Promenade Concerts at Her
Majesty's) with the good-natured and entirely novel idea
that he is a superb conductor—rather an important secret
to have kept itself for twenty years if there is really anything
very serious in it. The conductor at Covent Garden ought to
be nothing less than the greatest in the world; and the truth
is that Mr Harris's three conductors, with all their considerable merits, would not, if rolled into one, make a Richter or a Faccio. Therefore I am not going to trifle with an old
and sincerely respected public acquaintance by joining in
the latest chorus of "Good old Bevignani." I shall even venture to ask him why he takes an impulsive allegro like Mal
reggendo at an easy andante, and whether he really thinks
Verdi meant Perigliarti ancor as an allegretto when he
marked it *velocissimo*? But worse things than these befell
Verdi. The young bloods of the string band, nursed on the
polyphony of Wagner and Brahms, treated the unfortunate
Trovatore as mere banjo work. They relieved the tedium of
their task by occasional harmless bursts of mock enthusiasm,
usually ending in a smothered laugh and a relapse into
weariness, until they came to the hundred and forty bars, or
thereabouts, of slow and sentimental pizzicato to the tune of
Si la stanchezza in the prison scene. This proved too much
for their sense of duty. Languishing over their fiddles, they
infused a subtle ridicule into their toneless "pluck-pluck,
pluck-pluck" that got the better of my indignation. It was
impossible to help laughing. But why had not Bevignani
shewed these young gentlemen that there is room for their
finest touch and most artistic phrasing in Verdi's apparently
simple figures of accompaniment, and that a band which
cannot play a simple prelude of nine common chords with
even the prosaic virtue of simultaneous attack, much less

7

with the depth and richness of tone upon which the whole effect depends, is not in a position to turn up its nose at Italian opera, or any other style of instrumental composition? As for the poor silly public, it yawned and looked at its watch, quite ready to vote Verdi empty, stale, and played out, but incapable of suspecting perfunctoriness and tomfoolery in a precinct where evening dress is indispensable.

As to the singing, there was a tenor who was compendiously announced as "Signor Rawner, who has created so great a sensation in Italy," and who is undoubtedly capable of making an indelible mark anywhere. I listened expectantly for Deserto sulla terra, knowing that if the sensationist were a fine artist, his interpretation of its musical character would surround it with illusion, making it come from among the trees in the moonlight, soft, distant, melancholy, haunting; whereas, if he were the common or Saffron Hill Manrico, he would at once display his quality by a stentorian performance in the wing, putting all his muscle and wind into a final B flat (substituted for G), and storming London with that one wrong note alone. My suspense was short. Signor Rawner, knowing nothing about the musical character of the serenade, but feeling quite sure about the B flat, staked his all on it; and a stupendous yell it was. It is said that he can sing D; and though he mercifully refrained from actually doing so, I have not myself the smallest doubt that he could sing high F in the same fashion if he only tried hard enough. As may be inferred, I do not like Signor Rawner, in spite of the sensation he has created in Italy: therefore let me not do him the injustice of pushing my criticism into further detail. Madame Tetrazzini, with her tip-tilted nose, her pretty mouth, her ecstatic eyes, her delicately gushing style, and the intense gratitude of her curtsy whenever she brought down the house, did very well as Leonora, though I would suggest to her that D'amor sull' ali rosee might have been encored had she chosen her breathing places with some regard for the phrasing, and either restored Verdi's cadenza, or at least omitted that flagrant pianoforte sequence (G, B,

8

A, G, etc.) from the one she substituted.

As Valentine in The Huguenots she did not improve on her first attempt. Her Italian tremolo and stage hysteria were so intensified that but few of her notes had any definite pitch; whilst her playing was monotonously lachrymose from end to end. When she sings in the manner of a light soprano, and so steadies her voice for a moment, everybody is pleased; but when she becomes "dramatic" the charm vanishes. And yet you cannot get these Italian ladies to believe this. The more we shew by our encouragement of Miss Nordica, Miss Russell, and Miss Macintyre, and by our idolatry of Madame Patti with her eternal Home, Sweet Home, that our whole craving is for purity of tone and unwavering accuracy of pitch, the more our operatic visitors insist on desperately trying to captivate us by paroxysms of wobbling. Remonstrance, in English at least, is thrown away on them. For example, although Ravelli, who appeared as Elvino on Thursday, is no Rubini, yet the delight of the house at escaping from the detested tremolo, and hearing some straightforward, manly singing, was so extravagant, that he was recalled uproariously three times.

Miss Russell's Violetta, a part in which the tremolo rages throughout Europe worse than the influenza, is a triumph of good singing. Hard as it is to drag me to Covent Garden oftener than my bare duty requires, I would go again to hear her sing Parigi o cara as she sang it on Saturday last. Madame Fursch-Madi has not Miss Russell's youth and beauty, but she never wobbles and never fails. The idolized De Reszkes sing like dignified men, not like male viragoes. But do you supppose that Madame Tetrazzini or Signor Rawner will take the hint, or that Dufriche, the St Bris of Tuesday week, will cease to discount the beautiful quality of his voice by a laborious vibrato? Not a bit of it: they will only wonder at the simplicity of our insular taste, and modestly persist in trying to teach us better.

The Huguenots, admirably rehearsed, goes without a hitch. Ybos, another new tenor, with a much better fore-

9

head and brow (to put the point as delicately as possible) than the usual successor to Mario, appeared as Raoul; and though he did not attempt the C sharp in the duel septet, any more than Madame Tetrazzini ventured on the chromatic run through two octaves in the fourth act, he came off with honor, in spite of the shyness which hampered his acting. In the absence of a first-rate basso profondo, Edouard de Reszke was forced to repeat the double mistake of relinquishing the part of St Bris, which fits him to a semitone, and taking that of Marcel, which lies too low for him. He has to alter the end of the chorale, and to produce the effect of rugged strength by an open brawling tone which quite fails to contrast with the other bass and baritone voices as Meyerbeer intended. D'Andrade, too, whose voice is only effective (I had almost said only tolerable) when he is singing energetically between his upper B flat and G, repeatedly transposes passages an octave up, quite ruining the variety and eloquence of Never's declamation in the conspiracy scene. It is hardly necessary to add that every artist brought his or her own cadenza; but as none of them were quite so accomplished as Meyerbeer in this sort of composition, they only spoiled the effect they might have produced by sticking to the text. All these drawbacks notwithstanding, the performance reached a high degree of excellence; and the instrumental score was played (under Bevignani) with great spirit and accuracy.

Madame Gerster has grown mightily since June 1877. Her columnar neck and massive arms are now those of Brynhild rather than Amina; and I am afraid that her acting, though it was touchingly good, did not reconcile the Philistines to the incongruity. I see, too, that the comparative ineffectiveness of her Ah, non giunge, and a certain want of ringing quality in her extreme upper notes, are being cited as results of the loss of voice which placed her for awhile in the position of George Eliot's Armgart. But the Ah, non giunge fell equally flat in 1877; and her Astriffiamante in that year shewed exactly the same want of the delicate

10

tintinnabulation which was so enchanting in Di Murska's singing of Gli angui d' inferno. I could detect no falling off that the lapse of fourteen years does not account for; and the old artistic feeling remained so unspoiled and vivid, that if here and there a doubt crossed me whether the notes were all reaching the furthest half-crown seat as tellingly as they came to my front stall, I ignored it for the sake of the charm which neither singer nor opera has lost for me.

The pre-eminent claims of Covent Garden again compel me to leave the concerts aside for the moment; but next week St James's Hall and its legion pianists shall have their due without fail.

11 June 1890

I SEE that Bishop of Ripon's description of Mozart as "first in music" has been too much for Mr Labouchere, who intimates that it is quite enough to have to admit the pre-eminence of Shakespear in drama, and to leave uncontradicted the compliment paid by the Bishop in the department of morals. I do not blame Mr Labouchere for rushing to the conclusion that the Bishop was wrong; for Bishops generally are wrong, just as Judges are always wrong. Such is the violence of anti-prelatic prejudice in me (for the Bishop never harmed me, and may be, for what I know, a most earnest and accomplished musician), that though I happen to agree with him in the present instance, yet I take his declaration rather as a belated conventional remark surviving from the Mozart mania of the first quarter of the century, than as expressing an original conviction. The mania was followed, like other manias, by a reaction, through which we have been living, and which will be succeeded next century by a reaction against Wagner. This sort of thing happens to all great men.

I once possessed an edition of Shakespear with a preface by that portentous dullard Rowe, wherein Nicholas apologized for William as for a naïve ignoramus who, "by a mere light of nature," had hit out a few accidental samples of what he might have done had he enjoyed the educational advantages of the author of Jane Shore. I kept Rowe for a long time as a curiosity; but when I found a fashion setting in of talking about Mozart as a vapidly tuneful infant phenomenon, I felt that Rowe was outdone, and so let him drop into the dust-bin. Of course all the men of Rowe's time who knew chalk from cheese in dramatic poetry understood Shakespear's true position well enough, just as Wagner understood Mozart's, and laughed at the small fry who quite believed that Schumann and Brahms—not to mention Beethoven—had left Mozart far behind. For my part, I should not like to call Schumann a sentimental trifler and Brahms a pretentious blockhead; but if the average man was a Mozart, that is how they would be generally described.

Unfortunately, Mozart's music is not everybody's affair when it comes to conducting it. His scores do not play themselves by their own physical weight, as many heavy modern scores do. When a sense of duty occasionally urges Mr Manns or the Philharmonic to put the G minor or the E flat or the Jupiter Symphony in the bill, the band, seeing nothing before them but easy diatonic scale passages and cadences smoothly turned on dominant discords, races through with the general effect of a couple of Brixton schoolgirls playing one of Diabelli's pianoforte duets. The audience fidgets during the allegro; yawns desperately through the andante; wakes up for a moment at the minuet, finding the trio rather pretty; sustains itself during the finale by looking forward to the end; and finishes by taking Mr Labouchere's side against the Bishop of Ripon, and voting me stark mad when I speak of Mozart as the peer of Bach and Wagner, and, in his highest achievements, the manifest superior of Beethoven.

I remember going one night to a Richter concert, at which an overture or prelude to nothing in particular, composed in a moment of jejune Wagner-worship by Mr Eugene d'Albert, was supposed to be the special event. But it was preceded, to its utter ruin, by the E flat Symphony; and that

12

was the first time, as far as I know, that any living Londoner of reasonable age was reached by the true Mozart enchantment. It was an exploit that shewed Richter to be a master of his art as no Valkyrie ride or fire-charm could have done. And yet he has been kept mainly at the exciting obviousnesses of the Valkyrie ride and the fire-charm ever since, with Beethoven's seventh symphony for the hundredth time by special request for a wind-up to them.

Last week, however, came the announcement that the Richter concert would end with Mozart's symphony in C—not the Jupiter, but that known as No. 6. I left the Opera to hear it, and was fortunate enough to arrive just in time to catch the symphony, and to miss an attempt to give the thundering Gibichung chorus from the Götterdämmerung with a handful of feeble gentlemen, whose native woodnotes wild must have been cut to ribbons by the orchestra. The preformance of the symphony was a repetition of Richter's old triumph. The slow movement and the finale were magnificent: the middle section of the latter, which I confess had quite taken me in by its innocent look on paper, astonished me by its majesty, and by a combination of vivacity with grandeur.

I must add, by the bye, that the opera I left for the Symphony was Don Giovanni, as conducted by Signor Randegger. My compliments to that gentleman, with my heartfelt assurance that a more scandalously slovenly, slapdash, and unintelligent performance of the orchestral part of a great-work was probably never heard in a leading—it should be, and shall yet be, *the* leading—European opera-house. I hope the recording angel has put down to Signor Randegger, and not to me, the imprecations which the murder of that incomparable overture wrung from me. The other masterpiece of the Covent Garden repertory, Die Meistersinger, is the triumph of the season. Although dozens of details are neglected—although Lassalle still plays Sachs with the gestures of Benvenuto Cellini—although the cuts necessary to fit the performance in between half-past seven and half-past

13

twelve are mighty ones and millions, yet the work is such a wonder and a treasure of everything lovely and happy in music that it is impossible to grumble. The chance of hearing such a Walther as Jean de Reszke with such a Sachs as Lassalle (they both surpass themselves in singing the two parts) ought to set on foot a Wagnerian pilgrimage to London from the ends of Europe. Tavary, the new prima donna, is a hard-working and very capable German lady, a second-rate Donna Anna, but a satisfactory Eva, as far as singing and acting go.

Mr Kuhe's concert at the Albert Hall proved that Madame Albani cannot fill the Albert Hall as Patti can. The reason, I take it, is that the public only care for Madame Albani's voice as an instrument to make their favorite music for them; whereas Madame Albani, apparently, is only interested in music insomuch as it happens to be a means of displaying her voice. Certainly it is a very remarkable voice: the soaring of the upper notes is as wonderful as ever; the once faulty middle has been rounded and brought under control; the art of the singer has reached the limit of her capacity for art. But all this, instructive as it is to the singing-master, does not concern the public. If the net result for them is that Ah, fors è lui, as sung by Madame Albani, is a bore—and a bore it certainly was at the Albert Hall—then no mere vocal virtuosity, however seconded by the thousand little raptures, the wafted kisses, the effusions and unbosomings of the popular favorite, will avail one single encore.

Madame Trebelli's reappearance in so huge a hall was ill-advised. Those who try to persuade her that she is as good as ever shew how little they understood or appreciated her former excellence. She herself is misled, possibly, by her consciousness that the voice is there still, as well as the artistic subtlety that enabled her to use it to such good purpose. But the muscular control of the vocal machinery is impaired, and the days of C'est l'Espagne and Il Segreto are past. Even in her prime, Handel and Mozart were better

14

friends to her than Donizetti and Offenbach.

Mr Sims Reeves appeared, and attacked The Message with mingled guile and gallantry, though it was rather the guile that got him safely to the end. In spite of all his husbandry, he has but few notes left now; yet the wonderfully telling effect and unique quality of these few still justify him as the one English singer who has worked in his own way, and at all costs, to attain and preserve ideal perfection of tone.

The fact that Stavenhagen played a concerto of Liszt's at this concert reminds me of all the pianists I have neglected. There is Paderewski, a man of various moods, who was alert, humorous, delightful at his first recital; sensational, empty, vulgar, and violent at his second; and dignified, intelligent, almost sympathetic, at his third. He is always sure of his notes; but the licence of his *tempo rubato* goes beyond all reasonable limits. Sapellnikoff is never at fault in this or any other way in the domain of absolute music; but when the music begins to speak, his lack of eloquence is all the more startling. In such phrases as that which opens Chopin's Fantasia in F minor, or the first subject of the Appassionata, or the Pilgrim's Chorus in the Tannhäuser overture, he demonstrated how completely musical faculty may be divorced from dramatic sense. But his playing of the Polonaise in A flat was stupendous: the room woke up amazed, and recalled him again and again. Stavenhagen, on the whole, is the finest, most serious artist of them all: there is much less curiosity and more esteem and affection in the attachment of his audiences (not to mention that they are larger) than the others have attained or deserved. Of course there is the inimitable Sophie Menter, with the airs of an invalid and the vigor of a Valkyrie, knocking the breadth out of poor Schumann at the Crystal Palace, laughing Weber's delicate romance out of countenance at the Philharmonic, playing everything like lightning, and finishing always with a fabulously executed Liszt rhapsody for which all her sins are at once forgiven her. Madame

15

Teresa Carreño is a second Arabella Goddard: she can play anything for you; but she has nothing of her own to tell you about it. Playing is her superb accomplishment, not her mission. A newcomer, Pierre-René Hirsch, is clever and skilful; but he is not in the front rank, and will probably be better known in the *salons* than by the public if he settles in London. Clotilde Kleeberg, now recitalling at Prince's Hall, and Bertha Marx, again in her old place at Sarasate's Saturday afternoon concerts in St James's Hall, are as dexterous as ever. Buonamici, who played Beethoven's E flat concerto at the last Philharmonic, is a neat and finished executant, hardly as interesting, perhaps, as Albéniz, at whose recital on Saturday I was much scandalized on hearing the original version of Weber's Invitation replaced by that impertinent paraphrase of Tausig's, which I thought London had outgrown these many years. The Philharmonic directors, by the bye, have again attempted to float Moszkowski here as a serious composer. He landed them this time by a monstrous orchestral fugue—a sort of composite phonograph of all the fugues that ever were written, with the *point d'orgue* literally given to that instrument. The concert was otherwise worthy of the Society.

18 June 1890

BY the time I reached Paderewski's concert on Tuesday last week, his concerto was over, the audience in wild enthusiasm, and the pianoforte a wreck. Regarded as an immensely spirited young harmonious blacksmith, who puts a concerto on the piano as upon an anvil, and hammers it out with an exuberant enjoyment of the swing and strength of the proceeding, Paderewski is at least exhilarating; and his hammer-play is not without variety, some of it being feathery, if not delicate. But his touch, light or heavy, is the touch that hurts; and the glory of his playing is the glory that attends murder on a large scale when impetuously done. Besides, the piano is not an instrument upon which you can safely let yourself go in this

16

fashion.

Sophie Menter produces an effect of magnificence which leaves Paderewski far behind; but she balances the powerful bass of the instrument against the comparatively weak treble so as to produce a perfectly rich, full, and even body of sound, whilst with Paderewski the bass and middle elbow the treble into the corner in a brutal fantasia on the theme of the survival of the fittest. Again, Madame Menter seems to play with splendid swiftness, yet she never plays faster than the ear can follow, as many players can and do: it is the distinctness of attack and intention given to each note that makes her execution so irresistibly impetuous. At her recital she pleaded a broken finger-nail, from which inflammation had set in. But had it been possible to believe that those glissandos in the Strauss-Tausig waltz were played with a really bad nail, I should have flinched and fled. As usual, the Soirées de Vienne were superb, and the Beethoven sonata hardly recognizable. Beethoven defies her Austrian temperament.

At the Richter concert Berlioz' Carnaval Romain overture really came off. I am afraid the public is under the impression that performances of this sort come off every time they are put in the bill; but an expert can usually count on the fingers of one hand the number of performances at which he has felt that the composer would not have been more or less baulked and disappointed. At this very concert, for instance, the Egmont overture was heavy and forced, as it often is when placed first on the program. It was followed by the two great successes of the evening—the Good Friday music from Parsifal, the enchantments of which pass all sane word-painting, and the Carnaval, which slipped into the right vein after the first hundred bars or so, and finished to a miracle.

The Valkyrie Ride, which came next, excited the audience furiously; but it also made a lady on the orchestra put her fingers into her ears. The lady was quite right. The Valkyrie Ride requires above all things fine trombone-playing

17

—such playing, for instance, as Mr Manns seldom fails to get at the Crystal Palace from Messrs Hadfield, Geard, and Phasey, who generally contrive to stop short of that brain-splitting bark which detaches itself from the rest of the orchestra, asserting itself rowdily and intrusively in your ear, preventing you from hearing the music, and making you wonder, if you accept the hideous din as inevitable, how Berlioz could ever call such an ignobly noisy instrument "Olympian." No matter how many fortissimo marks the composer writes, there is no use in forcing the tone of the trombone, unless, indeed, you are to be intentionally hellish, as in Liszt's Inferno. But if you want to be majestic, as in the Valkyrie Ride and the Francs Juges overture, then it is not to be done by bawling like a mob orator who does not know his business. Why Richter permits forcing, and even encourages it, not only in the Valkyrie Ride but in the first movement of the Tannhäuser overture, can only be explained as the result of his share of original sin. It is not that his players cannot do better: they are always dignified in the Valhalla motif in the Nibelungen music.

I once heard Herr Müller, Richter's first trombone, play the *"oraison"* in Berlioz' Sinfonie Funèbre et Triomphale very finely. But on Monday week the only tolerable brazen sound in the piece came from the other side of the orchestra, where Mr Geard was playing the bass trumpet part on an alto trombone. During the few bars in which the theme was left to him the lady did not keep her fingers in her ears; and the volume of sound from the orchestra was greater instead of less than when his colleagues were blaring away, because the accompaniment could be heard through his transparent and musical tone, whereas the others drowned everything else with their distracting rattle. I am not squeamish about the quantity of sound that comes from an orchestra: the more thundering its fortissimo, the better I like it. I delight, for example, in Richter's tremendous handling of the Rienzi overture. But I am fastidious as to the quality of the tone, however voluminous it may be; and, frankly, the Valkyrie Ride might as well be conducted by Buffalo Bill as by Richter, if some regard is not paid to the artistic spirit, if not to the snobbish expression, of Sterndale Bennett's remark about treating trombone-players as gentlemen. I am aware of the full horror of recommending to Richter a precept by the Mendelssohnian Sterndale Bennett; but I cannot help that: much as I respect Richter, and appreciate the relief he brought us thirteen years ago in the midst of a dire music famine, I am not going to be tromboned out of my senses for him or any conductor alive when the remedy is so easy.

My temper was not improved by Brahms' Symphony in E minor, though I have no fault to find with the execution of it. Euphuism, which is the beginning and end of Brahms' big works, is no more to my taste in music than in literature. Brahms takes an essentially commonplace theme; gives it a strange air by dressing it in the most elaborate and far-fetched harmonies; keeps his countenance severely (which at once convinces an English audience that he must have a great deal in him); and finds that a good many wiseacres are ready to guarantee him as deep as Wagner, and the true heir of Beethoven. The spectacle of the British public listening with its in-churchiest expression to one of the long and heavy fantasias which he calls his symphonies always reminds me of the yokel in As You Like It quailing before the big words of the fool. Strip off the euphuism from these symphonies, and you will find a string of incomplete dance and ballad tunes, following one another with no more organic coherence than the succession of passing images reflected in a shop window in Piccadilly during any twenty minutes in the day. That is why Brahms is so enjoyable when he merely tries to be pleasant or naïvely sentimental, and so insufferably tedious when he tries to be profound. His symphonies are endured at the Richter Concerts as sermons are endured, and his Requiem is patiently borne only by the corpse; but Mr Orton Bradley, who gave a Brahms concert the other day at Steinway Hall, "his custom always of an

19

afternoon" in the season, was able to entertain us happily enough by reverently letting alone the more ponderous nothings of his favorite composer.

Pianoforte-playing is becoming an accomplishment most hateful to me. Death is better than eighteen recitals per week. I got only a glimpse of Madame Roger-Miclos, playing in her cold, hard, swift style on one of those wonderful steel dulcimers made by Pleyel. Then off to Steinway Hall to hear the opposite pole of the Pleyel instrument under the fingers of Mr Friedheim (now transformed from a wild-looking German student to a staid professor) and Mrs Friedheim. Also a young Polander named Leopold Godowsky, pupil of Saint-Saëns, who amazed us by substituting Beethoven's theme with the thirty-two variations for the first movement of the Appassionata, in which he proved a brilliant and all too rapid executant, but a frankly twenty-year-old interpreter of Beethoven, about whom, as might be expected, he has not learnt much from the composer of Ascanio. He next tried Schumann; and though the difficulties of the Etudes Symphoniques seemed to give him no trouble, a certain shyness, rather engaging than otherwise, prevented him from standing on his merits emphatically enough to get full credit for his performance. By this time, however, the audience had come decidedly to like him; and when he got on to Chopin, with whom his musical instinct and natural grace of expression had their way unembarrassed, his battle was won. I left him playing some excellent little *salon* pieces of his own in triumph, he and his audience on the best of terms.

The violinists are gathering to share the spoils of us with the pianists. Sarasate, less high-spirited than he was at that golden age which his only competitor, Isaÿe, has just reached, but perfect as ever, is playing at St James's Hall on Saturdays. Isaÿe is announced for the next Philharmonic (on the 28th); and as these two are now the greatest fiddlers in the world, as far as we know, it will be well for novices to hear them at once, instead of waiting for ten or twenty years and supposing that because the men are still there and their reputations undiminished, their powers must be in equally satisfactory preservation. And this reminds me, by an association of ideas which experts will find no difficulty in tracing, of a young pupil of Joachim's, named Felix Berber, who gave a concert on Thursday at which Sapellnikoff repeated his amazing performance of Chopin's Polonaise in A flat, the middle episode in which comes from his puissant hands like an avalanche. Felix Berber is a very remarkable executant; but he has succumbed so completely to Joachim as to have actually caught his intonation, which unfortunately means that in bravura passages every note is out of tune except the keynote. My advice to Herr Berber is: "Get another fiddle; and call no man master." I know the gratitude and devotion with which Joachim inspires his pupils; but gratitude never made anybody an artist yet; and a violinist needs all the artistic devotion of which he is capable for himself. Johannes Wolff is now to be heard in all directions, playing difficult pieces as if they were easy, and easy pieces (Raff's cavatina and the like) as if they were immensely important and difficult; but always coming off with distinction.

At the Opera, Madame Melba has appeared as Elsa, singing with great skill, but playing artificially and without the sensibility that the part requires. De Reszke's Lohengrin ought not to be missed, as the chances are heavily against any of us hearing a better if we put the matter off. The Favorita on Friday was terribly dreary. Mlle Richard sings perfectly in tune, avoids the tremolo, and has a mezzo-soprano voice of fair power and quality; but her old-fashioned operatic stage business is not acting, and her personal likeness to Titiens involves a quite conclusive unlikeness to La Favorita as fancy paints her.

25 June 1890

I HAVE been getting my mind improved at the Crystal Palace. Naturally that was not what I went for. My sole object in submitting to the unspeakable boredom of listening to St Paul on Saturday afternoon was to gain an opening for an assault on the waste of our artistic resources —slender enough, in all conscience, even with the strictest economy—caused in England every year by the perform- ance and publication of sham religious works called ora- torios. In so far as these are not dull imitations of Handel, they are unstaged operettas on scriptural themes, written in a style in which solemnity and triviality are blended in the right proportions for boring an atheist out of his senses or shocking a sincerely religious person into utter repudiation of any possible union between art and religion. However, there is an intermediate class in England which keeps up the demand in the oratorio market. This class holds that the devil is not respectable (a most unsophisticated idea); but it deals with him in a spirit of extraordinary liberality in dividing with him the kingdom of the fine arts. Thus in literature it gives him all the novels, and is content to keep nothing but the tracts. In music it gives him everything that is played in a theatre, reserving the vapidities of the drawing room and the solemnities of the cathedral for itself. It asks no more in graphic art than a set of illustrations to its family Bible, cheerfully devoting all other subjects to the fiend. But people who make a bad bargain never stick to it. These ascetics smuggle fiction under the covers of the Society for the dissemination of their own particular sort of knowledge; drama in the guise of "entertainments"; opera in scores labelled "cantata" or "oratorio"; and Venus and Apollo catalogued as Eve and Adam. They will not open a novel of Boisgobey's, because novels are sinful; but they will read with zest and gloating how The Converted Collier used to beat his mother in the days when he was an un- regenerate limb of Satan. They console themselves for

Coquelin by Corney Grain; and, since they may not go to Macbeth at the Lyceum, they induce Mr Irving to dress the Thane in a frock-coat and trousers, and transport him, Sullivan, Miss Terry, and all, to St James's Hall. It is just the same with music. It is wrong to hear the Covent Garden orchestra play Le Sommeil de Juliette; but if Gounod writes just such another interlude, and calls it The Sleep of the Saints before the Last Judgment, then nothing can be more proper than to listen to it in the Albert Hall. Not that Gounod is first favorite with the Puritans. If they went to the theatre they would prefer a melodramatic opera with plenty of blood in it. That being out of the question, they substitute an oratorio with plenty of damnation. The Count di Luna, grinding his teeth and longing to "centuplicar la morte" of his rival with "mille atroce spasimi," is a comparatively tame creature until he takes off his tunic and tights, hies to a "festival," and, in respectable evening-dress, shouts that "the Lord is angry with the wicked every day," and that "if the wicked [meaning the people who go to the Opera] turn not, the Lord will whet His sword and bend His bow." What a day Sunday must be for the children of the oratorio public! It was prime, no doubt, at the Crystal Palace on Saturday, to hear the three thousand young ladies and gentlemen of the choir, in their Sunday best, all shouting "Stone him to death: stone him to death"; and one could almost hear the satisfied sigh of Mr Chadband as St Paul's "God shall surely destroy them" was followed in due time by the piously fugal "See what love hath the Father bestowed on us." But to me, constitutional scoffer that I am, the prostitution of Mendelssohn's great genius to this lust for threatening and vengeance, doom and wrath, upon which he should have turned his back with detestation, is the most painful incident in the art-history of the century. When he saw Fra Diavolo, he was deeply scandalized at the spectacle of Zerlina undressing herself before the looking-glass on her wedding eve, singing "Oui, c'est demain," with the three brigands peeping at her through the curtains.

23

"I could not set such things to music," he said; and undoubtly the theme was none too dignified. But was it half so ignoble and mischievous as the grovelling and snivelling of Stiggins, or the raging and threatening of Mrs Clennam, which he glorified in St Paul and Elijah? I do not know how it is possible to listen to these works without indignation, especially under circumstances implying a parallel between them and the genuine epic stuff of Handel, from which, in spite of their elegance, they differ as much as Booth does from Bunyan. The worst of it is that Mendelssohn's business is still a going concern, though his genius has been withdrawn from it. Every year at the provincial festivals some dreary doctor of music wreaks his counterpoint on a string of execrable balderdash with Mesopotamia or some other blessed word for a title. The author is usually a critic, who rolls his own log in his paper whilst his friendly colleagues roll it elsewhere. His oratorio, thus recommended, is published in the familiar buff cover, and played off on small choral societies throughout the country by simple-minded organists, who display their knowledge by analysing the fugues and pointing out the little bits of chorus in six real parts. In spite of the flagrant pedantry, imposture, corruption, boredom, and waste of musical funds which the oratorio system involves, I should not let the cat out of the bag in this fashion if I thought it could be kept in much longer; for who knows but that some day I might get into business myself as a librettist, and go down to posterity as the author of St Nicholas Without and St Walker Within, a sacred oratorio, founded on a legend alluded to by Charles Dickens, and favorably noticed in the columns of The World and other organs of metropolitan opinion? But I fear I was born too late for this. The game is up; and I may as well turn Queen's evidence whilst there is some credit to be got by it.

As for the performance at the Crystal Palace, it was, with the three thousand executants, a rare debauch of its kind; and except that it was dragged out to twice its normal length by the slow *tempi* taken by Mr Manns—unnecessarily slow, I think—the effect was not so inferior to that of a performance on the proper scale as might have been expected from so monstrous a piece of overdoing. Edward Lloyd sang without a fault, and Mr Watkin Mills' vocal style was excellent. Madame Albani pulled the music about in her accustomed fashion by hanging on to every note that shewed off her voice, and her intonation, compared with that of her three colleagues, was fallible, but she was otherwise equal to the occasion. Madame Patey was at her best, as she generally is at such functions.

In the ordinary course of music, nothing more paradoxical could be imagined than Richter conducting a composition of Wagner's worse than Hallé, and at the same concert surpassing Hallé at a work by Mendelssohn. An adept will at once see that the Wagner piece must have been the Siegfried Idyll, which is music and nothing else, and the Mendelssohn one an overture (it was in fact Ruy Blas), which is music and dramatic poetry too. Ruy Blas has always hitherto appeared a weaker, if more refined, overture than that to Euryanthe; but at his last concert but one, Richter drew out Mendelssohn with a force that enabled him to sustain the comparison with Weber triumphantly. The performance was a remarkable example of the power of the sustained tone which Richter insists on from the orchestra, in contrast to the short-winded puffs and scrapes with which our own kid-gloved conductors are satisfied. Unfortunately, this splendid beginning was followed by a pianforte concerto by Brahms, a desperate hash of bits and scraps, with plenty of thickening in the pianoforte part, which Mr Leonard Borwick played with the enthusiasm of youth in a style technically admirable. The Siegfried Idyll followed, and was not a patch on the Manchester band's recent performance of it in London—was, in short, a downright blank failure, numbered by the Brahms boredom. Mr Borwick, by the bye, might be forgiven for venturing on a recital; for performances of concertos by Schumann and Brahms do not afford a sufficient basis for a critical verdict upon a player of his pretensions. This reminds me that Madame Teresa Carrñeo gave a third recital on Tuesday, treating us impartially to her Beethoven-Chopin repertory and to such arrant schoolgirl trash as I thought never to have heard again save in dreams of my sisters' infancy. It would not be strictly true to say that she went back to Prudent's fantasia on Lucia; but it is a positive fact that she substituted for Mendelssohn's Prelude and Fugue in E minor nothing less than a thumping scamper through Gottschalk's Tremolo. Certainly she is a superb executant, and her bow is Junonian; but Gottschalk!—good gracious! On Wednesday I went to hear Madame Haas play at Steinway Hall, and was glad to find in the program that most beautiful Beethoven sonata (Op. 110) which she has made so thoroughly her own. Paderewski should have been there to take a lesson in it from her.

At the Opera last week they put on the Figaro on an off-night; but the performance was a mere run through the voice parts and accompaniments: there was no attempt to bring the subtle and elaborate comedy to a serious representation. Dufriche, who appeared for the first time as the Count, at least stuck to the text; and since he did his best to keep his tremolo out of action, the disapproval manifested by the gallery and acknowledged by him in several ironic obeisances after Vedro mentr' io sospiro, was undeserved at that particular moment; but his notions of what he was on the stage for were evidently of the vaguest: he repeatedly bungled the business of the scene. Madame Scalchi slipped through the part of Cherubino with wonderful adroitness, and with a feeling for the music which was hardly sufficiently acknowledged. Miss Russell made a shocking interpolation in Perche crudel (high note, of course), and the Deh vieni, lying unfavorably for her voice, did not make its due effect; but, except for an occasional hardness of tone, her Susanna, vocally at least, was satisfactory, and her acting, as far as it went, was intelligent. Madame Tavary sang well as the Countess; indeed, the singing was good all round except in the case of D'Andrade, who took the greatest pains to be a failure as Figaro, and succeeded. The orchestra was not quite so bad as in Don Giovanni; but Signor Randegger did not induce them to take very much trouble with the score. On the whole, the critic who found Le Nozze "trite" was not far wrong; only he was mistaken in supposing that the triteness was Mozart's fault.

2 July 1890

THE concert last week in aid of the project for establishing a municipal band in London reminded me of the late Edmund Gurney's demand for an orchestra for the East End. If I had my way in the matter the money should not be raised by a concert and a subscription list, as if the London County Council were a distressed widow: a fitter course would be to levy the cost by the strong hand of the tax-collector on the thousands of well-to-do people who never go to a concert because they are "not musical," but who enjoy, all the same, the health-giving atmosphere which music creates. Just as the river is useful to men who do not row, the bridges to West Enders who never cross them, and the railways to the bedridden, so the provision of good music and plenty of it smooths life as much for those who do not know the National Anthem from Rule Britannia, as for those who can whistle all the themes in the Ninth Symphony. Now that we have renounced the hideous absurdity of keeping up Waterloo Bridge out of the halfpence of the people who actually go over it, it is pitiable to have to go back to that ridiculous system for a town band. We certainly want such a band, though not because private enterprise has been behindhand in the matter. On the contrary, it is because private enterprise every Sunday sends a procession, religious or Radical, past my windows every five minutes or so, each headed by a band, that I feel the need for some model of excellence to hold up to these enthusiastic instrumentalists. In Lancashire and Yorkshire there are, it is computed, twenty thousand bandsmen.

When I was in Bristol some time ago, a fifteen minutes' walk through the working-class quarter on Sunday morning brought me across three bands, two of them by no means bad ones. In London you can, on the occasion of a big "demonstration," pass down a procession miles long without ever being out of earshot of at least two bands. The cultured class sometimes, when suffering from an attack of nerves, wants the band-playing class to be dispersed and silenced; but this cannot now be effectively done, for the band-playing outnumber the cultured five to one, and two-thirds of them have votes.

Whether we like the bands or not, we must put up with them: let us therefore, in self-defence, help them to make themselves fairly efficient. It is certain that they are not so good as they might be at present, and that as long as they never hear anything better than their own music they will remain much as they are. Their instruments are not so bad as might be supposed. They may not come from the first-class stocks of Mahillon, Courtois, or Boosey; but the competition between instrument-makers has resulted in the production of fairly good brass instruments of the simpler types (cornets, saxhorns, etc.) at reasonable prices payable by instalments. Hence the fortuitous German bombardon with cylinders, bought at a pawnshop, and pitched nearly half-a-tone lower than its British companions in the band, is now scarcer than it used to be, though unhappily it is not yet extinct.

But even in bands in which the instruments are all manufactured to English military pitch and of endurable quality, with players whose ears are not satisfied until they have adjusted their tuning-slides and their blowing so as to get the notes made with the pistons tolerably in tune, chaos sets in the moment the music goes beyond the simplest diatonic harmonies. At the occurrence of one of the series of tonic discords which are so freely used in modern music, and which make the six old gentlemen who form the anti-Wagner

28

party in Paris put their fingers to their ears, the working-class bandsman not only does not know whether he is in tune or out, but he actually does not know whether he is playing the right note, so strange is the chord to his ear. Consequently he is limited to the banal quicksteps and tiresome Boulanger marches which confirm him in his vulgar and obvious style of execution. Even a Schubert march is beyond him, because the modulations, simple and brilliantly effective as they are, are not solely from tonic to dominant and back again. The only way to rescue him from his groove is to familiarize him with the sound of modern polyphony in all its developments. A gentleman can do this for himself at his pianoforte; but a wage-earner who has to buy a modest two-guinea cornet by laborious instalments is as likely to learn driving on his own four-in-hand as modern music at his own Steinway.

You must send round to Victoria Park, Finsbury Park, Battersea Park, Peckham Rye, Hampstead Heath, and Blackheath a numerous, well paid, honorably esteemed, highly skilled, and splendidly equipped band, with a conductor who puts music before applause, the chance of a knighthood, loyalty, morals, religion, and every other earthly or unearthly consideration—a municipal August Manns, in short. This is the only way to teach the bandsman of the street and his patrons how his quicksteps with their three chords and one modulation have been improved on by Schubert, Offenbach, Auber, and Rossini, by Weber, Mendelssohn, and Goetz, and finally by Beethoven and Wagner. Let him pick all this up through his ears, and he will come out with a much sounder knowledge than that of the literate person who knows that Wagner is "marvellous" by reading statements to that effect in the critical scriptures of the day. In the end he will pay back the outlay; for when he is qualified as a consumer and producer of good music, the resultant cheapness and plenty will bring down the exorbitant cost of even the Opera. Think of that, ye golden ones whose Oriental names I read on the box-doors as I

stroll about Mr Harris's corridors of an evening during the
entr'actes; and do not let the Municipal Band Fund fall
through for lack of subscriptions.

I cannot congratulate Lassalle on his Rigoletto last
Thursday at Covent Garden. A massive gentleman with all
the empty pomposity of the Paris Opéra hampering him
like an invisible chain and bullet tied to his ankle, and whose
stock-in-trade as an actor consists of one mock-heroic
attitude, cannot throw himself into a part which requires the
activity of a leopard; nor, by merely screwing up his eyes
in an ecstasy of self-approbation, convey the raging self-
contempt, the superstitious terror, the impotent fury, the
savage vindictiveness, the heartbroken grovelling of the
crippled jester wounded in his one vulnerable point—his
fierce love of his child, the only creature who does not either
hate or despise him. In such a character, burnt into music
as it has been by Verdi, Lassalle's bag of hackneyed Parisian
tricks makes him egotistical and ridiculous.

Further, he spoils the effect of the great scene with the
courtiers, and makes a most unreasonable demand on the
orchestra, by transposing his music a whole tone down, a
monstrous liberty to take. No one can blame a singer for
requiring a transposition of half-a-tone from our Philharmonic pitch; but where, as at Covent Garden, the French
pitch is adopted, a demand for "a tone down" could only be
justified in the case of a singer of very limited range, but
with sufficiently remarkable acting power to compensate for
the injury to the musical effect. As Lassalle has neither
excuse, it seems to me that we are entitled to expect that he
shall in future either sing the part as Verdi wrote it, or else
let it alone. At the same time, it is but fair to add that when
an unfortunate baritone has to sing fifty bars in what is
practically twelve-eight time, *andante*, on the four or five
highest notes in his compass, without a rest except for two
bars, during which he is getting out of breath in a violent
stage struggle, the composer has only himself to thank when
the same artist, who sings the much longer part of Wagner's

Hans Sachs without turning a hair, flatly declines to submit to the strain of Rigoletto.

As it was, the honors of the occasion were carried off by Madame Melba, who ended the famous quartet on a high D flat of the most beautiful quality, the licence in this instance justifying itself by its effect. Valero, if he did not realize the masterful egotist, full of *la joie de vivre*, as conceived by Victor Hugo and Verdi, yet played with such spirit and humor that he may put down the Duke as one of his London successes. His singing, to be sure, was only a tasty sort of yelling, without spontaneity or purity of tone; but it was pretty enough to bring down the house in La donna è mobile.

At the revival of Meyerbeer's Prophète many critics, including myself, were reduced to the humiliating necessity of buying books of the play, containing a French and an English version, both different in arrangement from the one used on the stage. I had never seen the opera except on paper. The three Anabaptists rather interested me when they started an open-air revolutionary agitation, as I am a bit of an amateur in that line myself; but when they turned out badly in the end I felt much as the mottle-faced man in Pickwick did when Sam Weller sang of the Bishop's coachman running away from Dick Turpin. "I say," said the mottle-faced man on that occasion, "that that coachman did not run away, but that he died game—game as pheasants; and I wont hear nothing said to the contrary." In a similar spirit I affirm that the Anabaptists died "game as pheasants," and that Scribe's history is trash.

But, indeed, Scribe never shewed his radical incapacity for anything deeper than his deadly "well-made plays" more conclusively than when he mistook for a great musical delineator of the passions of the multitude the composer who, in Les Huguenots, set forth the Reformation as a strife between a Rataplan chorus and an Ave Maria, the two factions subsequently having it out in alternate strains of a waltz. The Prophet, meant to be luridly historical, is in fact

31

the oddest medley of drinking songs, tinder-box trios, sleigh rides, and skating quadrilles imaginable; and even John of Leyden, whose part detaches itself from the dead mass of machinery as something alive and romantic, if not exactly human, is at the disadvantage of being a hero without having anything heroic to do, and of having finally to degrade himself by shouting a vile drinking song amid a pack of absurd nautch-girls. The orchestra seemed to feel this on Monday; for they brought the scene to an end in ruin and confusion by differing on the subject of the last cut in the score. Jean de Reszke, though a little hoarse, made as much as was possible of the part under the circumstances; and Mlle Richard's Fidès was at least more credible than her Favorita. Madame Nuovina, on the other hand, seems to have gone completely to pieces. The shrillness of her highest notes is worse than ever; and she has developed a tremolo which sounds like a burlesque of Madame Tetrazzini's. It is a pity; for her first appearance as Margaret in Faust promised better things.

9 July 1890

I AM inclined to think that the most important event of the past week is the revolt of the Private Man against the Philharmonic Society and the critics. As a rule the Private Man, conscious of the guilt of ignorance, submits to musical imposture without a murmur, and even pretends to like it. He writes to the papers if he is overcharged by an hotel proprietor, or if a lady is rude to him, or if the sandwiches at a railway refreshment room are stale; but when he pays to hear the Ninth Symphony at a Philharmonic Concert, and has that work served up in such a fashion that a whole meal of stale sandwiches would be ambrosial in comparison, he dissembles his loathing, and secretly deplores his own want of taste for the classic. And the critics chime in with a conventional compliment or two about "the celebrated Philharmonic orchestra," as if they did not know as well as I do that this band, potentially the best in the world, is actually as vapid and perfunctory an institution as ever drove a musician wild with disappointment by heartless trifling with great works.

But its last performance of the Ninth Symphony seems to have aroused the British lion. The critics said the usual thing; but one Edward Carpenter, an unattached essayist of credit and renown, declares, on the contrary, that the symphony was miserably unsatisfying. I was not at the concert myself, because, though I forewent Patti and the Albert Hall to attend, yet when I reached St James's Hall it was so full that I could only get one of those acutely uncomfortable stalls in the niches of the wall for my seven-and-sixpence. Now, for a good performance of the Ninth Symphony I would cheerfully sit the whole time on a sack of nails. For an average Philharmonic performance no seat, I regret to say, could be too comfortable—a fourposter would be best of all; so I looked askance at that ticket, with its discouraging "Row FF"; hesitated a moment; and—got my money back.

Therefore I cannot say from my own observation whether Mr Carpenter or the critics were right; but I implicitly believe Mr Carpenter. I have too often suffered from what he complains of to doubt him. Perhaps the society's directors will now wake up to the necessity of providing their band with a conductor capable of making it actually what I have said it is potentially. They once hit on a great conductor, no less a one than Richard Wagner; but instead of having the sense to hold on to him like grim death, as they should have done, they dropped him like a hot potato after one year, and clung to Mr Cusins (after eleven years of Sterndale Bennett) from 1867 until it became evident, a few years ago, that decomposition had set in; whereupon they tried Sir Arthur Sullivan, Dr Mackenzie, and Mr Cowen, only to find that these talented, polite, and estimable musicians take much the same view of Beethoven as Mr Andrew Lang (for instance) takes of Dickens or William Morris, and are about as competent to regenerate the British orchestra as he is to regenerate the British drama.

If they cannot find a true Beethovenian conductor, why can they not leave that much-abused genius in peace, and stick to the Moszkowski trivialities and the ballroom and jetty music which they play so prettily? An occasional old-fashioned Handelian allegro, consisting of rapid figurations, which only need to be played in strict time as fast as possible, could be thrown in to keep up the classical tradition; and Wagner and Beethoven could be left out on the ground that they were demonstrative and given to striving after effect (not to mention generally getting it)—in short, that they were no gentlemen.

Meanwhile the Richter concerts flourish by doing what the Philharmonic ought to do, and professes to do, and does not do, and probably never will do. There, if one cannot always avoid Wagner's *bête noire*, "the blessed Johannes," known to a long-suffering British public as Brahms, one can at least hear a Beethoven symphony or a Wagner prelude played with sympathy and understanding. That absurd body, the London branch of the Wagner Society, having nothing better to do with its superfluous funds than to endow Richter concerts which can get on perfectly well without it, was in St James's Hall in force last week, when Miss Pauline Cramer sang the closing scene from the Götterdämmerung. Over most German singers of her heroic build she has the advantage of a voice of very bright quality. She is evidently highly sensitive to the Wagnerian emotions —an enthusiast, in fact; but enthusiasm is dangerous in such mad bits as that when Brynhild springs on her horse and rides into the fire. Abandonment to a suicidal situation is impossible: the effect must be an illusion produced by skilful husbandry of force; and for this husbandry Miss Cramer has hardly sufficient sang-froid. She also falls occasionally into the common fault of her school: she emphasizes the high notes too much, somewhat in the fashion of the early Wagner singers, who made his vocal music sound like a succession of screams. If Miss Cramer would only pass from her middle to her highest register without a *sforzando* every time, I should have as much praise for her singing as for her admirable earnestness.

Of recent concerts I have lost count. Miss Zoe Caryll, whose position as a pianist cannot be ascertained from a performance of Liszt's Hungarian Fantasia under rather nervous conditions, promised to produce both the De Reszkes on the platform of St James's Hall; but Jean sent an apology; and as Edouard brought only one song (O lieti di from L'Etoile du Nord), a stupendous encore elicited nothing fresher than a repetition. Sarah Bernhardt was so hoarse that she barely contrived to read a dozen lines which no one could hear; Lassalle and Madame Fursch-Madi sang French routine music (Massenet and so on) which nobody cared a straw about; the celebrated orchestra did its worst; and if it had not been for Madame Melba's Caro nome, Brother Edouard's essay as aforesaid, and a skilful and artistic recitation by Paul Plan of the Gymnase, the concert would have been nearly as great a disappointment as all miscellaneous concerts deserve to be. The pianists are still active every afternoon and evening. I have, in spite of all my evasions, heard a young Dutchman named Zeldenrust, a neat player, with a certain individuality which is not exactly musical individuality; a Mr Ernest Denhoff, an expert who shewed little feeling for his business; Mr Schönberger, a born player, if not a very deep one; and Albéniz, who let an orchestra loose on his own compositions in the little Steinway Hall, where we all wished it outside, though we could not very well get up and say so. Albéniz will find the professors inclined to dispute his right to call his spontaneous effusions "sonatas" and "concertos"; but if he sits tight and does as he pleases in this respect, he will find himself none the worse. He is, so far this season, the most distinguished and original of the pianists who confine themselves to the rose-gathering department of music. There was also a Mr Leon de Silka, a young Spanish amateur, who invited the Spanish Ambassador and some other people to hear him play. Mr de Silka must not let his friends mislead

him as to his present position as a player. Just now young Mr
Leonard Borwick, for example, could play his head off. He
can hit the right notes dexterously enough; but he has all the
faults of an amateur—unevenness of finger, bad habits of
pouncing on every time accent in the bar, moments of irresolute artistic feeling scattered here and there between
longueurs of diffident prose, and a tendency to repress himself in the manner of a gentleman rather than to realize his
conception in the manner of an artist. If Mr de Silka asks me
whether he is a consummate pianist, I answer No. If he asks
whether it is worth his while to undertake the two or three
years' more hard study needed to make him one, I answer
Yes. My tale of pianoforte recitals ends with Miss Else
Sonntag, who has been carefully instructed in the school of
Liszt. In that school the race is to the swift and the battle to
the strong; and Miss Sonntag is neither the one nor the
other; but she does all the more credit to her school by the
measure of success she attains.

I did not know that there were twenty students of the
harp in England until I went to Mr John Thomas's concert
the other day and saw two score young ladies in white
twanging away at Rossini's Carita. In my childhood this
would have exactly embodied my notion of heaven, and
would consequently have terrified me out of my wits. Even
now that I am a grown-up critic I cannot pretend that I
faced them without misgiving; for beautiful as the notes of
the harp are when a cunning hand sprinkles them over the
orchestra, they are apt to get on the nerves when taken neat
in large doses. Miss Edith Wynne, still an admirable ballad
singer, helped; and so did Mr Ben Davies. All went well
until a sacrifice to pseudo-classicism was offered up in a tepid
trio by Spohr—Mozart-and-water, as usual. Miss Marianne
Eissler did not succeed in catching the pitch of the harp, nor
Mr Thomas the pitch of her violin; and Hollmann, with his
ears on edge, steered a middle course. Hollmann is a con-
necting link between Mr Thomas's concert and Mr Isidore
de Lara's, at which he played an aria of Bach's as only a great

artist can play that great composer's music. I am not fond of the violoncello: ordinarily I had as soon hear a bee buzzing in a stone jug; but if all 'cellists played like Hollmann, I should probably have taken more kindly to it. De Lara made his début as a dramatic singer and epic composer. Nothing is easier to write than a cantata, except, perhaps, a tragedy in blank verse; and I suppose people must go through the stage of thinking that all cantatas are music, just as they had to go through the stage of thinking that Hoole's translation of Tasso was poetry. When I was at Mr Grossmith's recital the other day, I could not help feeling thankful that he was born with a sense of the ridiculous. Lacking it, he would have strung his tunes into first subjects and second subjects, connected by a modulation to the dominant shewing the hand of the accomplished musician; hashed them up into a free fantasia to an accompaniment of their own fragments; and put them together again and re-capitulated them (after a masterly return to the tonic) with a coda or tail consisting of inversions of the common chord on the keynote. Then the whole would have been produced at a Philharmonic Concert as Symphony in C, by George Grossmith, Mus. Doc. Oxon.; and when the British public had been duly impressed by the description as above in a shilling analytical program, and had read the criticism in the morning paper (by the same gentleman who wrote the program), no eloquence of mine would ever have persuaded them that all this technical stuff bears no more vital relation to music than parsing does to poetry. However, this excursus is not meant for Mr de Lara, who avoids academics and simply gratifies his turn for writing voluptuous lyrics, which are none the worse for a little opium-eating orchestration, heightened by an occasional jingle of the *pavilion chinoise*. I did not care much for that part of the cantata where Miss Russell told the composer that the pity in his look was awful, and his visage a god's; but the audience were encoring it very heartily as I withdrew. Mancinelli looked after the orchestra and gave us some bits of an oratorio of his own (an amiable weakness in an Italian, although it would be a deliberate fraud on the part of an Englishman); and Tivadar Nachéz played Bruch's First Concerto. Nachéz is one of the most musically intelligent violinists we have; but his technique fails him in rapid and difficult movements. Talking of the violin, why on earth does not Isaÿe give a concert? At Collard's rooms, on Friday, two ladies, who announced themselves as "the sisters the Countesses Augusta and Ernesta Ferrari d' Occhieppo," sang several songs and duets in the popular outdoor Italian manner, which came rather as a surprise to those who were not familiar with our own music-hall school of vocalism. I never heard Miss Bessie Bellwood sing Beethoven's In questa tomba; but I think she could more than hold her own with the Countess Ernesta Ferrari.

23 July 1890

IT is a pity that a statistical department cannot be started at St James's Hall to ascertain how many of the crowd which the Ninth Symphony always draws really like the work. If a question to this effect were supplemented by another as to whether the catechumen had studied the symphony for himself or had derived his knowledge of it wholly from public performances, I am afraid that the answers (in the unlikely event of their being unaffectedly true) would shew that the line of cleavage between those whom it puzzles or bores, and those who cherish it among their greatest treasures, coincides exactly with that between the concert students and the home students. That terrible first movement is the rub. At the Richter concerts we are convinced but unsatisfied; at the Crystal Palace grateful but hardly convinced; at the Philharmonic wearied and embittered. The whole cause of the shortcoming in Richter's case is insufficient rehearsal.

Wagner assures us that the perfect performances which he heard in Paris by the Conservatoire orchestra under Habeneck in 1838 were achieved, not in the least by Habeneck's genius, for he had none, but because he had the perseverance to rehearse the first movement until he understood it. This took two years; but, in the end, the band had not only got hold of the obviously melodic themes, but had discovered that much of what had at the first blush seemed mere figurated accompaniment, to be played with the usual tum-tum accents, was true and poignantly expressive melody.

My own conviction is that if any band gets hold of this melody, the melody will get hold of the band so effectually that the symphony will play itself if the conductor will only let it, to ensure which it is necessary that he, too, should be equally saturated. But since the process does not pay as a commercial speculation, and the only national provision for orchestral music in this country is made by merely securing to every speculator full freedom to try his luck, a good performance of the first movement is never heard in London.

Richter himself is duly saturated and super-saturated; but in spite of all he can do in the time at his disposal, the perfect balance, the consentaneous inspiration, the felt omnipresence of melody in its highest sensitiveness, remain unachieved: you find the strings stumbling over the *forte* passages in a dry excited way, detaching themselves angrily from the turbid uncertain song of the wood and horns, and producing a worry which suggests that the movement, however heroic by nature, is teething, and cannot help going into convulsions occasionally. Richter strained every nerve to get it as nearly right as possible at his last concert, and he certainly got the uttermost that his material and opportunities admitted; but the uttermost was none too good. The rest was comparatively plain sailing. The Scherzo went perhaps a shade too slowly: he took it at from 110 to 112 bars per minute; and I stand out for 115 at least myself.

It was remarkable, by the bye, to hear the young people bursting prematurely into applause at the end of the Presto, before the repetition of the Scherzo. The reason was that the repeat is omitted in the familiar Peters edition arrange-

ment of the symphonies as pianoforte duets; and these
enthusiasts thought accordingly that the movement ended
with the little rally at the end of the Presto. Nothing could
be more welcome than a blunder which shewed that young
England is not depending on the Philharmonic for its
notions of Beethoven. The performance attained its highest
pitch during the slow movement. Obvious as the relation
between the Adagio and Andante sections seems, I have
heard it misconceived in all manner of ways by conductors,
from Mr Manns, who only misses it by a hair's breadth, to
Signor Arditi, who, on being confronted with it for the first
time one night at a "classical" Promenade Concert, went at
it with the greatest intrepidity, taking the Andante at a
supernaturally slow lento, and rattling the Adagio along at
a lively allegretto, the whole producing the effect of a
chastened selection from Il Barbiere for use on Sundays.
Richter made no such mistakes. At the *reprise* of the
Andante the movement was going so divinely that when the
first violins went at a passage with an unmistakeable intention of overdoing it, Richter flung out an imploring hand
with a gesture of the most appealing natural eloquence; and
they forbore. There was one other magical instant—the
announcement of the choral theme by the bass strings in an
ethereal *piano*. Then the choir was unchained and led forth
to havoc, in which I am bound to add that the four soloists,
who began merrily enough, did not escape scathless. But
badly as it was sung, this great hymn to happiness, with its
noble and heartfelt glorification of joy and love, was at least
better than an oratorio.

It may be that the tempest of evil passions roused by the
word oratorio disposes me to be unjust to Mr Lloyd, who is
so much associated with that dismal and immoral entertainment: anyhow, I do not think he struck exactly on the vein
of Lohengrin's declaration to the Brabanters and the farewell to Elsa, although Richter averted a repetition of last
year's flatfalling by enlarging the selection which proved
so ineffective then. Somehow, Mr Lloyd started senti-

mentally; tried a touch of jingoism at the climax, "Lohen-grin's my name"; rose to genteel piety for a moment; and finally relapsed into sentimentality. He sang well, and elicited shouts of "Bravo!" (imagine anybody daring to say "Bravo!" to a real knight of the Grail!); but he was not Lohengrin. Mr Max Heinrich delivered the two bits of public oratory from The Mastersingers (the speeches of Pogner and Hans Sachs) admirably, his enunciation being distinct and full of point. But I take the liberty of warning Mr Heinrich that much singing in that open sharp-edged way will soon cut off a couple of his top notes and damage the quality of the rest; indeed, there are warning signs of wear on them already. So fine an artist as he will easily find how to make a lighter touch and a rounder tone effective, instead of sacrificing himself to his ideal of force and dis-tinctness. There was a tremendous ovation to Richter at the end of the concert.

I have actually only heard one pianist since last week. That one was Madame Madeline Schiller, who has execu-tion in great abundance, but not of the first quality. Bang-ing through a string of Lisztian "studies of transcendent execution" does not make amends for simplifying the *pres-tissimo* of the Waldstein Sonata by playing the octave passages in single notes.

The performance of Cosi fan tutte by the pupils of the Royal College at the Savoy was much better than an average performance of Don Giovanni at Covent Garden. It had been assiduously rehearsed from beginning to end; and the performance was a great occasion for a company of green-horns, instead of a Worn-out bit of routine for jaded pro-fessionals. The despised book, after all, has some fun in it, though quite as good plays have often been improvised in ten minutes in a drawing room at charades or dumb crambo. The Royal College shewed progress in the or-chestral department. Last year, at The Taming of the Shrew, ordinary professional aid was largely drawn on; but this time there were only two outsiders and one member of the teaching staff in the orchestra, the rest being students. And they played very well, the romantic charm of the scoring for the wind in Soave sia il vento and the aria Smanie implacabile coming out with all possible delicacy. Indeed, Mr Villiers Stanford seems to have applied the smoothing-iron rather too diligently; for the point of the humorously majestic exordium to the overture was quite missed. The notes were played accurately enough; but the whole fourteen bars should have been declaimed so as to arrest the attention of the house at once. Surely Mr Stanford can see more in them than a mere conventional strum of chords by way of prelude.

I cannot say so much for the singing as for the playing. In academies, conservatoires, colleges of music, and the like, the instrumentalists are usually taught by professors publicly known as accomplished players on the instruments they teach. Bassoon and clarionet players get taught by Wootton and Lazarus, and pianists by Clara Schumann and Sophie Menter; but singers are as often as not handed over to gentlemen who, having tried in vain to make themselves sing, continue their experiments with undiminished ardor on others. I have come across a good many singing-masters in my time—delightful fellows, with the finest critical taste, full of enthusiasm—sympathetic accompanists, physiologists enough to have an original theory about the function of the so-called false vocal cords, overflowing with good advice about the mischief of tight-lacing and tobacco, tremendously down on all forcing and straining of the voice, and yet quacks, every man of them. Each could see that all the others were quacks; but each firmly believed too, that he himself had discovered the true Italian method as taught by Porpora.

When I call them quacks, I mean that they were mere theorists—a reason which would have greatly astonished them, as they all held that the theorist is the capable teacher, and the empiricist the quack. I remember one who taught very well until he came to London, where he found that

42

good teaching did not pay, because the only people who could afford to pay ten guineas for twelve lessons could not be induced to take more than the twelve. So he told them that he would in six weeks shew them how to sing like Patti; and he took care that at the end of their dozen lessons they should be able to make a much louder noise than at the beginning, which caused their friends to declare that their voices were immensely improved. One day I asked him how he learned the method he had discarded. At first he told me that he had arrived at it by an elaborate study of "the physiology of the vocal organs"; but I scoffed, and said that Huxley and Foster had done the same, but were not, as far as I knew, authorities on singing. He then told me that he had been thrown on his own resources by the discovery that the singing-masters to whom he proposed to serve an apprenticeship knew no more about the matter than he; whereupon, he added, "I pottered over anatomy, and experimented on myself and my pupils until I could tell by watching a singer exactly how he was doing it. Then I watched all the opera-singers, and found that those whose voices wore badly sang differently from those whose voices wore well. I heard old Badeali, when he was nearly eighty, sing with the freshness of a young man. Accordingly I taught my pupils to produce their voices as Badeali did, and to avoid doing what the others did. The plan answered perfectly—except in London, where they dont like it and wont do it, and expect to learn in a month what takes four or five years' hard work." I do not know whether it was all true or not; for my late friend had the artistic temperament; but the process he described was a perfectly scientific one. [His name, by the way, was George John Vandeleur Lee, of whom more hereafter.] After this I am rather at a loss as to the most delicate method of harking back to the Royal College of Music and Cosi fan tutte; for I do not know any of the professors of singing at that institution, and should be sorry to criticize them in ignorance. But somehow I cannot quite believe that the plan pursued by those six operatic pupils of the College is Badeali's plan. Of course I cannot be positive, for I never heard Badeali; and, anyhow, I am only a critic, and therefore do not profess to speak authoritatively on such questions. Besides, I do not wish to discourage the six, who came off very creditably.

27 August 1890

THERE is no month like August in London. I know nothing more soothing than a walk down Regent Street with all the social pressure off. A horrible story in the papers the other day told us about a marine excursion for the purpose of gratifying idle curiosity as to the sort of fishes that live in the profounder depths of the sea. Needless to add, the marine excursion called itself a scientific expedition, a title which covers a multitude of sins, especially that of unscrupulous cruelty. It has long been known that a Londoner, when suddenly relieved in August of the enormous pressure under which he has lived during the season, exhibits certain curious phenomena. He casts his gloves; his coats change from broadcloth to Scotch tweed; the gleaming black and white cylinders disappear from his head and wrists; and his appearance, considered as the index of his income, deteriorates by at least two hundred a year. The scientific gentlemen yearned to see what would happen to fishes in similar circumstances: hence the expedition. A netful of flattened-out creatures was hauled up from the bottom of the ocean, where they lived with the weight of the whole Atlantic on their backs, to the deck of the scientific ship, where the pressure was light as air. The fishes all burst; and it is now an established fact that the fish is inferior to the Londoner in capacity for adapting itself to circumstances. Let us hope that nothing will happen to that ship, lest the relatives of the exploded martyrs to science be tempted to burst themselves in another way without coming to the surface at all. However, this is somewhat of a digression. What I am trying to say, in as long a way as possible, is that August has set me free to do what a journalist ought to do all the year round—that is, wander in search of something interesting to write about, instead of, as at the height of the season, cramming his column with records of thousands of insignificant things for no better reason than that they are happening, and that people are supposed to want to know everything that is going on, whether interesting or not. That is why the papers now set to work in earnest to tell us in an artistic way the pick of the news between China and Peru, instead of mechanically choking us with the whole of the news between the Griffin and Hyde Park Corner, condensed in the style of the Exchange Telegraph tape.

The other evening it suddenly came into my head that a musical critic could not do better than go to a music-hall. The difficulty in the way was the memory of previous experiments in that direction, which had thoroughly convinced me that what makes one man merry makes another melancholy mad; and that I, as far as music-halls are concerned, belong to the melancholy mad section. Finally I compromised the matter by going to see the ballet at the Alhambra, and enduring a few of the preliminary "turns" with a view to observing the progress of the music-hall school of singing. For it is a distinct school, and in some respects a very striking one. Whether it has any regular teaching professors I do not know: possibly there may be Porporas, Bordognis, Romanos, Behnkes, and Lampertis who preserve the traditional renderings of What cheer, Ria? and Arsk a P'liceman; who teach pure Whitechapel English; and who are experts in developing that amazing *voce di petto*, five minutes of which would finish Patti's career for ever.

But more probably the music-hall prima donna, like the literary man, picks up her profession imitatively and intuitively. If a novice came to me for advice, I should recommend her to make the chest register of her voice strong and coarse by using it vigorously and constantly—even vituperatively on occasion—in public and private speech. The rest I take to be a matter of main strength. That chest voice has to be forced, with the utmost resonance of which it is

45

capable, an octave higher than the point at which the well-trained opera and concert singer drops it and betakes herself to her middle register. The thing is impossible; but, like many impossibilities, it can be accomplished at certain sacrifices—sacrifices which would disqualify an opera-singer (which *have* disqualified several, in fact), but which do not matter in a music-hall.

For instance, the effort cannot be sustained for long: two successive songs *con tutta la forza* can hardly be achieved without such restful devices as speaking, or rather shouting, several of the lines through the music, and occasionally subsiding into the comparative tranquillity of a step-dance. Again, the singer must forgo all power to use her voice sanely; for even if she could fall back on the artistic method, she dare no more face the tremulous squeaking sound of her own ruined upper registers than Edouard de Reszke dare chant Marcel's doxology in Les Huguenots in his head voice. She must vanquish her songs by going at them as if each verse were a round in a very fast glove-fight—which, by the bye, would be slightly less fatiguing to the performers, and, on the whole, decidedly less brutalizing to the audience. There are, however, certain gifted women who have mixed voices, shrill and ringing at the top, intensely telling in the middle, and flexible all over. With such an organ as this, a good ear, and such an abundance of *la joie de vivre* as may raise vulgarity to the pitch of genius, the lowliest lass (the lowlier the better, in fact) may become a veritable diva of the London Pavilion, and enter into the closest relations with the·Peerage.

I was not fortunate enough to come across such a star at the Alhambra; yet I heard artists who shewed an amazing capacity for taking infinite pains over any musical feat, provided only that it was clearly not worth doing. In the most eccentric ways and with stupendous virtuosity they played trashy tunes on all manner of unmusical instruments, from sticks and sleigh-bells up to banjos and mandolines. Where they live, and how they induce the neighbors to stand their

practising, baffles my acutest conjecture. If they amused me
more than the singers, they gave me less food for professional
reflection. I have spoken of the music-hall singer's reliance
for effect on the ardent abuse of a mere corner of the voice, at
the cost of the destruction of the rest of it; but I had no need
to go to the music-halls to learn that trick. Italian opera
familiarized me with it long before I ever knew what the inside of a music-hall is like. If you study the scores of Handel,
who knew how to treat the human voice, you will find that
when he was not writing to suit individual peculiarities he
recognized practically only two sorts of voices for each sex,
and that he insisted on an effective range of from an octave
and a sixth or thereabout to two octaves, the different registers relieving and contrasting with one another so as to
get the greatest variety of effect with the least fatigue. Turn
then to a score by Verdi, and see how the effective compass
demanded from a singer has been reduced to a minor sixth
at the extreme top, within which narrow bounds, however,
the most unreasonable and monotonous strain is mercilessly
enforced.

Anyone who knows how to sing can go through all the
solos proper to his or her voice in The Messiah, and feel not
only free from fatigue, but much the better for the exercise.
The same experiment on Il Trovatore or Un Ballo would
leave them tired and, as regards a considerable part of their
compass, almost toneless. The *reductio ad absurdum* of the
Verdi style is the music-hall style, which is simply the abuse
of a particular part of the voice carried to its furthest possible limit. Signor d'Andrade at Covent Garden, who can
shout all the high G's of the Count di Luna with the greatest
gusto, fails as Figaro in Le Nozze, exactly as the vivacious
lady who sang Woman, Poor, Weak Woman at the Alhambra the other night would fail if she were to try Eccomi
alfine in Babilonia, or Return, O God of Hosts. No doubt
she would protest that Rossini and Handel did not know
how to write for the voice, quite as vehemently as the Verdi
screamers did when Wagner went back to the old plan and

47

revived the art of singing for us.

The ballet, wherein we passed at a bound from the Utter Popular to the Ultra Academic—from the toe and heel crudities of the step-dance to the classical *entrechats* of the grand school—was dramatically weak. A ballet without a good story and plenty of variety of scene and incident is much like one of Handel's operas, which were only stage concerts for shewing off the technical skill of the singers. Now the deftest shake and the most perfect roulade soon pall unless they are turned to some dramatic purpose: we put up even with the nightingale only by giving it credit for poetic fancies that never came into its head. It is the same with dancing when somebody else is doing it: we soon weary of the few *pas* which make up the dancer's stock-in-trade.

We demand, first, a pretty dance (and composers of good dances are no more plentiful than composers of good songs); and, second, a whole drama in dance, in which the *pas seul* shall merge, as the aria and cavatina have at last merged in the Wagnerian music-drama. In opera this has been done by a gradual reduction of the independence and consequent incongruity of the soloist's show-piece until it became an integral part of the act. But I cannot say that I see much progress in this direction in the ballet. The solos are still often as absurdly out of place as those of Mr Folair and the Infant Phenomenon; and the old final cadenza and high note, which in opera is now either absorbed into the song structure or abolished altogether, flourishes in its choreographic form in the ridiculous teetotum spin round the stage with which every solo in a ballet ends. It is really a sort of taking round the hat for applause, as undignified in intention as it is unlovely in appearance.

The worst of it is that the only journalistic scrutiny as yet brought to bear on dancing is of a sort now all but obsolete in every other art. The very vilest phase of criticism is that in which it emerges from blank inanity into an acquaintance with the terms, rules, and superstitions which belong to the technical processes of the art treated of. It is then that you get asinine rigmaroles praising hopelessly commonplace painters for their "marvellous foreshortening," their knowledge of anatomy, their "correct composition" (meaning that every group of figures has the outline of a candle extinguisher), and so on; whilst great composers are proved to be ignorant and tasteless pretenders, because their discords are unprepared and improperly resolved, or their harmony full of fasle relations and consecutive fifths, or because *si contra fa diabolus est*. Why, I have myself been reproached with ignorance of "the science of music" because I do not impose on the public by hoggishly irrelevant displays of ignorance of the true inwardness of musical technology! Now it happens that in an evil hour the technology of the ballet has been betrayed to the critics by a friend of mine. Being a clergyman,[1] he found it necessary to disabuse his clients of their pious opinion that a ballet-dancer is a daughter of Satan who wears short skirts in order that she may cut lewd capers. He bore eloquent testimony to the devoted labor and perseverance involved by the training of a fine dancer, and declared his conviction of the perfect godliness of high art in that and all other forms. To this day you may see in the list of his works the title Art of Theatrical Dancing, immediately following Laws of Eternal Life. All this is much to his credit; but unfortunately his indiscreet revelation of how a critic with no artistic sense of dancing may cover up his incapacity by talking about *ronds de jambe*, arabesques, elevations, *entrechats*, *ballonnés*, and the like, threatens to start a technico-jargonautic fashion in ballet criticism, and whilst it lasts there will be no abolishing the absurdities and pedantries which now hamper the development of stage-dancing; for the critics will make as much as possible of any ugly blemish (the teetotum spin, for instance), provided only they can thereby parade their knowledge of its technical name.

I have left myself no room to speak more particularly of Salandra, as the Alhambra ballet is called: let it suffice that it

[1] Rev. Stewart Headlam.

is not so good as Asmodeus; that Legnani, young, intelligent, and not yet in her prime, holds her own against the memory of the superb and magnetic Bessone, more by a certain freshness and naïveté than by her execution, which is nevertheless sufficiently brilliant; and that Vincenti, the best male dancer I have ever seen, is as admirable as ever, though this ballet does not shew him at his best.

3 September 1890

I AM sorry I cannot describe the plot of Captain Thérèse. The outline of it in the "book of words," unbearably bald as it is, would, if quoted verbatim, occupy a column and a quarter of your space. Even then the reader would be no wiser; for though I have read this précis with close attention, and seen the performance into the bargain, I can make nothing of it. How much of it is Bisson and how much Burnand I know no more than the babe unborn. No doubt when Mr Monkhouse talks about grasping at the château and missing the substance, that is Burnand; and when everybody enters into inconceivable explanations as to the movements of an army which changes from French to Spanish and back again every fifteen minutes, getting a new commander-in-chief each time, and falling at last into such hopeless confusion that it arrests its own officer as a spy, and proceeds to court-martial the entire cast: that, let us patriotically hope, is Bisson. However this may be, one thing is clear: the first thing to do with Captain Thérèse is to cut out the plot. The next step will be to cut out the music, even at the risk of leaving somewhat of a hiatus in an entertainment which is, after all, advertised as an opera. I do not say that one or two of M. Planquette's numbers might not be retained to avoid any injury to his feelings; but he would, perhaps, himself prefer the entire suppression of a score which convicts him in every bar of an exhausted invention and a resourcelessly limited technique. Surely there was no need to go to France for these qualifications: have we not plenty of native composers who would be only too happy to oblige?

Certainly, if any of our young lions were allowed to try their hands, there would be serious danger of the audience being no longer able to remember the music phrase by phrase, progression by progression, as they listened, or to forget it with perfect indifference the moment it ceased; but this might be put up with for the sake of a dash of freshness, youth, spirits, fun, imagination, and possibly even of genuine musical originality. Nor need the work to which our musicians are now condemned be left undone, if they take to light opera. M. Planquette might undertake the oratorios, the symphonies, the cantatas for the provincial festivals: his talent is just ripe for them. Professor Villiers Stanford, Mr Cliffe, Mr MacCunn, and the rest could then follow the example of Sir Arthur Sullivan and fertilize their wasting talents by condescending to do as Mozart did—or as near as they can get to it.

There is nothing else in Captain Thérèse that I could wish to see excised, except perhaps all the incidents and most of the dialogue. The characters may be retained, though the only one who does not seem entirely extraneous, and obviously dragged in for the sake of the performer, is Madame Sombrero, who does not appear. And here let me drop the pretence of treating Captain Thérèse seriously as an opera, and put it on its own ground as a sort of variety entertainment to exhibit the popular aspects of Mr Hayden Coffin and Miss Phyllis Broughton. I say aspects advisedly, for I noticed no attempt to display their artistic gifts. Mr Coffin has evidently a great deal of capacity as a singer and actor; but it is running to seed for want of any real appreciation of its value on the part of the management, or on that of the opera purveyors whom the management delights to honor. Far be it from me to deny the grace of the stupendous flirtations, dancings, and kissings with which he and Miss Broughton gather the roses while they may; but I cannot help asking whether a young artist is to spend his whole life at this sort of thing. A new American prima donna was announced because a similar engagement had been successful in the case of Paul Jones. So much are the managers creatures of habit. The lady in question, Miss Attallie Claire, has a light soprano voice, not very voluminous, but of pretty and unforced tone. Perhaps it was made a condition of her engagement that she should be a contralto, because Miss Huntington was a contralto: at any rate, Miss Claire has been at some pains to cultivate her voice and extend its range downward rather than upward, not without success, as she sang a contralto song in the first act acceptably. But that does not at all alter the fact that she is neither a contralto nor even a mezzo, but a soprano. Mr Joseph Tapley is not a bad specimen of the English sentimental tenor. He lacks variety, like an organ with only one stop to it, though the one stop in his case is a popular one. As a speaker Mr Tapley breaks down. Vaguely conscious of difficulties in the way, and resolute not to be beaten, he rushes impetuously at his dialogue, and cries it about the stage as if his audience were deaf or a hundred yards away. His vocal tone in speaking, too, is poor, nasal, undignified, altogether out of the question, as if it had never occurred to him that quality of sound is as important in speech as in song. If the Daly Company were still in London, I should say to him, "Go to Miss Rehan, thou sluggard [if Mr Tapley will excuse that expression—not my own]: consider her ways, and be wise." But the sequel would have been a month's study with some competent guide, by which I do not mean an elocutionist of the Wopsle school, who makes his victims give speeches from Shakespear "off the chest," nor yet a pedant under the impression that it is correct to pronounce organ as "Orr Gann." Still further is it from my mind to find a job for any gentleman who may have had the misfortune to discover the universal principle which underlies all beauty. But if Mr Tapley can find a counsellor with the knowledge of an expert in phonetics, and the feeling of an artist for beauty of sound, he will be well repaid for a little attentive study by a considerable reinforcement of his own position. What is more —and this, of course, is what I am interested in bringing about—he will raise the artistic standard for his class of work, and make an end of the notion that a young opera-singer who can get his one or two cheap ballads encored every night has nothing more to learn. Those who know how slavishly the members of provincial touring companies copy their metropolitan prototypes, and how apt the provincial amateur is to buy the touring tenor's songs and imitate his ways, also know how appallingly true it is that theatres like the Prince of Wales, the Lyric, and the Savoy are more important as centres of artistic influence than St James's Hall and Covent Garden. Mr Tapley's national responsibility as an artist, in fact, is heavier than that of Jean de Reszke. However, if Mr Tapley must be taken exception to as a singer who is no speaker, what am I to say of those colleagues of his who are speakers but no singers? The barbarities which Mr Ashley inflicts on himself and his audience in the course of his experiments as a *basso cantante* are not to be described, and hardly to be endured. Mr Monk-house's long scena, "Two years ago, you understand," is so depressing that I could not help feeling that it would have been better for me had Mr Monkhouse never been born. But this feeling gave way to one of intense gratitude when I found that he was not going to make love to the elderly canoness who disguised herself as a soldier. I had mortally feared an attempt to revive the detestable Lurcher and Priscilla business from Dorothy; and it is something to be able to say that my fears were groundless. The comic business, if it is sometimes unnecessarily silly and vulgar, is at least not odious.

Somebody has sent me a cutting from which I gather that a proposal to form a critics' club has reached the very elementary stage of being discussed in the papers in August. Now clearly a critic should not belong to a club at all. He should not know anybody: his hand should be against every man, and every man's hand against his. Artists insatiable by the richest and most frequent doses of praise; entrepreneurs greedy for advertisement; people without reputations who want to beg or buy them ready made; the rivals of the praised; the friends, relatives, partisans, and patrons of the damned: all these have their grudge against the unlucky Minos in the stalls, who is himself criticized in the most absurd fashion.

People have pointed out evidences of personal feeling in my notices as if they were accusing me of a misdemeanor, not knowing that a criticism written without personal feeling is not worth reading. It is the capacity for making good or bad art a personal matter that makes a man a critic. The artist who accounts for my disparagement by alleging personal animosity on my part is quite right: when people do less than their best, and do that less at once badly and self-complacently, I hate them, loathe them, detest them, long to tear them limb from limb and strew them in gobbets about the stage or platform. (At the Opera, the temptation to go out and ask one of the sentinels for the loan of his Martini, with a round or two of ammunition, that I might rid the earth of an incompetent conductor or a conceited and careless artist, has come upon me so strongly that I have been withheld only by my fear that, being no marksman, I might hit the wrong person and incur the guilt of slaying a meritorious singer.)

In the same way, really fine artists inspire me with the warmest personal regard, which I gratify in writing my notices without the smallest reference to such monstrous conceits as justice, impartiality, and the rest of the ideals. When my critical mood is at its height, personal feeling is not the word: it is passion: the passion for artistic perfection—for the noblest beauty of sound, sight, and action—that rages in me. Let all young artists look to it, and pay no heed to the idiots who declare that criticism should be free from personal feeling. The true critic, I repeat, is the man who becomes your personal enemy on the sole provocation of a bad performance, and will only be appeased by good performances. Now this, though well for art and for the people, means that the critics are, from the social or clubable point of view, veritable fiends. They can only fit themselves for other people's clubs by allowing themselves to be corrupted by kindly feelings foreign to the purpose of art, unless, indeed, they join Philistine clubs, wherein neither the library nor the social economy of the place will suit their nocturnal, predatory habits. If they must have a club, let them have a pandemonium of their own, furnished with all the engines of literary vivisection. But its first and most sacred rule must be the exclusion of the criticized, except those few stalwarts who regularly and publicly turn upon and criticize their critics. (No critics' club would have any right to the name unless it included—but the printer warns me that I have reached the limit of my allotted space.)

15 October 1890

AND so we inaugurate the winter season by a comic opera at the Lyric! My first comment on the performance must be that not often among upwards of two dozen artists do we see a single comparatively subordinate player, during a bare ten minutes' traffic of the stage, and without having a word to utter, all but make a three-act opera a one-part piece, and that one part his own. But no intelligent critic will deny that this feat was performed on Thursday night by the donkey in the second act. If the tenor had only had that animal's self-possession and sagacity—if the second tenor had only imitated his golden silence—if Mr Brough, welcome as he was after the tedious and unconvincing drolls who have vainly tried to fill his place these many months, could have come up to his asinine competitor in grave elderly humor, La Cigale would run half a lifetime. The audience did not disguise their longing for some more of this gifted ass. The gentleman who sat in the stall next mine rent the air with maniac screams of laughter long after it had vanished.

The fable of the Grasshopper and the Ant is, to say the least of it, somewhat extraneous to La Cigale, having, in fact, no deeper connection with it than Millais' Bubbles has with Pears' soap: consequently, the annexation of La Fontaine not only causes the action to drag heavily in the last act for the sake of interpolating a far-fetched sentimental *tableau vivant*, but causes also a certain instability of *genre* throughout the whole work, which repeatedly threatens to turn serious, and then thinks better of it. Audran's rhythms are hackneyed, his tripping melodies rather short-winded, and his relapses into threadbare waltz-tunes much too frequent; but his workmanship is smart, his orchestration vivacious, and his musical vein harmlessly abandoned, as that of a comic opera writer should be. The finale contributed by Mr Caryll would be the best dramatic number in the score if only a dash of humor could be given to the music; for though the gradations which lead to the climax are not quite satisfactorily balanced, and there are a few disappointing bits of padding in it here and there, it is, on the whole, a success. I need hardly add that Mr Caryll discharged his responsibility as conductor in the most honorable artistic spirit. The work had been rehearsed to perfection; and it was a pleasure to hear his band. Miss Geraldine Ulmar made a tremendous hit as Marton. She would not rank as a prima donna at Covent Garden (though I have heard worse artists in that position) any more than Miss St Cyr, Miss Mabel Love, and their colleagues would be classed "assoluta" at the Alhambra; still, at the Lyric, with a trifle of natural facility, well backed by good looks, one passes easily for a Cabel or a Bessone. Miss Annie Rose tried to make Mr Scovel act by acting expressively herself; but he did not know his business well enough to respond effectively—and I admit that hardly any address could have saved the absurd situation in the third act, where the dramatic scene of Bernheim's confession is cut down in its prime by the twain suddenly walking off the stage to conclude it behind the scenes. But the fact remains that the easy expertness of Messrs Eric Lewis, Lionel Brough, and E. W. Garden stood out in merciless contrast to the amateurish posturing and unscholarly diction of the two operatic gentlemen, who will both need to polish themselves very assiduously if they mean to keep their places on the London stage.

22 October 1890

IFORGET the name of the distinguished actress who said, when the Infant Roscius was carrying everything before him at the theatres, that she began to see some excuse for poor Herod after all. Whoever she was, she was a woman of sense. Threatened as we are with a revival of the pianoforte mania of last season, it was some comfort to be promised a grown-up artist like Essipoff to begin with. In her stead we were offered Master Isidore Pavia, warranted only fifteen, of "wonderful talent" and "extraordinary abilities," and withal English born, taught by English masters, and free from all taint of foreign travel. Now I admit that Master Pavia's friends are right in looking on the career of a pianist as "a life not bad for a hardy lad" in the present dearth of opportunities: my only fear is that he will prove too hardy for the business until his youthful superabundance of stamina has found a more natural vent in the cricket and football field. On Wednesday afternoon he went at the Waldstein sonata like a young avalanche, *fortissimo sempre crescendo e prestissimo sempre accellerando,* keeping his feet cleverly over the straightforward bits, staggering gamely through the syncopated passages, going head-over-heels up and down the flights of octaves, and finishing, flushed but unbeaten, after a record-breaking neck-or-nothing "reading" that would have made Rubinstein gasp and Madame Schumann faint. When he got up to make his muscular bow, straight from his shoulder, how could an audience whose battles had been won on the playing-fields of Eton refrain their applause? For my part, I am glad to see that Mr Pavia (he is really too manly to be called Master Isidore) can come in to try the strength of his youth on a higher plane than that of the athletic barbarian; but though his natural turn for music, unspoiled and unforced as it is, is a gift upon which he and his acquaintances are to be sincerely congratulated,

he has not yet developed that depth of feeling and keenness
of artistic sensibility which alone can justify even the youngest of us in coming forward at St James's Hall as an interpreter of Beethoven. As to technique, let him take the next
opportunity of studying the Liszt technique as mastered by
Sapellnikoff or Sophie Menter; or if, as is unfortunately
quite possible, his English teachers have told him that
Liszticism is mere charlatanry, he has only to hear what the
Thalberg-Kullak-Wieck school has exacted from young Mr
Borwick and gained from Madame Schumann and Madame
Backer-Gröndahl to realize that, among European experts,
he would be described as having no technique at all. In short,
Mr Pavia, like most English beginners, will have to turn his
back on his first counsellors, and abandon premature recital-
ling for some years of hard study abroad.

The appearance of young Max Hambourg at the Pavia
recital reminded me that I had not exhausted the subject of
La Cigale last week. I want to know why the manager of the
Lyric Theatre, after making a parade of his sense of social
obligation by opening the season with a performance of the
National Anthem, proceeded to fill the stage with a troop of
children under ten, whose borrowed rouge and bedizen-
ments must, behind the scenes, have presented as grim a
contrast to their own pallor and shoddy as their unhealthy
excitement and delight did to the natural play of childhood.
I warn the Lyric management and my undiscerning fellow-
critics that if these senseless child-shows be not stopped by
the friends of the theatre, they will be stopped by the theatre's
enemies, whose vigilance committees are busily collecting
evidence which may be employed not merely to establish the
beneficent sway of the factory inspector, but to substitute
for him the Puritan censor.

I defy any person to invent a valid excuse, however far-
fetched, for the presence of a single child on the stage in La
Cigale. No doubt the ladies were charmed to see the little
pets enjoy themselves as if at a splendid children's party; for
what mother will not allow her darlings to dress in their best

and sit up late at a children's party "just for once"? Unfortunately, as La Cigale promises to have a long run, it will provide a children's party not just for once, but for hundreds of consecutive nights—perhaps until the inevitable hour when the Children's Employment Act will be shorn of that convenient clause by which a magistrate can license a child exceptionally in order that Shakespear's immortal masterpiece, Richard III, may not have to be presented without a sufficiently little Duke of York, and that Ibsen's Doll's House, so popular with the cultured classes in England, may not be lost to us by legal inhibition of the three tots of Nora Helmer's nursery.

Our magistrates have cheerfully accepted that clause as an express injunction to license as many children under ten as the stage will hold. No matter how unnecessary, how incongruous, how destructive to dramatic illusion their introduction may be, they are dragged in, in a sort of frenzy of wantonness, into every pantomime, every comic opera, every ballet, every circus, every spectacular display, as desperately as if the Act bound managers, under heavy penalties, to provide theatrical employment for all applicants of tender years; so that everybody who knows anything about the history of this sort of legislation now foresees that total and unconditional prohibition of the employment of children under ten (if not under twelve) as wage-earners will follow in a year or two as certainly as the stringent Factory Act of 1853 followed the loose one of 1848. And unless that result, as far as it concerns the stage, comes as a victory of the playgoers and of the critics over the managers, it will be a victory of our modern Jeremy Colliers over the theatre.

But I see no signs of action from either pit or press. As to the critics, they are hopeless novices in such questions. I verily believe that if they knew that Factory Acts prevent a benevolent employer, under heavy penalties, from putting Morris wall-papers on the rooms where women's work is carried on, and forbid him to serve up afternoon tea to relieve the toil there, they would be shocked into a clamor for immediate repeal. I am afraid they will leave me to play Cassandra single-handed until they suddenly find all their theatres under the control of a committee of the County Council, with Mr Hugh Price Hughes in the chair, and a *police des mœurs* commanded by Mr MacDougall.

Another matter which I may as well say my say about, before the gathering rush of performances reduces me to a mere chronicler of insignificant passing events, concerns all those singers, conductors, and managers who are either bewildered or indignant because French composers, whose music they have hitherto been able to lay hands on without payment, are now politely asking whether the Berne Convention, the International Copyright Act of 1886, and the Order in Council of 1887 do not mean that in future English bands must not play their music without paying a share of the *droits d'auteur*, or, if not, what they do mean? Mind, I do not express an opinion on the point myself: that would be contempt of court, as a decision is pending. I simply wish to remind the upholders of the old system that it is doomed in any case; for if his Honor Judge Martineau finds that the Act does not protect the foreign composer, then most assuredly further legislation will. What is more, Mr Alfred Moul, to whom the Literary and Artistic Congress accorded a vote of confidence, will not be in the smallest degree discredited if the decision goes against him. I am no great admirer of our system of providing for the subsistence and encouragement of producers by giving them property rights, which cost frightful sums to maintain and never work fairly; but I am, I flatter myself, all the better qualified to point out that there is a very important distinction between the man who would abolish the property system altogether as we have done in the case of our turnpike roads and bridges—and the man who holds on to his own property rights whilst disregarding those of other people. The first is a Communist: the second is a thief. It was one thing to abolish the toll-bars on Waterloo Bridge: it was quite another to sneak under them whilst other people were paying. If communism in works of art is to be the order of the day, let us by all means agree to allow our composers a reasonable subsistence out of the Consolidated Fund, besides compounding with the foreigner for a lump sum annually (no doubt Mr Moul will be happy to arrange terms), and then make all musical compositions common property; but, pending that readjustment, let us in common honesty give composers the same rights of property in their products as we claim for ourselves. What is to be said of the impresarios who want to produce the operas of MM. Massenet and Gounod without paying either of them a farthing, and then screw the top price out of the public for admission to the performance? And why do the theatrical and musical papers sympathize quite tenderly with projects of this description; whilst they imply, as clearly as they dare, that the man who seeks to enforce the author's claims is a blackmailer, a freebooter, an encloser of commons, a blocker of rights-of-way, a spoiler of the widow and orphan of the hard-working British bandmaster who "never paid nothink to no Frenchman for playing the Soldiers' Chorus from Faust, and aint a-going to begin now"? The sober fact is that the Société des Auteurs, Compositeurs et Editeurs de Musique is as necessary an institution as Stationers' Hall; and I presume Mr Alfred Moul was entrusted with its business in England because he was known to a sufficient number of reputable persons, as he certainly was to me, not only as a business man of capacity and credit, but as a musician and a gentleman. That it does not pay the society to sell its repertory in pennyworths is no more to the point than that Messrs Fortnum & Mason refuse to sell ham by the slice, or that the musician who buys The World only to read my criticisms has nevertheless to pay for those of W. A. Theoc, Q.E.D., and the rest of my colleagues into the bargain. And yet in a report of a test action, not yet decided, brought by Mr Moul against Herr Franz Grœnings, bandmaster of the West Pier at Brighton, I find our best musical paper, apparently convinced that Moul and Mephistopheles must be aliases of the same person, describing the demand for the *droits d' auteur* as a fact that was "admitted in cross-examination." This is exactly as if W. A., to whom I mentioned that a box for Aïda was placed at my disposal the other evening, were to state in his next article that "it has been elicited from the musical critic of The World that he made his way into Covent Garden Theatre without paying." I cannot believe that the critics and writers who have allowed themselves to be misled by the moans of their friends in the profession and the publishing trade can have ever given ten minutes' serious thought to the economic and social bearings of the copyright question. As soon as they do they will tell their indignant correspondents to pay and look pleasant, lest the Act of 1886 be amended by a more stringent one, which the French composers will be able to enforce without any of the timidity they evidently feel at present. In any case, I shall be able to say "I told you so," which is one of the chief joys of a wise man's declining years.

P.S.—I was present at the opening of Signor Lago's opera season on Saturday, but I prefer to wait and watch for another week before committing myself to an opinion. Besides, Sunday is hardly the day for one or two of the remarks I shall have to make on the treatment poor Verdi received from his compatriot Bevignani.

29 October 1890

SIGNOR LAGO'S enterprise at Covent Garden looked unpromising on the first night. The opera was Aïda: but the artists were nervous and unwelcomed; the dresses misfitted horribly; the chorus of Egyptian priests looked more like a string of sandwich-men than ever; the carpenters' department was so short-handed that the audience whistled "We wont go home till morning" and the Marseillaise whilst the last scene was being built; and there was a perfect plague of interruption from a contingent of Italians, who insisted on shouting *Brava*, and drowning the orchestral endings of all the songs by premature applause, in spite of smouldering British indignation. And Bevignani, as I hinted last week, did no more for Verdi than barely keeping the band and the singers together. In vain such written entreaties as $p\,p\,p\,p\,p$, "estremamente piano," and the like appealed to him from the score: the bluff mezzoforte never varied two degrees the whole evening. For crescendos we had undignified little hurry-scurries of accelerandos; and for the deep rich flood of harmony, which should sometimes make itself felt rather than heard through the silence, and sometimes suffuse everything with its splendor, we had shallow, blaring street-music and prosaic mezzoforte as aforesaid. Once or twice the real Verdi color glowed for a moment through the fog: for instance, in the accompaniment for three flutes in the fourth act; but that was due solely to the initiative of the players. When the conductor's guidance was needed, as it was very conspicuously by the gentleman who played the obbligato to Gia i sacerdoti adunanzi on a saxophone, and who quite missed the pathetic dignity of its tragic measure, the conductor galloped placidly after him as if the saxophone were doing all that could reasonably be expected of it. As to the majestic but tremendously grave and self-contained address of the captive Ethiopian King to his Egyptian conqueror, I turn in despair from Bevignani to Galassi, and ask him to consider the words—to listen for a moment to the music —and then to say whether he really considers that Verdi intended Amonasro to behave like a bedlamite Christy Minstrel. When one remembers Faccio and the Scala orchestra, it is hard to have to go back to the drum-slammings and blarings and rantings of the bad old times, which can only be mended now by their survivors, Signori Bevignani and Galassi among others, taking warning by the bankruptcy in which they ended. I hoped that fairer treatment might have awaited Il Trovatore; but I am afraid I shall appear smitten with Bevignanophobia if I dwell on what actually occurred. Whether the conductor had made a bet that he would get through the opera in the shortest time on record or not, I do not know: certain it is that the concerted music was taken at a speed which made all artistic elaboration, all

point, all self-possession, even bare accuracy, impossible.
Bevignani only drew rein once, and that was when, at the
end of the first scene of the second act, his eye suddenly
caught the word *velocissimo* in the score. At first the slipping,
scrambling, and bewilderment of the artists amused me;
then I became indignant; and at last the continual jarring
and baulking got on my nerves, so that I fled, exhausted and
out of temper. But for the relief afforded by the solos, during
which the band followed the singers, I should not have held
out so long. And I need hardly add that the burden of my
grumbling as I went home was that it is all very well to
appeal to the critics to encourage cheap opera, but that
opera without artistic interpretation is dear at any price,
and will soon drive the eighteenpenny god back to the
Lyric, where Audran as handled by Mr Caryll seems a great
composer in comparison with Verdi as handled by Bevignani,
who should really devote himself for the future to English
oratorio.

On Monday night there was a vast improvement. Arditi,
as alert as the youngest man in the band, and, what is more,
quite as anxious, conducted Les Huguenots, which only
needs a little better stage-management to be as presentable
as it is in the summer season. For instance, when Marcel
enters in the Pré aux Clercs scene, and the Catholics insist
that he shall take off his hat, whilst the Huguenot soldiers
maintain that he is right to keep it on, it is hardly reasonable
in the Catholics to remain covered whilst the soldiers carefully take off their helmets, under a vague impression that
somebody ought to do something of the sort. I am no bigot,
and have never complained of the Catholics first joining in
the Rataplan Chorus, with its gibes at "i Papisti," and then
returning to the bosom of their church for the Ave Maria.
Still I do not think that these things should be done when
there is no musical gain thereby. Perhaps I am inconsistent;
but it is odd how one strains at a gnat and swallows a camel
at Covent Garden. In Il Trovatore, for instance, it seemed
quite natural to me that a horde of bloodthirsty feudal re-

tainers should break into a convent-yard without causing
the assembled nuns to exhibit the faintest concern; because,
after all, the thing occurs every season. But when the gipsy
blacksmiths the other night deposited a glowing bar with its
red-hot end on a wooden chair, where it lay during the rest
of the act without either cooling itself or damaging the furniture, I could not help feeling that the illusion of the scene
was gone.

On the pecuniary prospects of Signor Lago's enterprise
I have only to say that if it fails, the failure will be due to the
superstition that the primary function of Italian opera is to
provide a means of passing the evening for a clique of dead-
heads in evening dress. The Covent Garden house is a vast
auditorium to which hosts of people would willingly pay
from two to five shillings a head to be admitted. But these
persons would drive out the deadhead, and cause his stalls
and boxes to be replaced by plebeian chairs or even benches.
On the other hand, ten "commercial gents," each with his
missis or young woman, at two shillings a head, would bring
in £2 solid cash (*non olet!*) into the treasury; whereas the one
languid deadhead, who keeps them out at present, brings
nothing. As to that crows' nest in the roof, where you can
now swelter and look at the crowns of the performers' hats
for eighteenpence, that is not cheap: it would be dear at a
shilling: sixpence is the proper price for such a place. It
seems to me that Signor Lago, like all his forerunners in this
direction, is trying to sit down between two stools. A cheap
imitation of the regular fashionable season is impossible.
It never pays to charge exclusive prices except when the
West End guarantees the inevitable loss for the sake of the
exclusiveness. Let me clinch the argument with one statistical fact. Only thirty-nine out of every thousand of us die
worth as much as £300, including the value of every stick
and shred we possess. The moment you propose to do without the West End subsidy this fact forces you back to Drury
Lane prices, no matter what the "traditions" of your entertainment may be.

Signor Lago's vocal artists are by no means ill selected. If he were as lucky in his stage-managers and conductors as in his singers, his performances would be rather better all round than three out of four of last season's subscription nights. Perotti is a vigorous and intelligent tenor, prompt and to the point with his stage business to a degree which contrasts very favorably with Jean de Reszke's exasperating unpunctuality and irresolution, and gifted with ringing high notes of genuine tenor quality. And if he would but reconsider his pink-and-white make-up, and tone down the terrible smile with which he expresses amorous sentiments, he would escape those incongruous reminiscences of the ballet which one or two passages of his Raoul evoked. Giannini is unsuited to heroic parts, much as Mr Tupman was unsuited to the costume of a bandit. He can shout high notes without wobbling; but he has so far shewn absolutely no other qualification for his eminent position. The sisters Giulia and Sofia Ravogli are two children of nature who have, by dint of genuine feeling for their art, contrived to teach themselves a great deal; but their Tuscan is full of nasal and throaty intonations abhorred of the grand school; and they indulge in unheard-of *naïvetés* (especially Giulia— Sofia has more *savoir faire*) when they come out of their parts to acknowledge applause, which they are apt to do at the most absurd moments. Further, they trust to luck rather than to skill for getting over florid difficulties; and their metrical sense is particularly untrained: they hardly ever sing a scale with the accents on the right notes. Giulia, the worse offender in this respect also, sang Strida la vampa as if every two bars of the three-eight time were one bar of common time. These are matters, fortunately, admitting of remedy. The main point is that Giulia thinks out her parts for herself and acts them courageously and successfully. Her Azucena was a striking performance, though I advise her to give up such little originalities, new but not true, as frankly presenting herself as a fine young contadina of eighteen, and laughing ironically as she repeats, "Strana pieta! Strana pieta!" Her voice is an ample mezzo-soprano, a little hollow and disappointing in the lower registers, where one expects the tone to be rich, but sympathetic all over, and very free and effective at the top. Sofia is a soprano, with much less spontaneity of utterance and dramatic expression, though she, too, feels her business strongly. Her voice, too, is smaller: indeed, it is hardly enough, used as she uses it, for so large a theatre. She was nervous in Aïda and over-weighted in Trovatore; so that she cannot be said to have done much more than hold her own; whereas her sister has made a decided success. Madame Stromfeld, who appeared as Marguerite de Valois in Les Huguenots, is blonde, plump, and over thirty. She has a phenomenal range upward, and is apparently a highly cultivated musician and experienced singer. It is a pity to have to add that the freshness of the voice is gone, except at the top, where some of the more impossible notes are remarkably brilliant. Mlle Maria Peri, aided by youth, screamed her way through Valentina, barely holding the C in the duet with Marcel for half its appointed duration, and occasionally forcing her chest register up to middle A, a fourth higher than she can afford, if she wishes to keep her voice. And here I must drop the Opera for this week, as I have other matters to record.

Sarasate, set up by the autumn holiday, left all criticism behind him at his first concert on Saturday week. He also left Mr Cusins behind by half a bar or so all through the two concertos, the unpremeditated effects of syncopation resulting therefrom being more curious than delectable. Bertha Marx gave a recital on Thursday. It was very brilliant, and brilliant in a sympathetic way; but O, Miss Bertha, if you would only mix just a little thought with the feeling now and then! Essipoff gave her first concert at Steinway Hall on the same evening. I see that Mr Kappey is going to give a lecture today (Tuesday) at the Chelsea Town Hall on military music. I hope he will, with Colonel Shaw-Hellier's assistance, succeed in wakening people up to the importance of having plenty of good wind bands among us. That is the

sort of music that really attracts the average Briton to take
up an instrument himself.

5 November 1890

ICANNOT say that the Covent Garden repertory has
been reinforced by La Gioconda, a mere instance of the
mischief which great men bring upon the world when
small men begin to worship them. Shakespear set all the
dramatic talent in England wasting itself for centuries on
bombast and blank verse; Michael Angelo plunged Italian
painting into an abyss of nakedness and foreshortening.
Handel plagued our serious music with a horrible murrain
of oratorio; Ibsen will no doubt open up the stage to all the
Pecksniffery and Tartuffery in Europe with his didactic
plays; and Verdi is tempting many a born quadrille composer of the South to wrestle ineffectually and ridiculously
with Shakespear and Victor Hugo.

To me, the kinship between La Gioconda and Ernani or
Rigoletto is hardly closer than that between Vortigern and
Macbeth; and I feel as comfortably superior to the critics
and musicians who cannot see much difference between
Ponchielli and Verdi as I do to those who could not see any
at all between the boyish forger Ireland and Shakespear. It
would have been kinder, even when Ponchielli was alive, to
tell him frankly that all his strainings at the bow of Ulysses
were not bending it one inch—that Donizetti's Lucrezia
and even Marchetti's Ruy Blas are better than his far more
elaborate and ambitious setting of Angelo. The choruses
and ballets in La Gioconda sound well: but they would
sound equally well and be more congruously placed among
the strings of Chinese lanterns at the French Exhibition. As
for the dramatic music, it is conventional, short-winded, full
of used-up phrases thinly disguised by modulations that
are getting staler and staler every year, and will soon stir
nobody's pulse; whilst the orchestration is invented rather
than musically imagined, and therefore, like much of the
harmony, remains absolutely inorganic; so that if the score

were to be lost, and someone—say Mancinelli—had to re-construct it from the voice parts alone, with the first violin copy thrown in, there is not the slightest reason to suppose that the result would be any worse than the original. Indeed, as Mancinelli writes for the orchestra better than Ponchielli did, it would most likely be better.

Imagine the effect of such an experiment on a work of Verdi's, or Gounod's, or Meyerbeer's, not to mention the inconceivable case of one by Wagner! Perhaps it is a providentially appointed compensation for the Ponchiellis, Ambroise Thomases, Drs Blank, and Professors Dash that their works need never be lost whilst any fragments of them remain. It is not from any wish to bear hardly on these gentlemen that I offer such observations; but I cannot forget that the enormous expenditure involved by operatic performances makes it imperative that we should insist on getting the best value for our money, which is hardly to be done by shelving the works of the great masters to make room for undesired resuscitations of Giocondas, Hamlets, and the like.

Having thus conveyed my opinion that La Gioconda was not worth doing, I am free to add that it might have been worse done. Miss Damian's début in opera was successful. She plays upon one string only, and that one is no *chanterelle;* but its tone is free and penetrating, a little lacking in color perhaps, but still capable of considerable intensity of expression. Suane, the tenor *à la* Gayarré without which no opera company is now complete, is thoroughly in earnest about his work, and shews much artistic feeling as a singer and actor. Those notes of his which are steady enough to have any recognizable pitch are by no means unmusical. But he is so afflicted with goat-bleat (*vibrato* is all nonsense—quite a different thing) that the house loses patience with him.

One lady, describing his Edgardo to me, averred that if he had sung the part of Faust to the accompaniments of Lucia, it could have made no difference in the effect, as it

would have been impossible to say what notes he was singing in any case. I think the lady was a little too hard on
Suane; but he would do well to take the criticism to heart; for
no tenor will ever conquer England if he cannot keep his voice
from splitting twenty times in every second. Let him listen
to Patti singing Home, Sweet Home, or to Sarasate playing an adagio, and ask himself whether they could improve
the effect by making the notes wobble. This much, however,
I will say: Suane's Gayarré wobble is not so bad as Peri's
"dramatic" wobble, which is one of the crudest Italian vulgarities, and should never be heard in Covent Garden. Giulia
Ravogli and Fiegna were unable to do much with their parts,
which are as cheap as even dramatic music can be made in
Italy. The *forlana* was the best thing yet done by the *corps de
ballet*, headed by Miss Loveday and Miss Smiles, one of
whom is, I suspect, only a step-dancer promoted from the
music-hall, whilst the other, though no great artist, comes
off with credit. Under these circumstances I am sorry that I
have not the remotest idea of which is Miss Loveday and
which Miss Smiles. For the Dance of the Hours Signor Lago
wisely called in Madame Katti Lanner, who brought twenty-
four of her pupils, and was, as usual, immensely equal to
the occasion. The work had been fairly rehearsed; and
Bevignani was good enough this time to give it a fair chance.

I hear that Meyerbeer's Robert the Devil, with Miss
Moody and Mr Manners in the cast, as well as Perotti and
Mlle Stromfeld, drew a full house on Saturday week; but
I was not in London that evening. Of La Traviata, which
served for Madame Albani's entry on Thursday, I also hear
encouraging accounts. I was in my stall punctually enough;
but the stall was in the St James's Theatre. That, however,
need not prevent me from giving a perfectly accurate description and sound criticism of Albani's Violetta, if I run
short of matter lower down the column.

Master Brahm Van den Berg is the latest infant pianist.
He is nearly as big as Pavia; but he dresses for his part in a
white sailor costume which would not be out of place in a

kindergarten. A hoop and a toy-gun, with a gushing lady confederate in the room to hand him a box of bonbons at the end, would have made the illusion complete. If I were Brahm's age, and could play as well, I would buy a tailed coat, and assert myself as a man in the teeth of parents and agents. All this infantile tomfoolery may amuse the ladies who support afternoon recitals in such hosts; but it puts me out of humor, and turns me crusty when I ought to be specially considerate. Young Van den Berg has a capital technique of the Brussels Conservatoire type, made familiar to us by such pianists as De Greef. Ambidexterity apart, he is not an extraordinary player. Essipoff, who is giving concerts at Steinway Hall, now has a rival in the first rank in the person of Paderewski, who on Saturday played Schumann's concerto at the Crystal Palace. And a very fine performance it seemed, coming so soon after Sophie Menter's reckless and unsympathetic onslaught last April on this most sensitive of concertos. Not a single point was missed throughout: Paderewski varied his touch and treatment with the clearest artistic intelligence for every mood and phase of the work, which could not have been more exhaustively interpreted. In the orchestra the great ebullition before the cadenza in the first movement was worked up magnificently, and Mr Manns did not conceal his delight at a success so perfectly after his own heart. It certainly was a concert of which he had every reason to feel proud.

The two volumes of Schumann's Letters, just issued by Bentley and translated by May Herbert, ought to be a fearful warning to critics and those who believe in critics. I once heard William Morris, on being suddenly asked why Haydon shot himself, reply promptly, "Because he found himself out." If I am ever asked why Schumann killed himself, I shall steal that pithy explanation. His case was more tragic than Haydon's, because it is not easy to believe that Haydon, even had he started with all possible enlightenment from without as to the true nature of art, would ever have succeeded in drawing a beautiful line or laying a square inch of

71

lovely color; but Schumann was a genuine artist before his restless intellect made him a quack and a pedant.

In these letters we find him again and again recommending some nostrum or another to young musicians—"pure four-part harmony," doses of Bach, and what not—or picking out trivial technical points from the scores of his composer friends, and gushing about them in the style of an analytical program. On the very next page he will be desperately trying to explain away the fact that the modern works which move him most also violate all his patent methods. He "analyses" a score of Wagner's, and immediately describes it to Mendelssohn as by a man who cannot write four bars that are melodious or even correct. There are consecutive fifths and octaves in it: Wagner lacks capacity for pure harmony and four-part choral composition: no permanent good can come from such a state of things. Then he goes to the theatre to *hear* the music whilst looking at the stage, and at once admits that he must retract; that he is impressed; that there is much that is deep and original in the work. Yet he learns nothing from this failure: the next time he delivers his opinion he explains as carefully as ever that though Wagner's music produces emotion, and has a mysterious charm that captivates the senses, yet it is demonstrably poor, repulsive, amateurish, and meaningless, because Wagner is "not a good musician," and lacks feeling for form and harmony.

Again, when a fine piece of poetry rouses the artist in him, he promptly sits down and writes to the author, asking him, not for a poem to set, but for something that can be finished up with a double chorus, because Handel has shewn in Israel in Egypt that double choruses are an infallible recipe for sublimity. Decidedly, if ever I write Advice to Young Musicians, the first precept in it will be, Dont take Schumann's. Indeed, the beginning and end of it will be, Dont take anybody's; for I had as soon wear another man's hat as take his advice, whatever other use I might find for it.

IS Gluck, the conqueror of Paris, at last going to conquer London? I hope so; for the man was a great master, one for whom we are hardly ready even yet. Hitherto our plan of sweeping together a sackful of opera-singers from Milan, Vienna, Monte Video, Chicago, Clapham, China, and Peru, and emptying them on to the Covent Garden stage to tumble through Trovatore or Traviata as best they can, has not succeeded with Gluck. This Orfeo, for instance! Anyone can see before the curtain is half-a-minute up that it grew by the introduction of vocal music, not into chaos, but into an elaborate existing organization of ballet. The opening chorus, S' in questo bosco, sounds nobly to people who are looking at groups of figures in poetic motion or eloquent pose, at draperies falling in graceful lines and flowing in harmonious colors, and at scenery binding the whole into a complete and single picture.

Under such circumstances, our old friend Monseigneur of the Œil de Bœuf, when he had a taste that way, no doubt enjoyed himself. But when we, to wit, Smith and Jones, with our suburban traditions, going to the Opera full of that sense of unaccustomed adventure which the fine arts give us, are dumfounded by the spectacle of our old original choristers appealing with every feature and limb against the unreasonableness of asking them to look like classical shepherds and shepherdesses—when their desperate Theocritean weeds have the promiscuity of Rag Fair without its picturesqueness—when even Katti Lanner's young ladies move awkwardly and uncertainly, put out of step by these long-drawn elegiac strains—when the scene suggests Wimbledon on a cold day, and Euridice's tomb is something between a Druidic cromlech and a milestone, bearing the name of the deceased in the tallest advertising stencil—then it must be confessed that S' in questo bosco affects its new acquaintances far from cheerfully.

These drawbacks were in full force at Covent Garden

last Wednesday; but Orfeo triumphed in spite of them. Gluck and Giulia Ravogli were too many even for the shabby sofa, apparently borrowed from a decayed seaside lodging, which was shamelessly placed in the middle of the stage, just outside the mouth of Hades, for Euridice to die conveniently on. It was the stage-manager's last insult; and when it failed, he collected all his forces behind the scenes and set them talking at the top of their voices, so as to drown the singing and distract the attention of the audience. What a thing it is to live in the richest capital in the world, and yet have to take your grand opera, at its largest and most expensive theatre, with the makeshifts and absurdities of the barn and the booth! And to add to the exasperation of it, you are kept waiting longer between the acts for the dumping down of this miserable sofa on the bare boards than would be required for the setting of the most elaborate stage-picture at the Lyceum or Drury Lane.

I am not sure that Gluck is not in a better way to be understood now than he has been any time since the French Revolution. Listening to the strains in the Elysian Fields the other night, I could not help feeling that music had strayed far away from them, and only regained them the other day when Wagner wrote the Good Friday music in Parsifal. No musical experience in the journey between these two havens of rest seems better than either. The Zauberflöte and the Ninth Symphony have a discomforting consciousness of virtue, and uphill effort of aspiration, about them; but in the Elysian Fields, in the Good Friday meadows, virtue and effort are transcended: there is no need to be good or to strive upward any more: one has arrived, and all those accursed hygienics of the soul are done with and forgotten. Not that they were without a priggish ecstasy of their own: I am far from denying that. Virtue, like vice, has its attractions. It was well worth while to slip through the Elysian hedge into the domain of Klingsor, and be shewn the enchantments of his magic gardens by Weber, plunged into his struggles and hopes by Beethoven, introduced to polite

74

society in his castle drawing room by Mendelssohn, besides being led by Mozart through many unforgettable episodes of comedy and romance—episodes producing no bitter reaction like that which was apt to follow the scenes of tragic passion or rapturous sentimentality which Meyerbeer, Verdi, and Gounod managed so well for Klingsor. I do not forget these for a moment; and yet I am glad to be in the Elysian Fields again. And it is because I have also been in the Good Friday meadows that I can now see, more clearly than anyone could before Parsifal, how exactly Gluck was the Wagner of his day—a thing that would have been violently disputed by Berlioz, who was, nevertheless, almost as good a critic as I. Listen to Orfeo, and you hear that perfect union of the poem and the music—that growth of every musical form, melodic interval, harmonic progression, and orchestral tone out of some feeling or purpose belonging to the drama—which you have only heard before in the cantatas of Bach and the music dramas of Wagner. Instead of the mere opera-making musician, tied to his poem as to a stake, and breaking loose whenever it gives him an excuse for a soldiers' chorus, or a waltz, or a crashing finale, we have the poet-musician who has no lower use for music than the expression of poetry.

Though it is easy to see all this in Orfeo during such numbers as Che faro? it might not have been so apparent last Wednesday in the ballet-music, although that never loses its poetic character, but for Giulia Ravogli, about whom I now confess myself infatuated. It is no longer anything to me that her diction is not always so pure as Salvini's, that her roulade is inferior in certainty and spontaneity to Signor Foli's, that the dress in which I first saw her as Amneris ought to have had ever so many yards more stuff in the train, that she would not put on the grey eyebrows and wrinkles of Azucena, and even that she is capable of coming out of a stage faint to bow to the applause it evokes. Ah, that heart-searching pantomime, saturated with feeling beyond all possibility of shortcoming in grace, as Orfeo came into those Elysian Fields, and stole from shade to shade, trying to identify by his sense of touch the one whom he was forbidden to seek with his eyes! Flagrant ballet-girls all those shades were; but it did not matter: Giulia awakened in us the power by which a child sees a living being in its rag doll. Even the *première danseuse* was transfigured to a possible Euridice as Giulia's hand, trembling with a restrained caress, passed over her eyes! And then the entry into Hades, the passionate pleading with the Furies, and, later on, the eloquence of the famous aria in the last act! I was hardly surprised, though I was alarmed, to see a gentleman in a stage-box, with frenzy in his eye, seize a substantial-looking bouquet and hurl it straight at her head, which would probably have been removed from her shoulders had not the missile fallen some yards short of its mark. Her success was immense. Nobody noticed that there were only two other solo-singers in the whole opera, both less than nothing beside her. She—and Gluck—sufficed. In the singer, as in the composer, we saw a perfectly original artistic impulse naïvely finding its way to the heart of the most artificial and complex of art forms.

Of the performance generally I have little to say. I intended to remonstrate about the Meyerbeerian cadenza which sounded so incongruously at the end of the first act; but I leave the remonstrance unspoken: Guilia shall do what she pleases, even if her next whim be to receive Eros in the first act with a strophe of L'Armour, ce dieu profane. But I submit as a matter for Bevignani's consideration—whilst acknowledging the care and thoroughness with which he has rehearsed the work—that the chorus Che mai dell' Erebo is hopeless at Covent Garden as an *andante*. His motley forces are utterly incapable of the Titanic tread with which this giant measure should march—"*ben marcato*," each crotchet a bar in itself. Under the circumstances it would be better to take it at exactly the same speed, and with the same strength and precision of accent, as the first movement of the Eroica Symphony. At this rate the groups of three *sforzandos* for the basses would sound like three gruff, fierce barks from the three-headed dog at the gate of hell (which is what Gluck intended), whereas at present they only suggest that Orpheus is a stout sluggish gentleman, giving his boots three careful scrapes outside the door *pour se décrotter.*

I will not chide Katti Lanner's maidens for being no more able than the chorus to move as gods to the noble measures of Gluck, which baffled "the many twinkling feet" even in the times of the old order in France, when the grand school was much grander than it is now. The tone from the strings in the orchestra left a good deal to be desired: it was sometimes weak and whining, and sometimes rough and obstreperous, never pure and dignified. Fewer instruments and finer playing would have produced a much greater effect. More justice was done to the scoring for the wind, which, far from growing old-fashioned, only becomes more admirable by the light of recent developments in orchestration. The oboes, of course, occasionally found it impossible to double the violin parts; but this mere *ripieno* function is no longer necessary or desirable, and the remark is only interesting as a technical record. On the whole, I must congratulate Signor Lago on a performance which gave me more pleasure than any I have tried this year. Maurel, by the bye, has arrived, and has begun his campaign by making a speech on the art of operatic singing. I shall have a word to say on his views when he delivers himself into my hands as Rigoletto next week.

Señor Albéniz, at his first concert at St. James's Hall last Friday, got together not only a good band, led by Hollander, and recruited from the Crystal Palace and Richter orchestras, but also brought into the field a new conductor, one Tomas Breton, born at Salamanca forty years ago, who at once shewed himself able to make our men do their best. Unfortunately the program was insanely long, containing practically three concertos, six orchestral movements, and a symphony by the conductor—an ingeniously horrible work, lasting forty-five minutes, full of what the program glozingly called syncopations, but which were in fact Procrustean torturings of two-four themes into three-four time. The programist further remarked, of the slow movement, that "there is just here a good deal of polyphony for the careful ear to distinguish." As if people went to concerts to sit carefully distinguishing polyphony! The whole affair, it appears, was only a *tour de force* in the style of Beethoven, produced by the composer as an exercise in his student days. It is as a capable conductor that I welcome Señor Breton; for we are at our wits' end here for men able to get first-rate work out of our bands, whereas we can all write symphonies. Albéniz was monotonously pretty in Mozart's Concerto in D major, playing without warmth, vigor, or variety of treatment. Then he tackled Schumann, but hardly did more than supply the orchestra with a very sweet and dainty accompaniment. In his solos he played some compositions of his own with his usual skill and charm.

19 November 1890

AS a rule, a musician in London, when he has had enough of chamber music from the Neruda quartet, cannot spend his Saturday afternoon better than at the Crystal Palace concert, if he can afford the six or seven shillings which the expedition costs. But he should take heed lest he stumble on one of those penitentiary Saturdays when they get Mr Edward Lloyd down, and turn on Mendelssohn; for then the land brings forth the oratorio public, who swarm over the room with Novello scores in all their borders. The orchestra, too, becomes a precipitous landslip of choristers, slanting up to the ceiling as if they had been conveyed in four cartloads of soprano, alto, tenor, and bass to the brink of the organ gallery, and successively tipped over into the abyss beneath. They shove the violins out on to the platforms, and squeeze the basses into the middle of the orchestras, where there is hardly room for a man's elbows, besides insulting the brass and drums for making a deafening noise in their ears. And they sing so woodenly that if the

78

very benches were to cry out—and I sometimes wonder that
they dont—the tone of that cry could not be more ligneous.
Had oratorio been invented in Dante's time, the seventh
circle in his Inferno would have been simply a magnified
Albert Hall, with millions of British choristers stolidly singing, All that hath life and breath, sing to the Lord, in the
galleries, and the condemned, kept awake by demons, in the
arena, clothed in evening dress.

It was on one of these dismal Saturdays that I went to
Sydenham to hear Madame Schmidt-Köhne, of the Royal
Opera, Berlin. She patriotically sang a song of Mozart's at
the Berlin pitch, whilst the orchestra accompanied her at
that of the Crystal Palace organ; so that really, as far as the
effect was concerned, she might almost as well have sung
out of tune. Then, after a few snatches of harvest tunes
worked up into a heavy overture by Grieg, and a "new tone-
picture" by Mr Cliffe, which contained nothing that was
new to me, we fell to at the Lobgesang, and sat out that
dreadful dreary symphony in the sure hope of attaining a
condition in which Watchman, will the night soon pass?
would exactly express our feelings. But in my opinion the
game was not worth the candle. I am for cutting out the symphony and the first four numbers *en bloc* (there is no need to
wait for the last three when the Lobgesang is at the end of
the program). The rhetoric of the programatical analyst
cannot much longer hypnotize people into imagining
that Mendelssohn succeeded in making a great symphony
out of materials barely sufficient for a sentimental pianoforte piece, by merely stretching them on the orchestral
rack. That abominable platitude for the trombones with
which the thing begins, and which is never dropped until
you are bored and worried out of your senses by it, will be
cited in times to come as a conclusive proof that there must
have been a pseudo-Mendelssohn: they will not believe
that the composer of Fingal and the Midsummer Night's
Dream music could possibly have perpetrated the Lobgesang.

79

There is an old story to the effect that the first time the symphony was rehearsed the trombone-player desperately tried to convert this platitude into music by introducing a *gruppetto*. The criticism was lost on Mendelssohn, who, deeply scandalized, sat upon the trombonist; and the story is now always told as instancing the severity and superiority of the composer's taste. As the man was perfectly right, I am glad to take this opportunity of doing him tardy justice in the matter. The truth is that the symphony would have been weak under any circumstances; but coming as it did after Beethoven's Ninth Symphony, it was inexcusable. As to following it up by going to the Albert Hall on Wednesday to hear Elijah, I would rather have died.

When I got to the Opera on Monday week, I found a troop of people coming out in the worst of tempers. Maurel was indisposed, and had retired in favor of Galassi, whose Rigoletto is not exactly a novelty. I stuck manfully to my post for half-an-hour or so to hear Dimitresco, the new tenor, who, without conspicuous qualities or conspicuous faults, sings acceptably in a style which is none the worse for owing something to the drawing room as well as to the theatre. After Questa e quella I left Rigoletto for the Monday Popular Concert, where I heard the last few bars of Paderewski's Schumann solo, and a trio by Rubinstein which made me wish myself back at Covent Garden. Paderewski's recital on Wednesday was much more entertaining, though there was certainly plenty to complain of. For instance, instead of giving us a poetic interpretation of the trio in Chopin's Funeral March, he used it in the most barefaced manner solely to shew how much tone he could get with one finger. Again, he threw himself so violently into Liszt's Erlkönig transcription that he not only made mere rampagious melodrama of it, swamping all the finer distinctions between the plaintive appeals of the terrified child, the grave reassurances of the anxious father, and the wanton fairy music of the Erl King, but actually came to grief manually at one point. Every piece in the program suffered more or less from a hurricane of superfluous energy which Paderewski will later on learn to use to the last inch, instead of letting half of it run to waste with a distracting roar through the safety-valve. He finished his recital by the Don Juan fantasia of Liszt, a work too composite to be described in a single phrase. In so far as it is a transcription it is only spoiled Mozart. As a set of variations it is redundant and over-elaborated. But as a fantasia it has some memorable points. When you hear the terrible progressions of the statue's invitation suddenly echoing through the harmonies accompanying Juan's seductive Andiam, andiam, mio bene, you cannot help accepting it as a stroke of genius—that is, if you know your Don Giovanni *au fond*. And the riotous ecstasy of Finch' han dal vino is translated from song into symphony, from the individual to the abstract, with undeniable insight and power in the finale, which Paderewski carried through triumphantly. If he plays it again—and he might do worse—I hope he will not put it at the end of the program, lest other duties should prevent me from waiting to hear it.

Maurel's Rigoletto, which came off in earnest on Thursday, will stand with Giulia Ravogli's Orfeo among the glories of Signor Lago's management. It utterly effaced Lassalle's heavy, stilted, egotistic, insincere attempt of last season. An operatic tragedian may be easily overrated at a period like the present, when it is still possible to follow a whole season attentively without meeting with any convincing evidence of even a superficial knowledge of the stories told in the operas on the part of singer, stage-manager, scene-painter, or anyone else in the house except those members of the public who bewilder themselves by referring to one-and-sixpenny books, containing an Italian and an English version, differing almost as widely from one another as from the stage version. Therefore, if I were to say that Maurel is a great actor among opera-singers, he might well retort, "Thank you for nothing: in the country of the blind the one-eyed is king." So I will put it in this way—that his Rigoletto is as good a piece of acting as Edwin Booth's Triboulet; whilst the impression it makes is deeper, and the pleasure it gives greater, by just so much as Verdi is a greater man than Tom Taylor, which is saying a good deal.

As to his singing, he does more with that French method which all baritones copied from Faure twenty years ago than I ever thought possible; and though he blurs the outline of the melody, and often, instead of striking the exact pitch of an E or an F, drags his voice laboriously up to just a hair's breadth under it, he has a remarkable command of the sort of vocal effects he aims at. If they are not the effects that please me best, yet I am not going to prove that they are "wrong" in the manner of a disciple of Maclise criticizing Monet or Monticelli.

Mlle Stromfeld's Gilda changed my opinion of her for the worse. When I heard her for the first time, as Marguerite de Valois, I confess I took her for an old hand, and a very clever one, making the most of a worn-out voice. I now perceive that her voice has never had a chance, and that her master, whoever he may be, has turned out, not a singer, but only an exponent of his method, which is, like most methods, a very bad one. Instead of teaching her to produce her voice freely, and leaving her to place it here or there according to the dictates of her instinct for musical beauty or dramatic expression, he has evidently proceeded on the theory that the voice "ought" to be placed just behind the upper teeth, and has not taught her to produce it at all. The result is that Mlle Stromfeld, in her constant effort (with which her whole artistic nature is at war) to pin every note to her hard palate, squeezes her throat and frays all the middle of her voice threadbare. Of what use was it to be able to finish Un di si ben with a high C that cut through the house like a knife, when she could not accurately pitch the preliminary G, which any soprano in the chorus could have managed without trouble?

Though this be method, yet there is madness in it. I am sorry to have to say these hard things; but if I refrain, what

will happen? Why, a dozen young ladies who read this
column, concluding that Mlle Stromfeld is an exemplary
singer, will find out who taught her; go to him or his pupils
for lessons; and be sacrificed to his views on the subject of
the hard palate. That, among other things, is what comes of
the "kindly" criticism which sees good in everything. I prefer to see sermons in stones—and to throw them. Let me
therefore add, before dismissing Rigoletto, that no human
quartet could have made anything of Un di si ben as Bevignani conducted it; and that though Dimitresco no doubt
honestly thought that he was singing La donna e mobile in
B natural at its final reprise behind the scenes, he actually
sang it in B flat and a quarter, the audience writhing with
anguish meanwhile.

Students of that curious disease, pianomania, which fills
St James's Hall with young ladies every afternoon during
the season, and puts countless sums into the pockets of
teaching virtuosos, will find such a treat in Bettina Walker's
My Musical Experiences, just published by Bentley, as
they have not enjoyed since Miss Fay's Music Study in
Germany. Miss Walker, like Miss Fay, went to Liszt, and,
on finding that he had no patent process for turning out
great players, went to Deppe, who had discovered that ar-
canum. Then she hurried—rather inconsequently—on to
Henselt, of whom she gives an interesting account. It is easy
to see that Miss Walker's impression of Henselt (giving a
lesson in Si oiseau j'étais) as "rising up in all his greatness—
suggesting to me a city rising by enchantment out of the
dust of ages," is as purely hypnotic in its origin as Miss Fay's
estimate of Liszt as "a two-edged sword." And to think
that of all those wonderful young fellow-students, with such
mysterious fascinations in their eyes and manners, who were
so sure to be Menters and Rubinsteins in ten years, more
than ninety-nine per cent must have been dowdy hobblede-
hoys and hobbledehoydens who will spend their lives as
obscure organists, casual accompanists, suburban teachers,
quadrille conductors, or high-school teachers getting up

performances of the overture to Zampa on six pianos for prize-day! Still the books are none the less worth reading —perhaps all the better—especially if you know how much of them to take seriously.

26 November 1890

THERE are few things more terrible to a seasoned musician than a miscellaneous concert. A ballad concert, a symphony concert, a pianoforte recital: all these are welcome when they are not too long; but the old-fashioned "grand concert," with an overture here, a scena there, and a ballad or an instrumental solo in between, is insufferable. Besides, it creates a discomfiting atmosphere by assembling a vast crowd of people without definite musical ideas, loosely strung good-natured creatures who are attracted solely by the names of the performers, and can distinguish between Edward Lloyd and Sims Reeves, but not between a Donizetti cavatina and a Bach fugue.

Now of all miscellaneous concerts a Patti concert is the most miscellaneous. Imagine Ernani involami, with Robin Adair as a ritornello, or Within a Mile tacked on to Ombra leggiera, or Home, Sweet Home introduced by Il Bacio! We had all three—I mean all six—at the Albert Hall last week; and that huge audience did not mind a bit—took these abysmal transitions with a complacency which shewed that all music was alike to them. Once upon a time there was some excuse for this. Though Patti has never been convincing or even interesting as a dramatic singer in the sense in which, for instance, Giulia Ravogli excels, yet in the old days we could not help wanting to hear those florid arias of the old school on that wonderful vocal instrument, with its great range, its birdlike agility and charm of execution, and its unique combination of the magic of a child's voice with the completeness of a woman's. And what a woman, too! A consummate artist, able to vanquish every technical difficulty as perfectly as Sarasate on his violin, and withal a shrewd and wilful negotiator, able to secure the full "rent" of her voice to the last farthing without ever letting herself to be seen in any character but that of the spoiled darling of Europe, the petulant, capricious little diva, singing, as the canaries do, without knowing a crotchet from a quaver or a sovereign from a sixpence. To earn five-hundred-pound notes with the skill and diligence of a Duran, to bargain for them with the tenacity of a Rothschild, and to pocket them with the fascinating *insouciance* of Harold Skimpole—surely this was the perfection of work and play, the highest achievement of *savoir vivre*. In those days it did not matter how a concert program was made up, provided the name of Patti headed the list of singers. But the extent to which this was taken advantage of to save the trouble of devising something better than the senseless hotchpotch program of the miscellaneous order always rubbed good musicians the wrong way; and for my part, I must say that I did not like it any the more because I felt how futile all protest must be in the face of immense commercial success.

But time is coming to my assistance at last. Patti now has to evade the full weight of Ombra leggiera, much as Mr Sims Reeves, who is just old enough to be her father, economizes his forces in The Message. There are dozens of young sopranos before the public who can sing Ah, non giunge better than she can count on singing it next time. Now that the agile flights up to E flat in alt have become too hazardous to be attempted, Patti, deprived of her enchantments as a wonderful florid executant, is thrown back, as far as operatic arias are concerned, upon her capacity as a dramatic soprano, in which she is simply uninteresting. Fortunately she has another string to her bow—one that has for a long time been its best string. She is a great ballad-singer, and I have no doubt that twenty years hence I, as a fogey of the first order, shall hear her sing Home, Sweet Home to an audience whose affectionate veneration I shall compare sadly with the ardent enthusiasm of the days when the black hair was not yet tinged with the hues of sunset. And I shall tell the youngsters, with the mellow good-nature of my age,

85

how she was the prettiest woman in Europe, and made fabulous heaps of money, and never learnt any new songs, and compelled even me to rave about her sometimes, though I always had it upon my mind that she had done no more than she could help for the art that did everything for her. But for the present all I can do is to say that I have been to the Albert Hall to hear her again, and that whilst I would not give twopence to hear Ernani involami and Ombra leggiera sung in that way and under those circumstances, in the ballads she has still no rival, except in our remembrances of herself. None the less do I insist that for the future the interest in Patti may as well be reinforced by the attraction of good music and artistically composed programs.

I must not omit to mention how Miss Gomez made amends for selecting an arrant piece of trash to begin with by a delivery of Hatton's Enchantress which melted all the criticism out of me, and was decidedly the greatest success of the concert, except perhaps Sims Reeves's introduction of a novelty entitled Come into the garden, Maud. As to the Chevalier Emil Bach's performance of Liszt's paraphrase of Weber's Polonaise in E, I will only say that I doubt whether I could have played it much better myself; and those who know my attainments as a pianist will need no further clue to my opinion.

The London Symphony Concerts began last Thursday. For one reason or another I have not been able to follow them very closely from their foundation. A glimpse of them in the earliest stage left on me the impression that the orchestra was somewhat undermanned and the conductor overparted. So, as the concerts were very much wanted, I decided, since I could not speak strongly in their favor, to let them alone and await developments. Returning on Thursday last to reconnoitre, I found matters quite changed. The band was fit for anything; and Mr Henschel was conducting without any of that nervousness about details and narrowness of survey which somewhat disabled him when he first left the drawing room piano-stool for the conductor's desk.

He still falls so far short of a complete command of the situation that sometimes, in approaching the grandest moments in a composition, when the steadiest calm is required to keep down all haste and excitement as the music broadens to the most imposing amplitude of tone and elevation of style of which the band is capable, he hurries in spite of himself, allows the impetus of the movement to carry him off his feet, and misses the imperturbable massiveness which Richter has taught us to expect at certain crises. I do not, of course, in the least mean that Henschel will not be complete until he is another Richter: on the contrary, the marked dissimilarity in their temperaments cannot but produce a differentiation of the most welcome kind if Henschel proves equal to Richter in originality and independence. We do not want that dead level which is so earnestly deprecated by the people who all wear the same shiny black hats and shiny white cuffs, who utter the same shiny moral sentiments, who keep the same hours, eat and drink the same foods, live in the same sort of houses in the same neighborhoods, marry the same class of lady, ride in the same class of railway-carriage, and dare no more be seen deviating by a hair's breadth from this routine when anyone is looking than they dare carry a leg of mutton wrapped up in a newspaper from St James's Palace to the Royal Institution. They would be down on me at once if I were to lose sight for a moment of the value of independent thought, individual initiative, active and free life, and even of occasional eccentricity; and I am bound to avoid offending them, for I assure you they are very influential. Therefore let me hasten to explain that I do not want Mr Henschel to slavishly adopt Richter's interpretation of, for instance, The Flying Dutchman overture; but I do want him to keep the hurry and tumult of the storm out of the Salvation *motif*—to hold back his forces like grim death just when they have rushed up to it, so that they may give it its proper sublimity of expression, instead of having barely time to scramble over it before the storm is on them again. Richter keeps himself in hand on such occasions by never letting a movement run away with him; never confounding crescendo with accellerando—indeed, he rather leans to allargando in such emergencies; and never flurrying himself by giving two beats in a bar when one would suffice, as in a two-four Mozartian allegro, for example. On points like these there is all the difference in the world between taking a wrinkle from a rival and imitating him. And now, lest I should quite overbalance my criticism by dwelling too long on what is, after all, only one particular, let me hasten to say that the Henschel performance was of remarkable excellence, far superior to anything ever heard now at an ordinary Philharmonic Concert, more finished in the details of execution than the Richter performances have been lately, and, on the whole, promising eventually to equal the Crystal Palace Concerts in musical value, and to surpass them in social value through their greater cheapness and accessibility. Even Mozart's Prague Symphony, a masterpiece which would have been a vapid failure anywhere else in England except under Richter, came nearer than I expected to suggesting what it might be if played by a whole band of Mozarts.

During the performance of an old overture composed by one of the minor Bachs I was annoyed by what I took to be the jingling of a bell-wire somewhere; but it turned out to be Dr Parry playing the cembalo part on a decrepit harpsichord. As, though the overture is a hundred years old, it was not written for a harpsichord of that age, Dr Parry might almost as well have played the Emperor Concerto on a Broadwood dated 1809.

At the Crystal Palace we have had two new concertos, one by Hollmann, for the violoncello and one by Paderewski for the pianoforte. Hollmann's was the better, because Hollmann is a violoncellist in a sense in which Paderewski is not a pianist. He finds music for a beloved instrument, without which he cannot satisfy his artistic impulse; whereas Paderewski uses the piano merely as a means to appease his musical rage or gratify his fancies, handling it with all the licence of a master who has hired it for his pleasure, and cares not a scrap for its feelings. He is a young man of prodigious but most uncompassionate ability, this Paderewski: a sort of musical Richard III. Hollmann, on the other hand, has been rather too effectually tamed in our drawing rooms; but Hercules is still Hercules, distaff or no distaff. If I have not much respect for composer Popper and his Papillons, I can at least appreciate the way in which Hollmann plays that air of Bach's from the Suite in D. After the tranquil boredom of Spohr's Consecration of Sound symphony, Bach was magnificent.

I have seen nothing of the Opera since Miss Russell's appearance as Elsa in Lohengrin, on which occasion I am glad to say that Arditi amended some of the most disgraceful cuts in the score—notably the fanfare behind the scenes in the introduction to the second act, and the dawn music. It is true that the restored pieces were execrably performed; but that can be remedied. They tell me that there have been rare doings since that night's performance of Tannhäuser, introducing Venus on Euridice's sofa, and so on; but the matter was carefully concealed from me until too late, perhaps wisely. So I am not in a position to do more than chronicle the event from hearsay.

3 December 1890

I MUST say that, after Signor Lago's exploits, I see nothing for it but a State Opera. Private enterprise is clearly not able for the work; and it remains for the critics and musicians to make everybody conscious that public opera-houses are as reasonable institutions as public picture-galleries and art-museums. At the same time I by no means pretend that the resources of private enterprise were exhausted by Signor Lago. To begin with, though the experiment was supposed to be in cheap opera, the performances, as I took occasion to say at the outset of the season, were only cheap to Signor Lago, not to the public. Even allowing for the fact that better dresses and more dancers were introduced as money began to come in, the staging of the operas, except in so far as it was borrowed from Mr Harris, was ridiculous. The preparation was so perfunctory that for the first week we had Bevignani rushing the performances through by racing the orchestra against the singers; whilst Arditi, who made the best of matters with astonishing tact and patience, must have been exhausted after every performance by the wear and tear of the vigilance required by his task. After seeing him pull Lohengrin through, I felt that he could be trusted to drive twelve horses tandem-fashion from Charing Cross to the Bank in the busiest hour of the day; and I am somewhat indignant at the brutalities of the little party which, for inscrutable reasons, is trying to persuade the public, by disparaging Arditi, that Bevignani is the operatic conductor *par exellence*.

But though Arditi succeeded in preventing the big operas from coming to open and irretrievable grief before the public, he was unable to secure anything approaching to steady and satisfactory performances. And I must add that, much as the adroit and sympathetic accompanist was to be preferred to the stolid and impatient one, a conductor in the full sense of the term would have been better than either. Under all the circumstances, it is odd that matters came off as well as they did. Without rehearsal, without stage-management, without organization, without authority, without definite artistic aim—in short, without time, money, or leadership, the performances tumbled through with a degree of success that was really amazing. When people are working together for individual but compatible ends frank anarchy is always lucky, because everyone may make an omission or a mistake without throwing the rest out of gear, or even particularly surprising them. But the result produced by a mob of artists, each bent solely upon getting through his or her part without an obvious breakdown, and incidentally picking up as much applause as possible on the way, falls very far short of the artistic whole which a complete operatic representation should present. That can only be achieved by highly disciplined cooperation; and this cannot in artistic matters (or indeed in many others) be established by the methods of the drill-sergeant, but only by spontaneous obedience to the authority of a convincing artistic purpose manifested by some central member of the company.

Thus, when Maurel was on the stage in Rigoletto, there was none of the chaotic disorder of Il Trovatore, in which the chorus looked on at the principals much as a crowd outside a soup-kitchen looks on at an altercation in which the parties are too respectable to take to their fists. Maurel seized their attention, and riveted them upon the drama with an authority that needed no reinforcement from the temporal powers that controlled the treasury. Giulia Ravogli did the same thing under ludicrously unfavorable circumstances in Orfeo. But neither Rigoletto nor Orfeo, as wholes, did credit to the management. Had there been a conductor with Maurel's strength and Giulia Ravogli's intensity, the season might have turned out differently, though no conductor can do as much with a scratch company, kept going on the hand to mouth system, as he could with the prestige, the permanence, and the assured resources of an opera-house supported by public funds and controlled in the public interest. And what likelihood is there of really great conductors preferring precarious jobs here to the safe berths, with pensions attached to them, available abroad? If Mr Harris, with his subvention from Mayfair, could not tempt Levi from Munich, Richter from Vienna, or Faccio from Milan, what chance have second-rate enterprises which begin with only barely enough money and credit to keep the chorus above the level of worsted tights and tinfoil daggers? This, let me add, is of course not the fault of Signor Lago, who will probably prosper on his provincial tour, to the rehearsals for which, London has just had the privilege of paying for admission.

Last Thursday it happened that I was thinking of these

things, and wondering whether we should ever have "the poor silly millions," as Marx called them, rescued from operatic imposture by a demand for a better state of things from the artists themselves. The vein was not a very hopeful one. My earliest reminiscence of an eminent operatic artist off the stage dates from a certain performance of Lucrezia Borgia, at which I, then in my teens, managed to get behind the scenes. The tenor was a fine young man from the sunny South, who was going to be the successor of Mario. At that time everybody was going to succeed Mario. The particular child of Nature in question made a deep impression on me as he went on to sing the interpolated aria Deserto sulla terra between the last two acts. As he passed me he cleared his throat demonstratively, and in the most natural and spontaneous way imaginable spat right into the midst of a group of women who were seated chattering just behind the proscenium. Immediately the question presented itself, Can a man look like Lohengrin, sing like Lohengrin, feel like Lohengrin, raise the Donizetti-ridden stage to the level of Lohengrin before he has himself reached the phase of having misgivings as to the considerateness of promiscuous expectoration? Since that time I have seen many other Italian successors of Mario—in fact, nearly all those who appeared between Mario and De Reszke—but I can hardly remember one who had any more of Lohengrin, or even of Raoul de Nangis, in him than this early Gennaro of mine. Anyhow, I made up my mind that no demand for a more serious view of the lyric stage would come from the Italian tenors.

As to looking to the enormously expensive star prima donnas for a move in any direction except that of an additional hundred a night, and a few fresh cuts to lighten their work, no such Utopian extravagance ever exercised my imagination. I should almost as soon have expected the critics to take the matter up. There was nothing for it but to wait for the whole Gye-Mapleson-Costa régime to collapse from inanition, which, to my savage satisfaction, it eventually did very completely. Judge, then, whether I had not some ground for the scepticism with which I pursued that train of thought on Thursday last.

Thursday, it will be remembered, was a dark day, cold as the seventh circle. I presently found myself prowling about a great pile of flats, looking for a certain number at which I had to make a call. Somebody else was prowling also; and I no sooner became convinced that he was looking for the same number as I, and was probably going to call on the same person, than I resolved not to look at him; because to look at a man under such circumstances is almost tantamount to asking him what the devil he is doing there. Consequently it was not until we got inside, and were introduced, that I recognized in the stranger no other than Maurel.

Imagine my feelings when I found that the business upon which he was bent was the formulation in some fashion of his demand as an artist for a more earnest treatment of his work and mission. "Of what value is your admiration of my Iago or Rigoletto," he said, in effect, "if you do not regard the opera as a serious entertainment? Besides, one of the conditions of a really admirable performance is that it shall be an organic part of a whole in which all the other parts are equally excellent in their due degree; and how can such a whole be organized except in a place where opera is taken seriously, both before and behind the curtain?" Maurel, having gone up and down upon the earth in search of such places, has wisely come to the conclusion that they do not exist ready-made, and that the artists must themselves set to work to create them everywhere, by rousing the critics and educating the public to appreciate theatrical art.

As a beginning, he wishes to submit his theory of art to criticism; to give sceptical dramatic critics illustrations of the dramatic resources of stage singing; and finally to assert the claims of operatic actors to weighty social consideration, founded on a sense of the importance and dignity of their function in society, instead of the capricious fashionable vogue which they now enjoy only when they happen to be phenomenal executants. This explains the speech he made

at the Hôtel Métropole the other day. He is anxious to
enlarge that after-dinner sketch into a carefully considered
address, giving practical examples of what he meant by
saying that one should not sing the part of Rigoletto with
the voice of Don Juan, and to deliver it to a select body of
the critics of London, who, as profound thinkers thoroughly
conversant with their subject on its philosophic, technical,
and social sides, and brimful of general culture to boot,
would at once seize his meaning and help him to convey it
to the public.

Modesty, and loyalty to my colleagues, restrained me
from warning him not to generalize too rashly from the
single instance with whom he was just then conversing; so I
merely hinted that though the London critics are undeniably
a fine body of men, yet their élite are hardly sufficiently
numerous to make up a crowded and enthusiastic audience.
To which he replied that an audience of two would satisfy
him, provided the two had his subject at heart. This was
magnificent, but not war: we at once agreed that we could
do better for him than that. However, prompt measures
were necessary, as he has to leave London next week. So we
then and there constituted ourselves an executive sub-
committee, fixed the date of the lecture for the afternoon of
Monday next, and chose for our platform the stage of the
Lyceum Theatre, on which, as Iago, he inaugurated a new
era in operatic acting. It was a cool proposal, especially as
Maurel altogether declined to proceed on a commercial
basis, and would only hear of putting a price upon admission
on condition that the proceeds should be given to some
charity. But the upshot shewed that we knew our Irving,
who promptly not only placed the theatre at Maurel's disposal, but charged himself with the arrangements. To the
Lyceum, therefore, I refer the critics, the students, the
amateurs, the philosophers, and the experts, as well as those
modest persons who only wish to hear Maurel sing again,
and to be shewn how he changes the voice of William Tell
into the voice of Don Juan.

SIR CHARLES HALLÉ has been unlucky this season so far. When I got to his last concert, on one of those horrible nights that nail a critic to his ain fireside, unless he is fonder of music than of vulgar comfort, I found the Manchester band gravely playing the Oberon overture to an audience every member of which might have stretched himself at full length along his bench without incommoding his neighbor in the least. Still, it was a picked audience: only enthusiasts would have braved such villainous weather. It will be a misfortune for us here if the Manchester orchestra is not supported sufficiently to ensure our hearing it from time to time. In London we are rather apt to think that one orchestra is the same as another; for, as we hear the same players wherever we go, we conclude that the differences must be all due to the influence of the conductors. The widest variation you get is between the Philharmonic band, which represents orchestral gentility, and the Richter band, which represents orchestral genius; yet their members are constantly playing with one another at the Crystal Palace and elsewhere: they cut their oboe reeds in the same way; they use the same delicate drum-sticks; in brief, they shape the physical features of their performances so exactly alike as to make them common to all orchestral concerts in London, just as Coquelin's turned-up nose is common to all his impersonations.

The public is as capable of appreciating physical differences in music as the experts are, although it cannot give a precise account of them as the experts can. Every man with an ear is differently affected by the oboe-playing of Horton and the piping of a pifferaro; by the clarionet of Egerton or Lazarus and the dingy boxwood instrument of his rival in the street, who produces a sound between that of a cheap harmonium and a cornet; by the drum-playing of Chaine or Smith and the flourishes of the trooper who "lets the kettle to the trumpet speak." Such differences are not necessarily those between good playing and bad, but between one sort of playing and another; both extremes, with all the intermediate gradations, have their peculiar emotional suggestiveness, and therefore their special artistic value. In Germany clarionet-players use reeds which give a more strident, powerful, appealing tone than in England; and the result is that certain passages (in the Freischütz, for example) come out with a passion and urgency that surprise the tourist who has only heard them played here by Egerton, Lazarus, or Clinton. But when it comes to the Parsifal prelude or the slow movement in Beethoven's Fourth Symphony, one misses the fine tone and dignified continence of the English fashion.

Again, the son of thunder who handles the drums in the Manchester band could hardly, with those mighty drumsticks, play the solo passage in the finale to Beethoven's E flat Pianoforte Concerto as delicately as Chaine does whenever the pianist gives him a chance; but then Chaine is equally at a loss when he comes to that final crescendo roll, with its culminating stroke upon the last note of the Trold King's dance, in the Peer Gynt suite, a moment which would be one of the highest in the life of his Manchester rival. Thus, though music be a universal language, it is spoken with all sorts of accents; and the Lancashire accent differs sufficiently from the Cockney accent to make the Manchester band a welcome variety, without counting the change from Cowen or Cusins to Hallé. Besides, the trip from the provinces to London freshens up the men, and does away with that staleness which so few conductors can supply stimulus enough to overcome without external aid from a change of circumstances. And it must not be omitted that the band, at home or on tour, is an excellent one. In forte passages it is superior to the Crystal Palace orchestra in power and to the Richter in quality, an advantage which enables it to produce certain effects in the scores of Berlioz which neither of the others can make much of. This alone would be sufficient to guarantee it a footing side by side with its rivals in London, if our amateurs had attained any real connoisseurship in the matter. It is true that Hallé's domain is that of "absolute music," whilst the fashion has been running of late strongly towards tone-poetry and music-drama. But this cannot last; every concert cannot consist of selections from The Niblung's Ring. And you never quite know where to have Hallé. When he conducted the Eroica Symphony last season for all the world as if it were a suite by Handel, nobody would have supposed him capable of coping with Beethoven's later works; and yet at this recent concert he finished with a performance of the Seventh Symphony as good as any I have heard—and I have heard Richter at it repeatedly. Earlier in the evening he had handed the bâton to Mr Willy Hess and taken his old place at the piano for Dvořák's concerto, which he played with enviable ease and spirit. The mere fact of his having in his repertory a long and elaborate work by a man twenty-two years his junior shews what sort of votary art has found in him. If Patti or Sims Reeves had been born pianists instead of singers, they would still be playing Mendelssohn's G minor Concerto at every concert, with Thalberg's Moïse fantasia for a solo, and an easy impromptu of Schubert's for an encore piece.

The day after the Hallé concert I heard Brahms' concerto played by Mr Leonard Borwick, the youngest representative of the Hallé school. He is a finished pupil, and can now play whatever any practical composer chooses to write down, however difficult it may be. So far, however, he has nothing to add: the composer's spirit does not attain reincarnation in him. No doubt that will come in time; and in the meantime there is no denying that his quick musical feeling and diligently earned technical accomplishment entitle him to take his place with credit among our foremost concert-players.

The latest infant phenomenon is a Belgian violoncello player aged twelve, one Jean Gerardy, concerning whom I am compelled to own, at the risk of encouraging the agents

to speculate in the phenomenon business, that he is one of
the best players I ever heard. His instrument, though the
maker has evidently spared no pains to make it as perfect as
possible, is new, and has the faults of that quality. Gerardy,
however, makes the best of it with a tact which is perhaps
his most surprising quality, considering his age. His execution is finished, his intonation hardly ever at fault, his touch
on the strings delicate and firm, and his taste irreproachable;
whilst his ways and manners are as thoughtful and dignified
as a boy's can be without making him insufferable. Another
violoncellist now busy in London is Julius Klengel, who
executes *tours de force* with great rapidity and accuracy, but
whose dry tone shews that he has cultivated his left hand at
the expense of his right. He was warmly applauded at
Essipoff's concert last Friday.

The performance of the Norwich Festival setting of
Milton's L'Allegro ed il Pensieroso at the Crystal Palace
last Saturday did much to soften the feelings with which I
have regarded the composer for some time past. Dr Parry
is so genuine an enthusiast, so thorough a workman at his
craft, so engaging an essayist, and, in short, so unexception-
able a musical fellow-creature, that Judith was a hard blow
to bear from him. Perhaps he was right—as a doctor of
music—to dissemble his artistic feeling; but why did he
write an oratio? I have hardly alluded to him with common civility since; but now that his genius, released from
an unnatural and venal alliance, has flown back to the noble
poetry that was its first love, let the hatchet be buried—and
Judith with it as soon as possible. This new cantata of his is
happy, ingenious, as full of contrapuntal liveliness as Judith
was full of contrapuntal deadliness, and genuine in feeling
throughout. The performance was admirable on the part of
the orchestra, and as good as could have been expected on
the part of the chorus. Mr Henschel did justice to Dr Parry
if not to Milton; but Miss Amy Sherwin displayed a virtuosity in the art of singing flat which no stretch of critical
indulgence would justify me in ignoring. In her first con-

tribution to the concert, Dove sono, she shewed that in slow melodies, with simple and carefully prepared modulations, she can keep fairly in tune; but when it came to Dr Parry's brisk movements and sudden modern transitions, she lost her way. As her voice is one of exceptional range and quality it is a pity that she should be practically disabled for work of this class by what may be only a bad habit, acquired in regions where people are rather more easily pleased in the matter of intonation than we in London.

As to Mr Hamish MacCunn's Cameronian's Dream, which was also performed under the composer's bâton, I must frankly say that a man might go on setting ballads in that way for a lifetime without making any real progress. Any ardent young musician can pick up those tricks of being solemn on the trombone, pastoral on the oboe, and martial on the side-drum easily enough nowadays. My comment on the Cameronian's Dream is that of the Sheffield gentleman at the Garrick Theatre: "Ive heard that before"; and I may add, as to Mr MacCunn's setting of line after line to the measure of Esperto nocchiero, that I have heard it quite often enough. The fiery chariot business at the end, with the ridiculous post-horn flourishes on the cornet, supported by a mechanical accompaniment which is as empty of poetic meaning and as full of prosaic suggestion as the tintinnabulation of an electric alarum, will probably end its days in ashes on Mr MacCunn's hearth, when he has come to see that when we all applauded Lord Ullin's Daughter so heartily we never intended him to make a habit of it.

17 December 1890

ONE cannot but admire Mr Richard Temple's independence and enterprise in trying back to Gounod and Molière as a relief to Cellier and Stephenson. His Mock Doctor company, however, shews how superficial are the accomplishments of the artists (save the mark!) who run about the country in light-opera companies. To perform all the latest works in their line no very great technical skill is needed: good looks, a certain felicity of address, and sufficient natural aptitude for music qualify any young person to play principal parts. At the Savoy we are highly amused by what we indulgently call the acting; but we have only to pronounce the magic word Molière, and think of the Théâtre Français, to recognize at once that this "acting" is nothing but pure tomfoolery—"jack-acting," the Irish call it—wittily turned into a stage entertainment by Mr Gilbert.

I was at the gala performance of The Gondoliers the other night, and noticed two things: first, that the music was much more familiar to the band than to the composer, who conducted on that occasion; and second, that the representation did not involve a single stroke of skilled stage-playing. Mr Frank Wyatt's success as the Duke of Plaza Toro does not afford the faintest presumption that he could manage three minutes of Sganarelle: Mr Courtice Pounds and Mr Wallace Brownlow might win unbounded applause as Marco and Luiz a thousand times without knowing enough to enable them to walk half across the stage and make a bow in the character of Leandre. I do not say this as an advocate of the French system: I have always maintained that the English actor who grows his own technique is much to be preferred to the drilled French actor with his borrowed regulation equipment. But if the finished English actor's original art is better than the French actor's conventional art, the Frenchman has still the advantage of the Englishman who has "gone on the stage" without any conception of art at all—who has not only an untrained body and a slovenly tongue, but who, having walked and talked all his life without thinking about it, has no idea that action and speech are subjects for artistic culture. Such innocents, though they do not find engagements at the Garrick or the Haymarket, unfortunately get before the public in light opera very easily if only they can achieve anything that will pass for singing. Indeed, I need not confine the statement to light opera.

The vulgarities and ineptitudes of Carl Rosaism pass

unrebuked at Drury Lane, although, if the culprits were only actors, Mr Harris would scornfully recommend them not to venture north of the Surrey or west of the Pavilion until they had made themselves commonly presentable. Light opera gets the best of it; for all the pleasantest, funniest, and most gifted novices get snapped up by the Savoy, the Gaiety, the Prince of Wales, and the Lyric, leaving the second-rate aspirants to the provinces for rough wear in grand opera (in English) or lighter work on tour with comic operas, according to their robustness and capacity. Under these circumstances I do not blame Mr Temple for failing to find a company capable of handling The Mock Doctor with the requisite skill and delicacy. No doubt he has done the best he could; but the result is not satisfactory. And I must say, even making the largest allowance for the incapacity of the performers, that I cannot see why so much of the concerted music should be absolutely discordant. It is always possible to be at least smooth and tuneful. Surely Mr Temple could obtain a more musicianly performance of that sextet if he cared enough for it to assert his authority. Still, on Thursday last, when I dropped unobtrusively into the pit, the audience, put in good humor by the irresistible flavor of Molière which hangs about Kenny's libretto, were very willing to be pleased. If Mr Temple's enterprise fails, it will not be the fault of the piece.

Maurel's lecture was, as everybody by this time knows, a great success. That is to say, everybody was there, and everybody seemed delighted. Nevertheless, my private opinion is that very few of the audience appreciated the situation sufficiently to feel the least urgency in what Maurel had to tell them. A certain eminent dramatic critic whom I consulted as I left the Lyceum said, with the air of a man who does not wish to be unkinder than he can help, that the lecture was "free from paradox." By this he meant that it struck him as truistic, not to say platitudinous. Happy man! to have to deal with a department of art in which the

petty warfare of the critic is fully accomplished, leaving him
free to devote his energy to the demand for a higher order
of subject now that there is no further question of the necessity for intelligent and unified treatment of that subject, no
matter what its order may be. After his round of the Lyceum,
the Princess's, Haymarket, the Criterion, the Alhambra,
the Olympic, and Drury Lane this pampered scribe hears
Maurel insisting that operatic actors should study the
psychology of their parts, and that the designers of stage
costume and scenery should aim at producing an appropriate
illusion as to the place and period assigned by the dramatist
to the action of the piece; and his only comment is, "Who
disputes it?" How I should like to see him doing six weeks
Italian Opera without the option of a fine! There he would
find only one period, "the past," and only two places, "an
exterior" and "an interior." In costume the varieties might
prove more definite and numerous. I have often seen Marta,
in which Queen Anne is introduced alive, with the ladies in
early Victorian Archery Club dresses, the Queen's retinue
in the costume of feudal retainers of the Plantagenet period,
the comic lord as Sir Peter Teazle, the noblemen in tunics
and tights from Il Trovatore, and the peasants with huge
Bavarian hats beneath their shoulders, reminding one of the
men in Othello's yarns. As to La Traviata, with Violetta in
the latest Parisian confections, and Alfredo in full Louis
XIV fig, that is familiar to every opera-goer. Yet this by
itself might matter no more than the Venetian costumes in
Paul Veronese's Marriage in Cana, if it were ignorance,
naïveté, convention, poetic licence, or anything but what it
is: to wit, sheer carelessness, lack of artistic conscience,
cynical conviction that nothing particularly matters in an
opera so long as the singers draw good houses.

When a special effort has to be made in the case of a
practically new work, such as Romeo, The Mastersingers,
or Othello, the exception only brings the rule into more
glaring prominence; and too often the exception is in point
of scenography (as Maurel puts it) rather than of psycho-

logy: that is, the scene-painter and costumier, stimulated by lavish managerial expenditure, think out their part of the opera, whilst the principal singers and the stage manager (if there is one) jog along in their old grooves. Clearly, then, Maurel's appeal, granted that from a dramatic critic it would be a mere knocking at an open door, is in the opera-house a sort of Childe Roland's blast on the slughorn.

So much I have said to spare the feelings of the dramatic critics. Now I may add privately to Maurel that average dramatic criticism here is simply confusion made articulate, expressing the critic's likes and dislikes unintelligently and therefore unsystematically. It is all very well to say to Maurel, "Well, what then? We knew all this before you were born." Suppose Maurel were to produce a sheet of paper, in the manner of Mephistopheles producing his bond, and to say, "In that case, oblige me by allotting a hundred marks to Mr Beerbohm Tree, or any other actor whom you have criticized, in such a manner as to shew the proportion between his technical, his psychological, and his scenographic accomplishments; and append an estimate of the allowance to be made for your idiosyncratic bias for or against him." How many dramatic critics would be able to do more than exclaim piteously with Barnacle junior, "Look here: you have no right to come this sort of move, you know"? If these gentlemen as much as suspected the exist-ence of half the things that I have to pretend to know all about, and that Maurel has actually to do, they would trans-pose their remarks a tone or so down at future performances.

For my own part, I have no fault to find with the lecture, except on a point of history. All that about the Dark Ages and the barbarous Middle Ages is a modern hallucination, partly pious, partly commercial. There never were any Dark Ages, except in the imagination of the Blind Ages. Look at their cathedrals and their houses; and then believe, if you can, that they were less artistic than we who have achieved the terminus at Euston and the Gambetta monu-ment. And to think that Maurel, of all men—Maurel, who

was an architect before he went over to the lyric stage—
should believe such a thing! However, he does not really
believe it; for instead of following it up in the sequel, he
turned right round in his tracks, and practically assumed
that art has been going to the deuce ever since the Re-
nascence.

I have no other exception to take to the lecture or to the
vocal illustrations. The rôle of lecturer was never better
acted since lecturing began. As far as one man, limited by a
peculiar vocal technique and a strongly marked meridional
temperament, could make his case complete he made it
complete. The Verdi *nuance* he utters as if he were native
and to the manner born; the Wagnerian *nuance*, like the
Mozartian, he has to translate; and intelligently and skil-
fully as the translation is done it is to me still a translation.
Iago and Rigoletto, with their intense moods and swift
direct expression, come to life in him; but Wolfram and
Don Juan, with their yearning northern abstract sentiment
flowing with endless inflections, only find in him a very
able proxy.

I must return to the subject of the Hallé orchestra to
chronicle a magnificent performance of Berlioz' Fantastic
Symphony. At present no London band can touch this
work at all, because no London band has learnt it thoroughly.
We can get the notes played, and we sometimes do; but, as
in the case of the first movement of the Ninth Symphony,
only confusion and disappointment come of the attempt.
Now the Manchester band, knowing the work through and
through, handles it with a freedom, intelligence, and spirit
which bring out all its life and purpose, and that, too, without giving the conductor any trouble. It is especially to be
hoped that the orchestral students of the Royal College of
Music who had a turn at the Harold Symphony in St
James's Hall two days before were at this concert. If so, it
must have helped them to realize how completely they were
beaten, in spite of the highly praiseworthy degree of skill
they have attained in using their instruments, and the

excellent drill they are getting in *ensemble* playing.

The singing of the Royal College pupils bore eloquent testimony to the fund of negative advice available at the institution. One could see with half an eye how earnestly the young vocalists had been told what not to do—as, for instance, not to press on the notes with their breath, not to force the tone, not to sing with effort, and so on. If the College only succeeds presently in securing some teacher who can also tell the pupils what to do, they will soon begin to shew signs of knowing how to sing. At present they seem to me to be hardly more advanced than M. Jourdain was in fencing after his instructor had informed him that the two main points in practising that art are—first, to hit your adversary, and second, to avoid being hit by him.

Mr Boscovitz's recital at Steinway Hall last week was unusually well worth hearing. He had a spinet and a harpsichord, both of them really fine instruments of their sort; and on them he played a number of old pieces, from Bull's Carman's Whistle to the Harmonious Blacksmith, occasionally repeating one, with detestable but interesting effect, on a Steinway grand, which is about as like a harpsichord as an oboe is like a Boehm flute, or a bassoon like a euphonium. If Mr Boscovitz repeats this recital, or lecture, he will do well to complete it by also using a clavichord, if he can get one, as well as by securing a double harpsichord for Bach's Italian Concerto. His omission of the last two movements from this work considerably astonished the audience, in whose powers of endurance he seemed suddenly to lose faith. The *pianos* and *fortes* marked by Bach can only be produced on a harpsichord with two manuals. If Mr Boscovitz cannot obtain such an instrument, he should explain the matter in defence of his own playing; for I confess I did not know what was wrong until Mr Fuller Maitland told me; and without this warning I should certainly have ignorantly pitched into Mr Boscovitz for not attending to Bach's directions.

24 *December* 1890

THE musical season is turning out badly for orchestral concert givers. Mr Henschel, who began by declaring that he would trust the public, and venture without a guarantee, has now sorrowfully announced that he is beaten, and cannot complete his series of symphony concerts unless more stalls are subscribed for. And Sir Charles Hallé was abandoned at his first two concerts in a way really discreditable to London amateurism. Hereupon Mr Arthur Symons, in the Pall Mall Gazette, endeavors to sting London into doing its musical duty by declaring that we can no longer pretend to be a musical nation. As to that, it cannot be said that symphony concerts have ever been much of a national matter; so long as St James's Hall suffices for our needs in that department, it is hardly worth discussing its fullness or emptiness from the national point of view. But for the few of us who require good music as part of our weekly subsistence, the cutting off of our opportunities by no less than two concert series out of a total of four is not to be borne without remonstrance. No doubt the weather has been partly to blame: thick boots and a warm coat buttoned up to the neighborhood of the chin are indispensable in St James's Hall just now for people who wish to enjoy their music without a castanet accompaniment from their own teeth; and as the ordinary patron of the stalls is condemned by custom to garnish himself with indoor fireside wear, he naturally shirks his concerts unless the attraction is exceptionally strong. Still, I do not see why the subscriptions should not be forthcoming, whether the subscribers attend or not. Many very rich people in London seem to me to suppose that they have nothing but their own private whims to consult in the disposition of their incomes. I demur to this, and contend that they are as much bound to support orchestral concerts by their subscriptions as they are to support hospitals. That they may dislike music and never go to a concert when they can help it is clearly no more to the point than that they dislike being ill, and would not go to a hospital on any terms. If concerts of high-class music are vitally necessary, as I believe they are, and if they cannot be kept on foot without the support of the rich, why, the rich must do their duty.

As a plebeian, I demand *circenses*, if not *panem*, to that extent. And it cannot be urged that there is at present any difficulty in finding worthy enterprises to support. Hallé has long been above suspicion in this respect; and though Henschel is comparatively a beginner, the value of his concerts is already beyond question. And it must be remembered in estimating the general effect of their labors that they have only asked the public for a shilling where Richter has demanded half-a-crown, whilst the scale of their performances is equally expensive.

The Bach Choir gave a concert on the 16th. I was not present. There are some sacrifices which should not be demanded twice from any man; and one of them is listening to Brahms' Requiem. On some future evening, perhaps, when the weather is balmy, and I can be accommodated with a comfortable armchair, an interesting book, and all the evening papers, I may venture; but last week I should have required a requiem for myself if I had attempted such a feat of endurance. I am sorry to have to play the "disgruntled" critic over a composition so learnedly contrapuntal, not to say so fugacious; but I really cannot stand Brahms as a serious composer. It is nothing short of a European misfortune that such prodigious musical powers should have nothing better in the way of ideas to express than incoherent commonplace. However, that is what is always happening in music: the world is full of great musicians who are no composers, and great composers who are no musicians.

In his youth, Brahms when writing songs or serenades, or trifles of one kind or another, seemed a giant at play; and he still does small things well. I listened to his cleverly harmonized gipsy songs at the last Monday Popular Concert of the year with respectful satisfaction, though I shall

107

not attempt to deny that fifteen minutes of them would have
been better than twenty-five. This last remark, by the bye,
shews that I am full of malice against "holy John," as
Wagner called Brahms, even when he does what I have
admitted his fitness for. Consequently my criticism, though
it relieves my mind, is not likely to be of much value. Let me
therefore drop the subject, and recall the attention of the
Bach Choir to a composer of whom I entertain a very
different opinion, to wit, John Sebastian Bach himself. It is
the special business of this society to hammer away at Bach's
works until it at last masters them to the point of being able
to sing them as Bach meant them to be sung. For instance,
there is the great Mass in B minor. The choir has given
several public performances of that; but all have been timid,
mechanical, and intolerably slow. And when the elderly
German conductor who got up the first performances was
succeeded by a young and talented Irishman, the Mass
became duller and slower than ever. The public did not take
to the work as performed in this manner. It satisfied its
curiosity, received an impression of vast magnitude, yawned
and felt no great impatience for a repetition of the experience. If the society thinks that this was the fault of Bach, it is
most unspeakably mistaken.

Nothing can be more ruinous to the spirited action of
the individual parts in Bach's music, or to the sublime
march of his polyphony, than the dragging, tentative, unintelligent, half-bewildered operations of a choir still in the
stage of feeling its way from interval to interval and counting one, two, three, four, for dear life. Yet the Bach Choir
never got far beyond this stage with the B minor Mass.
Even at the great bi-centenary performance at the Albert
Hall no attempt was made to attain the proper speed; and
the work, as far as it came to light at all, loomed dimly and
hugely through a gloomy, comfortless atmosphere of stolid
awkwardness and anxiety. The effect the slow movements
would make if executed with delicacy of touch and depth of
expression, and of the quick ones if taken in the true Bach

major mood, energetic, spontaneous, vivid, jubilant, was left to the imagination of the audience; and I fear that for the most part they rather declined to take it on trust. All this can be remedied by the Bach choristers if they stick at it, and are led with sufficient faith and courage. There is more reason than ever for persevering with their task at present; for Bach belongs, not to the past, but to the future—perhaps the near future. When he wrote such works as Wachet auf, for example, we were no more ready for them than the children for whom we are now buying Christmas gift-books of fairy tales are to receive volumes of Goethe and Ibsen. Acis and Galatea and Alexander's Feast, the ever-charming child literature of music, were what we were fit for then.

But now we are growing up we require passion, romance, picturesqueness, and a few easy bits of psychology. We are actually able to relish Faust and Carmen. And beyond Faust there is Tristan und Isolde, which is at last music for grown men. Mr Augustus Harris has never heard of it, as it is only thirty years old; but as he goes about a good deal, I cannot doubt that in the course of the next ten years or so he will not only have it mentioned to him by some ambitious prima donna who aspires to eclipse Frau Sucher, but may even be moved to try whether a performance of it would not be better business than a revival of Favorita. Now the reaction of Tristan on Wachet auf will be a notable one. The Bach cantata, which seemed as dry and archaic after Acis and Galatea as Emperor and Galilean would after Cinderella, will, after Tristan, suddenly send forth leaves, blossoms, and perfume from every one of its seemingly dry sticks, which have yet more sap in them than all the groves of the temple of Gounod. Provided, that is—and here I ask the ladies and gentlemen of the Bach Choir to favor me with their best attention for a moment—provided always that there shall be at that time a choir capable of singing Wachet auf as it ought to be sung.

Messrs Richard Gompertz, Haydn Inwards, Emil Kreuz, and Charles Ould, honorably associated as "The

Cambridge University Musical Society's String Quartet,"
have given a couple of concerts at Prince's Hall, at the
second of which I enjoyed myself without stint until they
began to play Brahms, when I precipitately retired. Mr
Edward German's symphony, performed at the last Crystal
Palace concert, shews that he is still hampered by that hesi-·
tation between two distinct *genres* which spoiled his Richard
III overture. If Mr German wishes to follow up his academic training by writing absolute music in symmetrical
periods and orderly ingenuity of variation, let him by all
means do so. On the other hand, if he prefers to take
significant *motifs*, and develop them through all the emotional phases of a definite poem or drama, he cannot do
better. But it is useless nowadays to try to combine the two;
and since Mr German has not yet made up his mind to discard one or the other, the result is that his symphonic movements proceed for awhile with the smoothness and regularity of a Mendelssohn scholar's exercise, and then, without rhyme or reason, are shattered by a volcanic eruption
which sounds like the last page of a very exciting opera
finale, only to subside the next moment into their original
decorum. I can but take a "symphony" of this sort as a bag
of samples of what Mr German can do in the operatic style
and in the absolute style, handsomely admitting that the
quality of the samples is excellent, and that if Mr German's
intelligence and originality equal his musicianship, he can
no doubt *compose* successfully as soon as he realizes exactly
what composition means.

At the last Monday Popular Concert of the year Madame
Neruda distinguished herself greatly in the slow movement
of the Mozart Quartet (No. 3 in B flat) and in Grieg's
Sonata in F. In the quick movements of the quartet poor
Mozart was polished off with the usual scant ceremony.
Madame Haas, who is always happy with Beethoven, played
those variations on an original theme (in F), an affection for
which is a sure sign of tenderness and depth of feeling in a
player. The audience acted wisely in recalling Madame

Haas twice, as her only fault is an occasional timidity in
expressing herself fully—a timidity which must be caused
by doubt as to whether her relations with Beethoven are
being understood or appreciated.

THE music publishers of London owe me their ac-
knowledgments for having devoted Christmas Day
to examining sundry parcels of music with which
they have from time to time favored me of late. It was a rare
way of enjoying the season. I cannot say with Shelley that

> I sang of the dancing stars,
> I sang of the dædal earth,

but I sang of the love of yore, and the coming years, and the
whispered prayer, and the twilight shadows, and the sweet
long ago, and the parting tear, and the distant bells, and the
old cathedral, and the golden gates, and the moon shining
o'er Seville, and the hour before the battle, and the eager
eyes looking out for Jack, and a floating home on the world
of foam being the home of homes for me, and goodness
knows what else. Most of them had waltz refrains, except
Seville, which was a bolero, and the pious ones with harmonium obbligato culminating in shouts of "Hosanna" or
"Miserere, Domine." When I finished it was late in the
evening, and I felt that I had done something to avenge the
unfortunate cows and turkeys of whose blood I at least am
guiltless.

When I came to turn it all over in my mind, satanic glee
at the sufferings I had inflicted on my gormandizing neighbors gave way to wonder as to why these ditties had been
sent to me. At the first blush it seemed as if the publishers
expected me to review them, and yet how could any sane
man of business suppose that there was the faintest chance
of my recommending the public to sing:

> Will he come? Will he come? O, my heart!
> I am waiting and watching in vain.

Ere twilight's soft shadows depart,
O, come to me, come once again!

WALTZ REFRAIN
Just (*tum tum*)
Once (*tum*) a-
Gain (*tum tum*),
(*Tum*) When the," etc. etc.

One publisher sent me, not this particular song, but some dozens exactly like it, without one redeeming piece to save me from feeling that my time had been utterly and wantonly wasted. Yet I should not be surprised if he feels positively swindled because this column does not contain the titles of all his detestable compilations, with a note certifying them as "a tuneful melody to flowing words, compass G to D, for soprano or tenor, or E flat to B flat, for contralto or baritone." It is certain that space is cheerfully given up to "reviews" of this sort by editors who would fall into convulsions if they were asked to as much as mention the literary equivalents of such songs in their columns. What is more, these reviewers' verdicts are heartily indorsed at hundreds of suburban pianos, where Sullivan is shirked as difficult, Blumenthal given up as abstruse, and Schumann repudiated as hideous and bewildering. For my part, however, I must say once for all that there is no use asking me to take that point of view at Christmas or any other season. People in search of trash will get no assistance from me, unless I take to composing it myself.

The Doctor of Music who sent me the full score of his motet for double chorus to a couple of phrases from the Psalms, all done in strict Mendelssohnese with the meaning carefully extracted, and beginning with two vigorous minims to the words "Lord Howe," must have meant to have a rise out of me. He may esteem himself fortunate that he has failed. Messrs Chappell send a couple of songs by Battison Haynes, one of which, Hey nonny no, is being popularized by Mr Plunket Greene. The music is full of point; but the

words, described as "of the Elizabethan period," are almost
as void of sense as if they belonged to the Victorian period.
They will suit any *basso profondo* who wishes to enliven a
drawing room by a fortissimo upon such couplets as

> Is't not fine to dance and sing
> When the bells of death do ring?

although, after all, that is a matter of taste. A French serenade, by Francis Thomé, is on the usual lines—three-eight
time, pizzicato accompaniment, minor mode changing to
major, "si tu savais, ma toute belle," etc. It served the turn
of so good a singer as Liza Lehmann at the Crystal Palace
the other day. Of songs which claim more serious consideration I have four sets. The first, a couple of songs by Mr Goring Thomas (Chappell), and the second, a series of settings
of Tennyson by Mr Alfred Cellier (Metzler), are in the
politest vein, delicate in sentiment, elegant and finished in
workmanship, shewing the influence of Sterndale Bennett,
modified in Mr Thomas's case by the fascinations of Gounod.
Nothing could suit Tennyson better. The other two are
much fresher. One is a little cycle of songs by Marshall-
Hall, with a rhymed preface containing some strong observations as to the sort of encouragement the author received
in this country, "where Truth and Art seek bread and home
in vain." Australia has now offered Mr Marshall-Hall a
professorship, which will, it is to be hoped, establish some
sort of truce between Truth and Art and their natural enemies, the baker and the landlord. But these songs will not
make Mr Marshall-Hall so popular in Australia as Mr Milton Wellings, for they are no simple tunes with every strain
repeated and furnished with an obvious complement. They
run into dramatic monologue of the latest Wagnerian type,
rather a serious matter for the ordinary amateur. Two or
three of the songs, however, can be turned to account by any
really cultivated amateur. They are published by Mr Joseph
Williams.

The Album for Song, by Agatha Backer-Gröndahl, the

Norwegian pianist, published by Warmuth of Christiania and Breitkopf & Härtel, is full of that steadfast poetic feeling and beautiful taste which so ennobled her playing. The pianist's hand is apparent in the vocal parts of the songs; not that pianoforte traits are anywhere substituted for vocal traits, but that a considerable demand is made on the performer for pure cantabile singing and delicacy of vocal touch whereas there is little conceded to what may be called the personal conditions of singing. Pure soprano voices, capable of being used in the upper register pretty continuously without fatigue, will find in Madame Gröndahl's songs just the opportunities they need. Tito Mattei, from whom I dreaded some unscrupulous *pièce de salon*, has surprised me with a song, Treasured Violets (Doremi & Co.), remarkably happy in its sincerity of expression and the perfect relation between its musical form and Mr Oxenford's little poem. The same merit, though in an absurdly trivial degree, may be claimed by M. Piccolomini for his Madelina (Orsborn & Tuckwood). Le Portrait (Metzler) is one of those quaintly sweet and naïve old French songs with which singers like Mrs Henschel and Miss Lehmann can score so effectively against the gushing modern drawing room song, of which I have received a fair example in Mr Lawrence Kellie's Sleeping Tide, which goes on to a most fervent and effective climax about nothing that I can discover. Of a couple of songs by Kate Elston, the earlier, For Dear Love's Sake (Marriott), is cruder in workmanship than On the Moonlit Sea (Reid); but it is also more deeply felt and forcibly expressed, an advantage which is well worth the sacrifice of a little conventional smoothness in the harmony. Mary Carmichael's songs (Metzler) are still daintily pleasant, but they are losing all pretence of thoroughness. Charles Ernest Baughan, on the other hand, in setting some lines of Lowell's entitled A Lover's Dream (Hopkinson), has elaborated his harmonies to the point, as it seems to me, of producing a discrepancy between them and the melody, most of which belongs clearly to the old tonic and dominant school. Nevertheless, the song is a promising one. Roeckel's Breton Slumber Song (Enoch) is a tender and pretty lullaby, in which Mr Baughan's error and his promise are alike avoided.

Bad as most of the vocal music sent me has proved, it is classic in comparison to the instrumental pieces. Most of these are waltzes and quadrilles introducing the refrains of all the silliest and most hackneyed of the songs. I believe it would be found quite easy to train circus horses to compose dance music of this sort, if any ringmaster could infatuate himself into the belief that the public would care two straws about such an accomplishment. I do not say that the stuff should not be written if it is wanted; but why send it to be reviewed? Of what interest can it be to anybody to know that I find the picture on the cover of The Chappies' Polka passably comic? In the whole bundle I find just one Valse Caprice, by Hamilton Robinson (Joseph Williams), which I can play without a sense of extreme indignity. There is absolutely nothing else, except Mr Isidore de Lara's Rêveuse (Mocatta), which has a definite poetic intention adequately and characteristically expressed. All the same, it is emptily sensuous, lacking in the intellectual vigor which goes, as a matter of course, with the higher kinds of artistic vigor; and I altogether decline to do violence to my own temperament by celebrating these languors, however featly they may be expressed in tone-poetry. Finally, I have to ask the publishers who send me arrangements of famous works for "the Liszt organ" to be kind enough to send the instrument as well, as otherwise it is impossible for me to say whether the transcriptions are effective or not.

I forgot to mention that Mr James Fleming sends me a number of a magazine entitled The Violin, published at 71 Paragon Road, Hackney, and containing a couple of photographs of a beautiful long-pattern Stradivarius violin, with —considering the subject—some unusually sensible letterpress concerning it.

21 *January* 1891

CHRISTMAS being the season of mirth, music, the
great English killjoy, with its intolerable hypocrisies,
is gladly put away until it is time to return to work
and duty and mental improvement and other unpleasantnesses; consequently my critical machinery has got out of
gear somewhat. I might have kept off the rust by attending
the regulation Christmas performance of The Messiah; but
I have long since recognized the impossibility of obtaining
justice for that work in a Christian country. Import a choir
of heathens, restrained by no consideration of propriety
from attacking the choruses with unembarrassed sincerity
of dramatic expression, and I would hasten to the performance if only to witness the delight of the public and the
discomfiture of the critics. That is, if anything so indecent
would be allowed here. We have all had our Handelian
training in church, and the perfect churchgoing mood is one
of pure abstract reverence. A mood of active intelligence
would be scandalous. Thus we get broken in to the custom
of singing Handel as if he meant nothing; and as it happens
that he meant a great deal, and was tremendously in earnest
about it, we know rather less about him in England than
they do in the Andaman Islands, since the Andamans are
only unconscious of him, whereas we are misconscious. To
hear a thousand respectable young English persons jogging
through For He shall purify the sons of Levi as if every
group of semiquavers were a whole bar of four crotchets *a
capella*, or repeating Let Him deliver Him if He delight in
Him with exactly the same subdued and uncovered air as in
For with His stripes we are healed, or lumbering along with
Hallelujah as if it were a superior sort of family coach: all
this is ludicrous enough; but when the nation proceeds to
brag of these unwieldy choral impostures, these attempts
to make the brute force of a thousand throats do what can
only be done by artistic insight and skill, then I really lose
patience. Why, instead of wasting huge sums on the multi-

116

tudinous dullness called a Handel Festival does not somebody set up a thoroughly rehearsed and exhaustively studied
performance of The Messiah in St James's Hall with a
chorus of twenty capable artists? Most of us would be glad
to hear the work seriously performed once before we die.

However, if I did not go to The Messiah, I ventured on
a pantomime, although in London we are unable to produce
an endurable pantomime for exactly the same reasons that
prevent us from achieving an endurable performance of
The Messiah. Therefore I did not make the experiment in
London. I found myself one evening in Bristol with nothing
better to do than to see whether pantomime is really moribund. I am bound to say that it seems to me to be as lively as
it was twenty-five years ago. The fairy queen, singing In
Old Madrid with reckless irrelevance at the entrance to the
cave where Aladdin found the lamp, was listened to with
deep respect as an exponent of the higher singing; and in
the cave itself The Bogie Man, in about fifty verses, took
immensely. A street scene at night, with Chinese lanterns
and a willow-pattern landscape, were stage pictures with
just the right artistic quality for the occasion; and the absurdity of the whole affair on the dramatic side was amusing
enough from an indulgent holiday point of view. There were
no processions presenting one silly idea over and over again
in different colored tights, until a thousand pounds had been
wasted in boring the audience to distraction. And—though
here I hardly expect to be believed—there was not a single
child under ten on the stage. I told Mr Macready Chute,
the manager, that he should come to London to learn from
our famous stage-managers here how to spend ten times as
much money on a pantomime for one-tenth of the artistic
return. I bade him, if he thirsted for metropolitan fame, to
take for his triple motto, Expenditure, inanity, vulgarity,
and that soon no spectacular piece would be deemed complete without him. With these precepts I left him, assuring
him that I felt more than ever what a privilege it was to live
in a convenient art-centre like London, where the nearest

pantomime is at Bristol, and the nearest opera at Bayreuth.

Stavenhagen, about whom I need say nothing pending his concert on Thursday, was the pianist at the Monday Popular Concerts from the New Year until last Monday week, when a wild young woman named Ilona Eibenschütz made her first appearance. Coming on the platform immediately after Miss Marguerite Hall, whose *savoir faire* is so superb that nervous people secretly long to throw things at her head, the newcomer, stumbling hastily up the stairs, and rushing at the piano-stool with a couple of strange gestures of grudging obeisance, as if she suspected some plot among us to be beforehand with her, produced an unmistakeable impression on the matronhood of the stalls. Backs were straightened, elbows drawn in, lips folded: in that moment Ilona, it seemed to me, was friendless in a foreign land. But when she touched the first chord of Schumann's Etudes Symphoniques, the hand lay so evenly and sensitively on it, and the tone came so richly, that I at once perceived that I was wasting my sympathies, and that Ilona, however ingloriously she might go to the piano, would come away from it mistress of the situation. And she certainly did. She is too young to have yet acquired the sang-froid necessary for the complete management of her great musical energy: she has to use that energy itself for self-control; but in spite of her not being yet at her best, she left the platform amidst such a storm of applause that, after two more outlandish bows, she dashed at the piano again and gave a brief but terrific sample of her powers of mechanical execution. As to Miss Marguerite Hall, I got laughed at by a critic of a younger generation for admitting that I had never heard her before; but the loss was my own: she uses her voice admirably.

By ill-luck, I was performing in public myself on the night of Mr Henschel's first London Symphony Concert of the year; and as he did not come to hear me, I do not think he can reasonably complain of my not having been to hear him.

28 *January* 1891

THE thaw came just in time to make Stavenhagen's concert comfortable for the nobility and gentry. Nevertheless, as the audience hardly outnumbered the ordinary Stavenhagen recital attendance far enough to cover the extra expense of the band, we all, I hope, felt that we were to some extent sponging on his preference of artistic satisfaction to pecuniary profit. And even the artistic satisfaction must have been qualified by the impossibility of getting a good performance of a concerto out of a scratch orchestra, however well manned, with a casual conductor, however eminent. Only those orchestras which, like the Crystal Palace, the Richter, the Henschel, and the Manchester, are organized by a permanent conductor as going concerns, can achieve really good work in this department. All that could be said was that Stavenhagen was as well served as the circumstances permitted. His old fellow-student in the Lisztian school at Weimar, Arthur Friedheim, himself a pianist of exceptional ability, conducted with a knowledge of the works in hand sufficient to enable him to dispense with a score throughout; and the band was of the best. Poor Madame Stavenhagen had to face the English public for the first time under rather nervous conditions. It was bad enough to brave the personal criticism provoked by her having ventured to carry off one of the few marriageable young men of genius in Europe, without also being compelled by circumstances to assume the character of Potiphar's wife, and sing a tremendously long dramatic soliloquy demanding powers of tragically passionate expression which are foreign to her temperament. This soliloquy, too, was her husband's maiden effort in the sublimely romantic style of composition, so that her anxiety as to her own reception was complicated by uncertainty as to how the composer of Suleika would strike the critics in his new capacity. And I cannot help thinking that there were other misgivings at work. Stavenhagen's hair had been carefully brushed for this con-

119

cert for the first time within the memory of man; and if I know anything of human nature, he had been lectured on his inveterate habit of putting his hands in his pockets the moment he gets away from the piano. Now, as the evening wore on, his hair visibly fell out of cultivation into its primitive condition; and whenever his hands were idle they wandered in the forbidden direction, and once or twice went all the way. Add to these preoccupations a doubt about the stability of the bow of his tie, which caused Madame Stavenhagen, in the very midst of a sustained high note—and a very sweet one, as it happened—to steal an anxious glance at his neck, and it will be apparent that our minds were confused by two incompatible planes of consciousness—one of being *en famille* with the Stavenhagens, and the other of wandering with Potiphar's wife in the desert under the eye of the eternal Sphinx. However, the music, which is in The Niblung's Ring manner, and contains nothing of which the composer need be ashamed, was well received, and Madame was encored. Later on she sang Leise, leise; but here she certainly did not do herself justice. The Adagio—that incomparable Adagio—should never have its steady, tranquil movement disturbed by the slightest *rubato*; but Madame Stavenhagen, I am sorry to say, pulled the latter half of it about badly. And she gave an illustration of what Diderot was driving at in his paradox by almost losing her self-control at the approach of the finale. Far be it from me, nevertheless, to complain overmuch of this. I only wish some more of our singers ran any risk from an excess of sensibility. Stavenhagen, whose reception may be described as affectionate, played the C minor Concerto of Beethoven, but hardly succeeded in getting quite back to its date. He did not take it seriously enough. The first movement, which made hardly any effect, is, when properly handled, grand in the old-fashioned way; and the Largo is anything but trivial, though it sounded a little so on Thursday. He was more at home in the Liszt Concerto in A, its genuine organic homogeneity being particularly welcome after the formal inco-

herence of the earlier work. In The Erl King transcription
he did not hit off the heavy father happily. Let him play me
that gravely tender and reassuring phrase, "Mein Sohn, es
ist ein Nebelstreif," as Schubert intended it, and I will not
ask to hear his present interpretation of the piece further
improved upon; for the rest was admirable—far better than
the blind passioning of Paderewski, who is yet, in some respects, the riper man of the two. Indeed, Stavenhagen, with
all his strength, intelligence, skill, fine taste, and artistic
sensibility, is by no means full grown as an artist: the last
word cannot be said about him for some years more.

One or two of the comments on Santley's condition after
his Australian tour, as displayed at the Popular Concert of
the 19th, shew the dangers of becoming the idol of unintelligent critics. When a singer attains fame in England, the
person whom *naïfs* mortally offend by describing as "the re-
porter" proceeds without further consideration to praise
him or her for every conceivable excellence that a singer can
possess. The raptures of the knowing critics over Ravogli's
dramatic depth are picked up and reproduced at second-
hand in the next puff of Patti; whilst the authentic descriptions of Patti's roulade and Marimon's shake are boldly laid
at the feet of Ravogli, whose powers of florid execution are
hardly greater than mine. This goes on until the advancing
age of the famous one makes the critic feel that it is time to
discover a falling-off somewhere; and then you have him
gravely remarking that Patti no longer sings with her old
fire and grandeur, just as he will tell us some day that Ravogli's superb voice, though the hand of Time has impaired
its once faultless flexibility, still remains, etc. In the same
way we are now being informed that Santley has left behind
him in Australia merits that he never possessed. I was conscious of no such deterioration on Monday week as others
pretend to have discovered. Certainly the voice is not so
smooth and young as it once was: he no longer, for instance,
sings G with the ease of a tenor. But that was the case long
before he went to Australia. Again, the rough Lancashire

diction, the nervous haste, the ineptitude of his attempts to throw himself from one character into another in such dramatic narratives as The Erl King: these shew that he is no Coquelin; but when was he ever a Coquelin? On the other hand, the qualities to which he owes his great reputation— the perfectly placed voice, the unforced, unspoiled tone, the fine vocal touch, the natural quality of his typical (and therefore exceptional) baritone: all these were as conspicuous last week as they were when he sang the same songs just before his departure. To shut our ears persistently to all a singer's imperfections in order to proclaim him a phœnix, and then to take advantage of his going to Australia to suddenly open them and proclaim him a wreck, is neither generous nor sensible. As far as my judgment goes, the voyage has done him much more good than the lapse of time has done him harm.

A desperate attempt has been made to get an autobiography out of Rubinstein by setting a shorthand writer at him. The idea was that he should make a full confession to the stenographer, who should, on his part, maintain an impassive attitude and take him down verbatim. Now Rubinstein is an impatient man, and withal so uncommunicative that his own account of his private correspondence is: "It has absolutely no existence. I am not partial to the pen; and I particularly dislike writing letters." Consequently, though the stenographer escaped with his life, the autobiography is not a success. Still, its failure has a certain characteristic value. As might be expected from Rubinstein's work as an artist, he reveals himself as a hugely energetic man, of no great breadth of sympathy or clearness of intelligence; behind our time (and indeed hardly up to his own) in musical development, though extraordinarily intense in that development as far as it goes; and deeply convinced of the religious nature and function of art. "If the theatre is to be a means of education," he says, "let it be above the people." And again: "It needs no prophet to foretell the beneficent influence of a permanent opera in the provinces. The standard of morality cannot fail to rise." The much-discussed passage about our musical backwardness runs as follows: "Of the German people at least fifty per cent understand music; of the French not more than sixteen per cent; whilst among the English—the least musical of peoples—not more than two per cent can be found with any knowledge of music. Even the Americans have a higher appreciation of music than the English. I speak frankly, but without malice; for I have always been most hospitably received in England. But whilst I am deeply sensible of this kindness, I cannot refrain from saying that their ignorance of music is only exceeded by their lack of appreciation. The children of Albion may resent this candor. Perhaps it would have been wiser to have reserved my opinion." Do not dream of apologising, friend Rubinstein: your remarks may do the children of Albion some good.

4 February 1891

ON second thoughts I have resolved to suppress my notice of Ivanhoe. I was upon my high horse last week when I wrote it; and when I went on Saturday, and saw how pleasantly everything went off, and how the place was full of lovely and distinguished persons, and how everybody applauded like mad at the end, and, above all, how here at last was an English opera-house superbly equipped for its purpose, I felt what a brute I had been to grumble—and that, too, after having been indulged with peeps at the proofs of the score, admission to rehearsals, and every courtesy that could pass betwixt myself and the management, without loss of dignity on either side. Just as a sort of penance, and to shew what I am capable of, I give a couple of paragraphs from the discarded notice. Here they are:

"Proceeding then at once to the faults of Ivanhoe, I maintain that it is disqualified as a serious dramatic work by the composer's failure to reproduce in music the vivid characterization of Scott, which alone classes the novel among the masterpieces of fiction. It would hardly be reasonable to

demand that Sir Arthur should have intensified the work of
Scott as Mozart intensified that of Beaumarchais and even
of Molière; but he might at least have done as much for him
as he has done for Mr Gilbert in Patience and its forerunners:
that is, before the Savoy operas became machine-made like
The Gondoliers. Take for example Scott's Bois Guilbert,
the fierce Templar, the original 'bold, bad man,' tanned
nearly black, disfigured with sword-cuts, strong, ambitious,
going on for fifty, a subject for Verdi or Velasquez. Is it possible to sit patiently and hear the music of the drawing room,
sensuous and passionate without virility or intelligence, put
into the mouth of such a figure? Not with all the brass and
drum sauce in the world. Then there is that gallant scamp
De Bracy, for whom we all have a sneaking fondness because he broke down ignominiously when Rowena began to
cry, and then went out and stood up like a man to King
Richard's terrific horseplay. Did he deserve nothing better
than to be treated as a mere fop out of Princess Ida? And
Richard himself, whose occasional attempts to behave like
a king were so like Mr Pickwick's famous attempt to sneer:
surely, though it is quite conceivable that he should be singing the same sentimental ballad whenever he is neither drinking nor killing anybody, yet the ballad should not be a mere
paraphrase of the Wandering Minstrel song in The Mikado,
as if Cœur de Lion had picked up that subtle strain by ear,
and not picked it up quite accurately. As to Cedric singing
the most arrant modern tum-tum in honor of the Crusaders
—no, Sir Arthur: it may be very pretty and very popular;
but it is not Ivanhoe."

"I have here condemned the composer, and not the book-
maker, because, with Scott's novel to work upon, it was
clearly the composer's business to dramatize it musically
himself, resorting to a librettist's aid only for the filling in of
the lyrics, and of such speeches as could not be taken verbatim from Scott. The task would not, I grant, have been an
easy one; for though the material of the story is dramatic
enough, yet, being a story, it is told with a disregard of stage

conditions which no playwright's ingenuity could entirely overcome. It is true that the resources of music-drama surpass those of narrative in some respects: the castle of Torquilstone might have been exhibited in three compartments, with the scene between Rowena and De Bracy in one, that between Bois Guilbert and Rebecca in another, and Front de Bœuf and the Jew in the cellar, all three couples proceeding simultaneously to the point at which they are interrupted by the horn of the besiegers. Some polyphonic skill would have been required in the composition of the music; and only a comprehensive *coup d'œil* and *coup d'oreille* could have taken it all in; but then Sir Arthur is an accomplished contrapuntist, and the London public has had some training at Barnum's in the practice of watching several shows at the same time. Yet this disposes of but one difficulty. The tournament—and what would Ivanhoe be lacking the tournament?—is obviously impracticable without adjourning to the Agricultural Hall. Still, though the jousting must perforce be done by description, it is hard to have to exchange the inimitable commentary of Isaac of York—'Father Abraham! how fiercely that Gentile rides!' etc.—for alternate characterless fragments of recitative from Locksley and Friar Tuck, officiating as a pair of bawling showmen. This, however, is but a trivial sample of the way in which the story has been gutted of every poetic and humorous speech it contains. Here is a piece of Scott's dialogue in the scene in the lists in Templestowe, with Mr Sturgis's 'restorations' (in the architectural sense) of the same:

'REBECCA. Say to the Grand Master that I maintain my innocence, and do not yield me as justly condemned, lest I become guilty of mine own blood. Say to him that I challenge such delay as his forms will permit, to see if God, whose opportunity is in man's extremity, will raise me up a deliverer; and when such uttermost space is passed, may His holy will be done!

'GRAND MASTER. God forbid that Jew or Pagan should

impeach us of injustice! Until the shadows be cast from the west to the eastward will we wait to see if a champion shall appear for this unfortunate woman.

'BOIS GUILBERT. Rebecca, dost thou hear me?

'REBECCA. I have no portion in thee, cruel, hard-hearted man.

'BOIS GUILBERT. Ay, but dost thou understand my words? for the sound of my voice is frightful in mine own ears. I scarce know on what ground we stand, or for what purpose they have brought us hither. . . . But hear me, Rebecca: a better chance hast thou for life and liberty than yonder knaves and dotard dream of. Mount thee behind me on my steed—on Zamor, etc., etc.

"Mr Sturgis 'adapts' the above to the stage as follows:

'REBECCA. I am innocent. Now, if God will, even in this last dark hour He will appoint a champion. But if no champion come, I bow before His holy will and am content to die.

'GRAND MASTER. Sound trumpets! . . . Now, since no champion makes answer here, draw near and bind the maiden to the stake, for surely she shall die.

'BOIS GUILBERT. It shall not be! Fools, dotards, will ye slay the innocent? Butchers and burners, she is mine, I say! I say she shall not burn! Back, as you hope to live! . . . Swear to be mine, and I will save thee now. My horse is nigh at hand, etc., etc.'

If the noble dialogue of Scott is not more suitable for English music than the fustian of Mr Sturgis, then so much the worse for English music. Purcell would have found it so. I protest, in the name of my own art of letters, against a Royal English Opera which begins by handing over a literary masterpiece for wanton debasement at the hands of a journeyman hired for the job."

Now all this was evidently mere temper. Poor Mr Sturgis, I suppose, knew no better: he unquestionably meant to improve on the book; and if, when he came forward hand in hand with the composer amid thunders of applause on Saturday night, nobody had a brickbat to break on him for love of Scott, why should I spoil the harmony of the occasion by striving to belittle him? But the fact is, I must have been possessed by a demon when I wrote that notice, for I find lower down in it that even the building did not please me.

"The scene-painters," I wrote, "have alone dreamt of going to Scott for inspiration; and they stand forth as gods in consequence; though even to them I will say that if Mr Ryan will go round to the front, and look at that pointed doorway under the Norman arch in the scene where Rebecca describes the siege from the window, he will agree with me that it was not a happy thought. Otherwise, the Torquilstone architecture contrasts most favorably with the curious absence of any architectural idea in the auditorium. The view of the stage from all parts of the house, as far as I was able to test it, is capital; and the acoustical conditions are of the happiest. Also the upholstery and materials are luxurious and costly to excess; but as to any beauty of form or individuality of design, I have been in hydraulic lifts of much higher excellence in these respects. Even the exterior has been disfigured by a glass and iron rain-shelter, which I can hardly believe to be the work of human hands, so utterly destitute is it of any trace of the artist's sense. But people who are not particular about these matters will find every comfort and convenience that money can buy; and the majority, I fear, will find that a sufficient recommendation. Indeed, I should not go out of the way to complain myself if it were not for the ostentation of artistic effort everywhere, challenging me at all points to give my opinion—as a musical critic—whether the building is not really handsome."

But enough of this unsociable document. The truth is that the theatre is very pretty; and so is the opera. I do not say that the ceiling is equal to that of Henry VII's chapel in Westminster, or that the score is in any essential point an advance upon that of Macfarren's Robin Hood, which had a long run at Her Majesty's thirty years ago; but who ever said they were? My business is to praise them for what they are, not to disparage them for what they are not. Ivanhoe, then, has plenty of charming songs in it; and the crash-bang and the top notes in the exciting situations are as stirring as heart could wish. The score is as neat as a new pin. The instrumentation, from the big drum upwards, is effective, practised, and stylish, with all the fullness given by the latest improvements; the tone-colors, though rich, are eminently gentlemanly; there is no Bohemian effervescence, no puerile attempts at brilliancy or grandiosity; all is smooth, orderly, and within the bounds of good breeding. There are several interesting examples of that coincidence of inspiration which is so common in music. For instance, the third act of Ivanhoe begins like Berlioz' Faust, with a scene before sunrise for the tenor. And the musical expression found by both composers is practically identical. Again, when Rebecca presently comes in, and sings Ah! would that thou and I might lead our sheep! we hear through the music a delightful echo of that other *pastorale* in the first act of Orphée aux Enfers. Then the hag Ulrica no sooner begins her invocation of Zernebock than we recognize her as first cousin to Ulrica in Un Ballo, with her Re dell' abisso affrettati. The rousing prelude to the Friar's drinking song might be a variation on Vivat Bacchus from Mozart's Seraglio. The chief stroke of humor in the opera is the patriotic chorus in the tournament scene, to which, with a sly reference to Mr Macdermott, Sir Arthur has imparted an unmistakeable music-hall swing, which must have sorely tempted the gallery to join in.

As there is a double cast, I must be careful not to fall into such an error of taste as to draw comparisons; for, after all, a critic is expected to be a gentleman. Therefore I shall keep to myself my opinion that Miss Macintyre is a stronger and more intelligent Rebecca than Miss Thudichum, who is, on the other hand, more sympathetic and yields more readily to musical inspiration than Miss Macintyre, besides having the more suitable voice in point of tone-color. Nor must I hint that Miss Lucile Hill, if her performance was looked forward to with less curiosity than that of Miss Palliser, is a much more credibly Saxon Rowena, in voice as well as in appearance, interesting as Miss Palliser is in her own way. And if I permit myself to remark that Mr Norman Salmond is a more congenial Richard than his gloomy and remorseful rival, it is not that I wish for a moment to contrast the two to the disadvantage of either.

As to Mr Ben Davies, the robust and eupeptic Ivanhoe, who sets to with the mailed Bois Guilbert at Templestowe in a comfortable immensikoff of the period, and gets beaten because he is obviously some three stone over his proper fighting weight, his obstreperous self-satisfaction put everybody into good humor. But unless he tones himself down a little at future performances, Mr O'Mara, from the artistic point of view, will leave him nowhere. I do not care how good a voice a man has: I object to his rushing out of the stage-picture and bawling at me—not to mention that it sets everybody else bawling too. The Templar of Mr Sturgis' version is a pirate king sort of personage, of whom nothing sensible can be made. Mr Noije did not dress at the rehearsal at which I saw him play; and as Mr Oudin was in full war-paint both at rehearsal and of course at the first performance, it is not surprising that I have a penny plain impression of Mr Noije, and a twopence colored one of Mr Oudin. But I applaud them both for their struggles with the worst and most difficult part in the opera. Further comment I must defer until I have seen a public performance by the second cast. I may, however, confirm the good reports of the chorus and the orchestra, especially the orchestra.

Several other performers and composers—Albéniz, Henschel, Mozart, Wagner, etc.—may be safely postponed to next week, their lasting qualities being better ascertained than those of Ivanhoe.

MAID MARIAN, the new opera at the Prince of Wales Theatre, is a good deal better than anyone dared to expect after Captain Thérèse and its fore-runners. Naturally we all dreaded that the book would prove an incoherent series of pretexts for exhibiting the principal favorites of the company as nearly as possible in the costumes and business of their previous successes. In devising these things, men of established literateness have over and over again fallen into such abysses of futility and wearisomeness as to make outsiders doubt whether whey knew how to read and write, much less to invent and compose. If I were a manager, I would harden my heart against all veterans who know the stage and know the public and know the people they have to write for. When a man has eaten of that tree, the sooner he is driven out of the garden the better. It will always be found that his reputation is based on triumphs achieved when he was a novice, and dreamed that the public wanted to forget themselves in a pleasant story at the theatre, and not to yawn over stale theatrical gossip illustrated by *tableaux vivants*.

All my hopes of Maid Marian were founded on the fact that I had never in my life heard of Mr H. B. Smith, the librettist, or Mr Reginald de Koven, the composer—though so jealously do I guard my innocence of such matters that this by no means argues them unknown. The result justified my attitude; for seldom has man been less bored of late years by a comic opera than I on Thursday last. Mr de Koven's selection from the general stock of tunes and rhythms has been made with taste and intelligence—always with ease and vivacity, and sometimes with real feeling. The song of the bells in the third act is quite charming: in spite of the lateness of the hour, the double encore was endured without the slightest impatience; and Miss Violet Cameron sang it with an artistic grace of which I confess I had hardly thought her capable. Indeed, to see Miss Cameron for once in an opera in which the author has not deliberately treated her as a mere beauty in a shop window, forcing vulgarity upon a talent that is naturally quiet and sympathetic, and exploiting her beauty in such a fashion as to betray an utter lack of any true artistic sense of its great value: this alone would be worth a visit to Maid Marian, even if Allan-a-Dale were the only pleasing figure in it.

But none of the artists have this time to brazen out a struggle against degrading and dehumanizing parts. The fun is not unbecoming to those who make it: even where the play is flimsiest there are none of the arid wastes of inanity, feebly favored with blackguardism, which have made many a modern comic opera depressing even to those who were beneath being revolted by it. Mr Coffin appears to greater advantage than ever in a part which allows him to be natural and manly without incongruity; and Miss Attalie Claire as Annabel does far better than was possible in the odiously silly rôle in which she made her first appearance. Miss Manola keeps Marian going with credit, though, as the part is the weakest in the opera, and she not particularly well fitted by it, she is unable to make as much of the occasion as her colleagues, who are suited to a hair's breadth. Mr Monkhouse, as the Sheriff of Nottingham, succeeds in shewing that he has a touch of the true comedian in him; and if Mr Le Hay does not venture beyond tomfoolery, it is not for lack of opportunity. Madame Amadi and the gentlemen who fill the minor parts are all efficient. The numbers which proved most popular in the score are the tinkers' chorus, the burlesque glee, a capital quartet in the second act, a serenade warbled by Mr Coffin in his most seductive mezza voce, and the song of the bells as aforesaid. Mr Clement Scott has contributed a lyric which begins:

O, promise me that some day you and I
Shall take our loves together to some sky,

and goes on prettily about "those first sweet violets of early spring which come in whispers."

I am sorry to have to add that Mr Sedger again permitted Mr Charles Harris to send a handful of unfortunate little children on the stage at the latest possible hour. They were not pretty children; they could only dance in the most childish fashion; they were in the way of the other dancers; they detracted instead of adding to the artistic effect of the stage picture; in short, Mr Harris's motive in allowing them to be present was clearly a philanthropic desire to give them some money to take home to their parents. However, as the children can be withdrawn from the stage and paid all the same, he can easily gratify the humanitarian instincts of the public in this matter without stifling his own.

I ventured on a couple of acts of Ivanhoe again last week; and I must say I saw no sign of the falling-off in public interest which was said to have been apparent on the second night. The house seemed to me as good a one as any manager could reasonably expect or desire. The only reaction that has really occurred is a reaction in feeling after the extravagant hopes raised by the puffery with which the Royal English Opera was inaugurated. A comparison of the newspapers of 1876 with those of 1891 would lead anybody who knew no better to conclude that the opening of the Bayreuth Festspielhaus with The Niblung's Ring was an insignificant event in comparison with the opening of the Shaftesbury Avenuehaus with Ivanhoe. The innocent people who believe whatever they see in print—and among these are still a considerable section of the playgoing public—are convinced that something magnificent and momentous beyond all parallel in the annals of music has just happened. And no wonder! Editors have given their space, critics their superlatives, with reckless profusion, apparently for the sake of Mr Carte's *beaux yeux*. Dissentients have been intimidated by the unanimity of the cheering; and the fuglemen have been shameless in their disposition to make themselves agreeable. There has never been anything like it since first the press began to notice music.

And now to improve the occasion. First, I would ask Mr

Carte whether all those silly columns which soddened the Monday papers have convinced anybody that Ivanhoe is a greater work than Don Juan, than Les Huguenots, than Der Freischütz, than Faust, than Die Meistersinger—and I contemptuously submit that if they do not mean this they mean nothing. Well, the adept, who knows that on these terms they must mean nothing, is justly incensed at being trifled with on so gigantic a scale; whilst the novice, who swallows the stuff and rushes to the theatre, comes away deeply disappointed, whereas if he went with any sort of reasonable expectation he would find a good deal to please him. The truth is Mr Carte is not a master of the art of advertisement. With all his experience he has fallen into the beginner's error of thinking that praise cannot be overdone, and that nothing else is of any use.

Now it is quite true that over-puffery is impossible; but over-praise is not puffery at all, because it neither interests people nor convinces them. I yield to no man in the ingenuity and persistence with which I seize every opportunity of puffing myself and my affairs; but I never nauseate the public by getting myself praised. My favorite plan is to select some gentleman who has a weakness for writing to the papers, and who writes rather well when his blood is up. Him I provoke, by standing on his tenderest corn, to write to the papers saying that I have no sense of humor, of morals, of decency, of art, of manners, or what not. This creates an impression that the national feeling on these points runs so strongly the other way as to require urgent correction; and straightway many people who never heard of me in their lives become ashamed of their ignorance. Then all the enemies of my assailant constitute themselves my partisans; and so I become famous to a degree that goads those who see through the whole puff to write fresh letters and paragraphs denying that I am famous at all, thereby making me more famous, or infamous, or what you will; for any sort of notoriety will serve my turn equally. All this would be the easiest thing in the world did not so much depend on the adroitness and opportuneness of the original provocation; and here, no doubt, my well-known critical insight, developed by profound economic, historic, artistic, and social studies, gives me an advantage. But if Mr Carte will study my method, he will, I think, profit by seeing how the damaging recoil after the Ivanhoe boom might have been avoided, and much ineffective fulsomeness converted into invaluable stimulant, if only an element of attack and controversy had been provided.

There is another point in the recoil which specially concerns Sir Arthur Sullivan. The score of Ivanhoe is far superior to the libretto; and if it be true, as I affirm, and as even the most abandoned of the laudatory critics hint between the lines, that nearly half the second and third acts—that is, the last two scenes of all, and the second scene of the second act —would be better out than in, the fault is entirely Mr Sturgis's (although I still think it serves Sir Arthur right for not having constructed his own libretto). But, according to the press, Mr Sturgis has risen to the full height of the occasion, and has given the composer the utmost opportunity of exercising his powers. Consequently Sir Arthur has not only been baulked in his artistic effort by the weakness of the libretto, but he has to bear the blame of the shortcoming himself in order that nothing may be said against his colleague. It really does not do to spread butter on both sides of the bread. However, the balance of dramatic criticism will soon be redressed. Next Monday week there will be performed, for the first time in England, Rosmersholm, one of the masterpieces of Henrik Ibsen. We shall see how the papers which have just proclaimed Mr Sturgis a great dramatic poet will take it out of Ibsen. The dramatic critics sometimes jibe at us, their musical brethren, because we came so frightfully to grief over Wagner. I should not be surprised if we found a *tu quoque* presently to console ourselves with.

I see that Reményi, whose eminence as a violinist is almost as great a secret as Dante Rossetti's eminence as a painter was for a long time, announces an afternoon concert for Thursday, just before his departure from England. As it is to take place at Colonel North's, at Eltham, and the tickets are a guinea apiece, inclusive of special train, I am afraid the news is of little interest to the general public.

18 February 1891

ON the 10th, the Bach Choir, which has improved as a singing body since I last heard it, gave us rather more Bach than it was quite able for. The cantata, Ich hatte viel Bekümmermiss, went well; and I can hardly believe that even the densest Philistine in the room was left quite unmoved by the religious love-duet—just such another as that in Wachet auf—and by the trio and chorale following. But the motet was a mere exhibition of incompetence. It is true that the physical difficulty of getting through a long and complicated unaccompanied work without breaking down or dragging the pitch into impossible depths was triumphantly mastered; but the preoccupation caused by the arduousness of the feat hindered all attention to beauty of tone or sensibility of treatment. For the first minute or two all the buzzing noises which attend awkward and hasty singing rose to such a din that a blind listener might have guessed that only a dozen of the choir were singing through an animated conversation carried on in whispers by the rest. Further on the tone became a little cleaner; and the tenors and basses occasionally sang up spiritedly in the true English choral fashion, as if to call attention to their being a fine body of men; but the motet might just as well have been a bare exercise in counterpoint for anything else that the performance brought out.

The Whitsuntide cantata, O, Ewiges Feuer, finished the concert, which was too long, considering the great strain made on the attention by music of such fullness and sublety of detail. Mr Morrow attacked the original first trumpet part with the greatest gallantry; but it was too high for him. The strain was obvious, and the tone forced and hard. Still, it would be a pity to give up the highest register of the trumpet as a bad job again. Julius Kosleck's performances have shewn us the great orchestral value of those silvery ringing notes which seem to come from the sky; and he is a living proof that a nineteenth-century trumpeter able to touch high D, and to hold out through a performance of a long work like the Mass in B minor, is not an impossibility. Who has not occasionally heard an amateur of the posthorn display powers of lip sufficient to cope with the most unreasonable demands of "the heroic art," as kettledrum and trumpet-playing used to be called? Mr Morrow, though he falls short of Kosleck, is able at least to improve on the effects produced by re-scoring the trumpet parts for clarionets, or transposing them. The solo singers were Mrs Hutchinson, who excelled herself in the soprano part; Mr Hirwen Jones, who, with a little more practice at Bach, would soon supply that want of quality in the lower part of his compass which was the chief drawback to his performance of the tenor music; Mr Plunket Greene, who was fairly equal to the occasion in the wonderful duet; and Miss Hilda Wilson.

On the following Friday I went to St Anne's, Soho, at half-past seven, to hear the St John Passion. These services take place every Friday evening, and will continue until Good Friday. Let me, by the bye, counsel a careful avoidance of tickets marked "Special," and conferring the privilege of admission between a quarter and half past seven at the Dean Street door; for they also confer disabilities of the most exasperating character. On presenting mine, I was admitted by a policeman to the almost empty church, and referred to a churchwarden for a seat. I should have preferred dealing with a pew-opener, whom I could have corrupted by a tip. The churchwarden, with the natural human impulse to part with his dearest treasures last, deliberately selected the worst seat in the church, and told me I must sit there. Sit there accordingly I did until half-past seven, when the unspecialized ticket-holders entered riotously and spread themselves over the seats which I had idiotically supposed to be reserved. Then the bell began to din a certain keynote into our heads; and when, after half an hour's ding-dong, it was firmly fixed there, the organ stole upon our ears with a soft melody in a key exactly a tone and three-quarters sharp to that of the bell, which still jangled solemnly on. Never since I was baptized have I felt less in harmony with consecrated walls than whilst listening, with my teeth on edge, to that execrable discord.

When the bell stopped, I found myself, not a worshipper, but a critic. As such, I cannot refrain from informing the gentleman who intoned the service that he has not the most elementary notion of how to do it. He produced his voice from the throat much as Mr Penley does, but without that gentleman's eye to humorous effect, and also without his intelligible articulation; for I could not distinguish a solitary word. I recognized the Lord's Prayer by the help of the choir, and noted that it fell about half a tone as it went on. The lesson was read quite distinctly by another gentleman: he was no artist; but he gave it out like a man who was not disposed to stand any nonsense. On the whole, I must say that the service was treated in a way that shocked me. Granted that the paganism of my profession has so got into my bones that I cannot help looking at a service just as I look at an opera (and I should be a very poor critic indeed if I did not take my function to be as religious a one as man can discharge, and one which, if it is not fit to be exercised in a church, is not fit to be exercised anywhere), yet surely I ought not to be asked to tolerate from a clergyman at the altar a wilful neglect of the technical part of his business that I should never be expected to tolerate from a ballet-dancer. Have these clerical gentlemen ever noticed how the noblest music becomes ridiculous and noxious when uttered by the sort of amateur who is too self-satisfied or too slovenly to cultivate his powers carefully?

If so, has it ever occurred to them to consider what effect a chapter of the Bible may produce under the like treatment —and I estimate the difficulty of doing justice to a chapter of Isaiah as about equal to that of singing an aria by Gluck? Why, Talma said it required eighteen years' work to finish him as a master of diction. There was only one really impressive passage in the entire service at St Anne's; and that was the singing of "It is finished" by a boy—a profane, unordained boy with an alto voice. If my recollection serves me aright, the Church has some warrant beyond my word for admitting that even babes and sucklings may make better ministers than gentlemen who do not seem to know the difference between a collect and a gargle. I may add—though this matter is less important—that the St John Passion, or what they did of it, has been carefully rehearsed, and is as well done as the artistic material available admits of. It contains some curiously jejune flights of fancy on Bach's part, and is, as I presume all the world knows, almost trivial compared with the great St Matthew Passion.

Arbos, the Spanish violinist introduced to us by Albéniz, has made no very deep impression on London so far. At his first appearance he tried over the Kreutzer Sonata, and did not seem to think much of it, though here and there a passage evidently struck him as rather good. Then he polished off Bach's Chaconne in D minor very neatly, but yet in a take it or leave it sort of manner that half provoked the audience to leave it. He is a player of no mean address and general intelligence, this Señor Arbos; but he has no intention of giving himself away to the public or to the composers, and I am afraid that they, being by this time rather spoilt in that respect, will return his coldness. Joachim is back again in much better preservation than he was two years ago. He played the E major Partita at the Bach concert admirably; and at the Popular Concert the night before nothing could have been more enjoyable in its way than the pretty Brahms trio which he played with Miss Davies and Paersch, whose horn-playing is fine enough to raise rents in any really musical capital. The concert ended with the Beethoven septet, always popular. But though I can enjoy it still with the youngest, I fled precipitately on this occasion before the end of the first section of the Allegro. Whether Joachim was impatient of the staleness of the work, or in a hurry to get home, or too tired to do anything but fall back on the habits of his shallow-genteel school, I cannot say; I can only vouch for the fact that he took that broad, free, elate theme with an empty haste that made the whole movement impossible from the outset. There were no such reverses at Reményi's concert at Eltham on the 12th.

It is useless to compare Reményi with Joachim: they are both fiddlers, it is true; but then John the Baptist and the late Archbishop Tait were both preachers, yet to weigh one against the other was always admittedly out of the question. If there is to be a comparison at all, Sarasate must be the other term of it. In negative excellence—freedom from blemish—Sarasate's playing is certainly superior. In academic qualities of execution, too, the prolonged serenely perfect note that Sarasate makes his violin utter with a single delicate stroke of the bow would take a gold medal from the white-hot sound that Reményi sends whirring at you with at least four full strokes, much as Wilhelmj used to. Again, Sarasate, in his quiet and certain mastery of every sort of passage, shews himself the more highly trained player. But in the intensity of life in the tone—and this affords a cardinal test of a player's force—in vigor and originality of conception, in alertness of interest and unhesitating belief in his own way of doing it, Reményi often makes Sarasate appear a mere musician by contrast. In the concerto (with a piano for orchestra) he woke up Mendelssohn out of his customary pale Philharmonic politeness in an astonishing way. His playing of the last movement, which Sarasate treats as a mere record-breaking exhibition of speed, was a masterpiece of creative execution; he transfigured it with innumerable broken lights touched in with infallible judgment.

To declare Sarasate a better or worse violinist than Reményi is about as sensible as declaring Claude a better or worse painter than Constable; but I am not sure that it might not be worth while to open the question—not here or now, though, if you please—whether in Reményi the artist has not gained as well as the man by his refusal to sacrifice all other interests and activities to the cultivation of his violin-playing machinery. His very appearance among musicians is stimulating: he has nothing of "the professional" about him; he might be anything active, from a Chancellor to a shoemaker. Colonel North wound up the concert by a blunt and warrior-like speech, in which, after remarking that this classical music was all very well, but that we wanted something that we knew something about, he called upon Reményi to give us Home, Sweet Home, which was accordingly done with imperturable complaisance, and with a penetrating charm that would have consumed Patti with jealousy. Our millionaire host could hardly conceal his emotion at the line, "Be it ever so humble," of his favorite air.

25 February 1891

I HAVE to announce an important move on the part of the London branch of the Wagner Society, which has almost led to a reconciliation between me and that body. The misunderstanding came about in this way. I once gave them a guinea for the good of the cause; and they spent thirteen shillings of it on a horrible evening party. Then, to appease me, they bought a ticket for a Richter concert, and made me a present of it—a pretty treat for a man who was almost dead of concerts, and was throwing half a dozen tickets per day into the waste-paper basket. Naturally, I received an application for a second guinea with speechless indignation. It may be asked what they did with the other eight shillings. Well, they sent me four numbers of their quarterly, The Meister, for half of it—and I admit that The Meister was good value for the money—but they sent the remaining four shillings to the Bayreuth people, who had just cleared a profit out of a series of performances to which I had contributed four pounds. This was enough to make any man mad; and as there was nothing to prevent me from getting The Meister from Messrs Kegan Paul for four shillings

paid across the counter (not to mention that I always get review copies), I forswore the Wagner Society, as I thought,
for ever. Now, however, the Society makes a fresh bid.

The translations of Wagner's writings in The Meister
have deservedly proved a success; for they are good Wagner
and good English, being made by men who understand the
language of the philosophy of art in both tongues. But as
The Meister does not run to a hundred and twenty pages a
year, it would take half a century to complete a translation of
Wagner's ten volumes in such quarterly doses. Therefore
the Society proposes to issue, besides The Meister, six instalments per year of translation, in separate numbers, which
can be bought for a shilling apiece by outsiders. And this
raises the question, Shall I subscribe again to the Society, or
shall I simply pay five shillings a year to Kegan Paul for the
translations (there is to be a reduction of a shilling when you
buy six together), and four for The Meister, thereby saving
eleven shillings a year? I wish I could make up my mind
about it. As to the evening party, I object to that entirely:
the sort of recruit that gets caught in such traps now goes to
the Meistersingers, the Ballad Singers, the Grosvenor Club,
etc., where he can have half a dozen lively concerts for every
one dull evening which the Wagner Society can offer him.
The German subsidy I also repudiate, because we are immeasurably worse off than the Germans in musical matters.
I have to sit in our vulgar diamond-show at Covent Garden,
listening to scratch performances of Faust and Les Huguenots, whilst Mottl is producing Les Troyens in Carlsruhe,
Levy conducting Siegfried at Munich, and Richter using
his left hand at Vienna to conduct Carmen, because his right
is fatigued with perpetual Wagner. Next autumn I shall
have to pay £20 to hear Tannhäuser properly done at Bayreuth because I have not the remotest chance of hearing it
even decently done at home. Of course there is Ivanhoe; but
even Ivanhoe is not everything. I shall have to subsidize not
only the Festspielhaus at Bayreuth, but the London, Chat-
ham and Dover, or Great Eastern Railways, with other lines

whose names I forget—except that vile Links-Rheinischer
with its string of joggling dustbins—and the hotel-keepers
of Brussels, Cologne, Mayence, Nuremberg, and Bayreuth
itself. Now there is no fun in all this for me. The sea passage
makes me ill; Cologne Cathedral, as "restored" by the German empire, brings on a relapse; and the carnivorous *table
d'hôte* which wiles away the Rhine for those who have been
there before, fills me with nothing but loathing. And in the
meantime I am spending all my holiday time and money,
without getting a holiday. The moral is obvious. If there
were a Festspielhaus on Richmond Hill, charging fifteen
pounds for admission to the regulation Bayreuth cyclus of
four performances, I should pay willingly and consider myself a gainer by the transaction. And since there must be
many others of the like mind, why in the name of common
sense does not this London branch of the Wagner Society
declare itself an autonomous English Wagner Society, and
save up the fifty pounds a year which it now spends in sending coals to Newcastle, to form a fund for placing a Wagner
Theatre on Richmond Hill? The only objection to it is that
it is impossible. What of that? The Bayreuth theatre was ten
times as impossible when it was first conceived; yet it has
been an accomplished fact these fifteen years. Besides, it
does not become gentlemen who propose that the English
people should keep their Wagner theatre in Bavaria to talk
about impossibility. The arrangement to which they are
contributing 4s. per head per year is not only impossible,
but impracticable, which is a real objection.

On the whole, I am inclined to conclude that I can do no
good by holding one opinion and backing the other to the
extent of 12s. a year. I had rather give the money to Mr
Grein's Théâtre Libre, which is likely to help Wagnerism
more than all the £20 pilgrimages in the world. When the
Bayreuth reserve fund is replaced by the Richmond Hill
reserve fund, then it will be time enough to open my hand.

Whilst I am on the subject of Bayreuth, I may as well
give the particulars of the autumn arrangements. There will

be twenty performances—ten of Parsifal, seven of Tannhäuser, and three of Tristan—from July 19th to August
19th, both inclusive. It will, therefore, be possible to see
either Parsifal or Tannhäuser twice within four successive
performances, but not Tristan. The first and last sets contain two Parsifals, with a Tristan in each; and the two beginning July 26th and August 9th each contain two Parsifals
and two Tannhäusers. It is by no means too soon to secure
seats now. The Festspielhaus is so admirably constructed
that people are apt to think that it does not matter where
their seats are, so perfect is the view from all parts of the
auditorium. But the distance of the back seats from the stage
makes a considerable difference to all but very long-sighted
persons. If you want to see the facial play of the artists, take
my advice and secure tickets in the front half of the house.

The Crystal Palace concerts began on the 14th with an
overture by Miss Ellicott—a pretty piece of writing which
left no impression. The symphony was Schumann's in D
minor, about which one hardly knows exactly what to say. It
is a failure, like most of Schumann's orchestral works; but it
is too interesting to be left always unheard on that account.
Here and there, indeed, it surges up to momentary success.
The beginning is imaginative and full of promise; but at the
end the abuse of the full wind, and the general want of clearness and variety in the instrumentation, make the last chord
more welcome than it ever could be in a work with sufficient
matter in it. The Carmen suite was, perhaps, the most satisfactory number of the program. It consists simply of the
preludes to the acts taken in reversed order, except that the
working up of the jealousy motive from the end of the first
prelude is placed at the beginning of the whole as an exordium. The suite was most delicately played; and the prelude to the fourth act, usually omitted in the theatre, proved,
as might have been expected, a particularly poetic little tone
picture.

At the concert last Saturday, Stavenhagen invited us to
enter into his recent fancy for Beethoven's early concertos

143

by playing the second, just as he selected the third for his own concert. Of course it is easy for a Lisztian champion to execute these works with prodigious smartness; but if he has no respect for them—if he is only indulging a passing fondness for children of a bygone age, he can make no effect with them. I dare not say that Stavenhagen has no respect for the early concertos; but I do say that it is only a theoretical respect: it does not get into his fingers; and the net result is a depreciative misrepresentation of every part of them except the pretty final rondos. Stavenhagen, by the bye, must not be judged by his performances this season. When he was last over here, though he was very ill on the day of his recital, he played at least six times as well as at his recital the other day, when there was nothing specially the matter with him. I have heard many second-rate players handle the Chopin polonaise in A flat better than he did. The transcription of Isolde's death song brought him up to the mark for a moment; but the Erl King, which he had given brilliantly a few days before, went to pieces so absurdly that he could hardly help laughing at himself. He really owes it to us to pull himself together and give another recital in something like the form he displayed when last he played the Todtentanz at the Crystal Palace. Returning to that institution, I have to record that Neruda, having played the Mendelssohn concerto with great glory at the Hallé concert on Friday (which I was unable to attend—to my loss, as I am told and can well believe), declined to venture again for Mr Manns on the following afternoon. Ilona Eibenschütz accordingly came to the rescue with Chopin's F minor concerto, in which she more than justified all the favorable things I said of her on the occasion of her first appearance at the Popular Concerts. At the back of the room, however, the instrument she used was felt to be not quite what was wanted for the concerto. I say this with the less reserve because it is no longer true of the Boardwoods, as it was twelve years ago, that they had fallen so far behind the time as to make their then virtual monopoly of the concert platform a nuisance to themselves, to the public, and to the artists, upon whose gratitude they had strong and perfectly honorable claims. The monopoly is now broken down; the full force of the competition of Steinway, Erard, Bechstein, and Pleyel has been brought to bear on them; and the result is that they have enormously increased the power of their instruments without sacrificing the artistic individuality and homogeneity of tone which always distinguished their pianofortes from the massive overstrung machines which first put them out of countenance. Nevertheless, it did happen on Saturday that Miss Eibenschütz would have been better equipped, as far as her more remote hearers were concerned, with a good Steinway than with the instrument she had. The orchestra was not at its best except in the quieter parts of its work. In the climax of the first movement of the eighth symphony, and in the Tannhäuser overture, it flagged and fell short just at the very points where a miss was as bad as a mile. Miss Rosina Isidor followed up the Chopin concerto by Come bello from Lucrezia. Poor old Come bello! If Miss Isidor had only realized how ridiculous a figure it cut between Chopin and Beethoven, she would have thought twice before bringing it down to the Crystal Palace. The trumpery Italian vocal waltz with which she subsequently favored us was still more out of place. Miss Moody and Mr Manners were more judicious in confining themselves to Gounod and Meyerbeer at the previous concert.

4 *March* 1891

ON Wednesday afternoon last I went into St James's Hall at one minute before three o'clock to hear the Albéniz concert, intending to have the usual twenty minutes or so over the evening paper before business began. To my amazement Albéniz appeared at the stroke of three as if he had been sent up on the platform by electric wire from Greenwich. This is the sort of thing I have been resolving to do all my life without having succeeded in any single instance; and I shall henceforth regard Albéniz not only as one of the pleasantest, most musical, and most original of pianists, but as a man of superior character. These concerts of his deserve support. They are short; they are cheap; they are enjoyable; the music is light and varied enough for afternoon digestion without any compromise as to artistic quality; and the programs, which strike the happy medium between the bare list of pieces and the heavily manufactured "analysis" with quotations (so useful in keeping your eyes on the music and your ears off it), are given without fee. If the experiment fails, it will only shew that the public has not as much good sense as Albéniz. On the afternoon in question Arbos played the Mendelssohn concerto with pianoforte accompaniment, which, played by Albéniz, was by no means the least interesting part of the performance. Arbos is a smooth, finished executant, seldom at fault in his intonation. Once it is understood that he is not a first-rate player, such as Isaÿe, Sarasate, or Reményi, he will disappoint no reasonable person. Madame Belle Cole and Mr Hirwen Jones sang the charming old duet from Spohr's God, Thou are Great; and Albéniz played Chopin's Berceuse and Impromptu in his own manner, dainty without triviality. Why, I wonder, has he dropped those Brassin transcriptions of the rainbow bridge in Das Rheingold, and the fire charm and Valkyrie ride in Die Walküre, which the Wagner Society made him get up? His performances of these were highly effective; and Stavenhagen's success with the Liszt transcription of Isolde's last song shews that the public appetite for Wagner is so sharp for the moment that they would rather have transcriptions than nothing; whilst the hit Paderewski made with the Don Juan fantasia suggests the possibility of reviving that form of composition. I fancy that this is the field in which Albéniz might find the largest and freshest scope for his peculiar talent. He has not the temperament for Beethoven and Schumann, nor the inhumanity to visit Brahms upon us. With Mozart he is not at home except when bringing out the exquisite prettiness of the shallowest end of his work. I almost wish he would try a fantasia of Thalberg's just to see how a modern audience would stand it. I mean, of course, one of his own audiences, and not a crowd of those aborigines who unexpectedly descended on St James's Hall last year, when Madame Teresa Carreño began to slash away at Gottschalk's Pasquinade, Tremolo, etc., as though some superb Junonian contemporary of Arabella Goddard's had shared the fate of Rip Van Winkle. They say that Madame Carreño is so pleased with her success that she is coming back to us this season. If so, I shall be happy to go to see her play.

In spite of all the precautions that have been taken to keep the news from me, I accidentally discovered, in the course of a walk up Bow Street the other night, that Mr Harris has been secretly performing oratorios at Covent Garden. My attention has been kept off these pious orgies by a skilful parade of masked balls. Would I could hope to be treated always with the consideration shewn me in this matter! I am spared the oratorios, in deference to the well-known inadequacy of my constitution to sustain such penitential exercises; but next season, when Mr Harris changes his mind about producing Siegfried, and serves up La Favorita instead, with Mlle Richard to give matronly propriety to the title part, I shall be led to a stall in the front row like a lamb to the slaughter. I have no faith in that lazy Parisian contingent taking the trouble to get up anything that has not been a stock dish at the Opéra for the last ten years.

There are many ways of proving that the social atmosphere of West London is unhealthy; and I have most of them at my fingers' ends. But the most convincing to me is the baneful effect upon musical artists of a run through the drawing rooms. Young Gerardy, who was quite a wonderful artist when he first came, shewed a melancholy falling-off at his last recital. Not that the execution of the ornamental passages was less finished than before; it was rather more so: all the pretty bits were prettier than ever. But the normal playing—the lengths of straightforward work between these delicacies—that was where the deterioration shewed itself. The tone then became comparatively common, careless, valueless—as different as possible from the thoughtful, sensitive touch on the strings that was so remarkable before. Perhaps it only set his private admirers chatting and yawning; anyhow, the boy is the worse for his London experience —more shame for London.

Let me here say determinedly that if we are to have any more 'cello virtuosos, someone must really compose a little new music for the instrument. Goltermann and Popper are all very well; but they are not Mozart and Beethoven. What with Hollmann, Klengel, and Gerardy, I have heard that Mazurka Caprice of Popper's not less than fourteen thousand times within two seasons. It has been encored each time; and the encore piece has always been Popper's Papillons—a pleasing title, but one which now strikes terror into me. Kol Nidrei is quite a novelty after Popper; but even Kol Nidrei palls as the years roll on. I am now always in two minds as to putting myself in the way of hearing Hollmann. On the one hand, there is the chance of his playing a melody by Bach or Schubert, a chance not to be lightly lost. On the other hand, one never can feel sure that those Papillons will not pop out at the last moment and make me wish I had never been born.

Henschel has just brought his six symphony concerts safely into port, having judiciously kept the public up to the mark by announcing shipwreck when he was halfway across. At the fourth concert he tried the attractions of Albani, with great success as far as the filling of the hall was concerned. No doubt the lady was expensive; but Henschel certainly took it out of her (pardon the expression) by putting both the great aria from Der Freischütz and Isolde's death song in the program. The Leise, leise, got pulled about as usual; and the other would have fared no better had it not been too difficult to take many liberties with. But on these great occasions, when Albani is rapturous, and almost everybody is near enough to see the shining of her eyes, she gets on the very softest side of her audience; and criticism only mutters between its teeth when she drawls down the scale of E natural like a woman who will not come downstairs sensibly because she wants to shew off her diamonds. At this concert there was produced a symphonic poem by Mr Percy Rideout, modestly entitled Epipsychidion. It begins with some vague extracts from Tristan, and presently settles down into a sentimental ballad refrain, in the manner of Mr Milton Wellings, set forth with a surprising but second-hand splendor and effusiveness of orchestration. Mr Rideout, though he is younger than most symphonic poets, is man enough, I hope, to excuse my frankness if I tell him that Epipsychidion is not worth a rap, though it is quite the right thing for him to have begun with. The fifth concert, at which I was not present, was a Wagner concert; and so, indeed, was the last one, as far as I heard it. The orchestra has not improved during the season. I do not think the wit of man could move such players to a worse performance of the Tannhäuser overture than that with which the final concert ended. Henschel was in his most perverse humor, beating the pilgrims' march in an impossible fashion, and rushing the rest through headlong, besides deliberately urging the trombones to blare most horribly. Altogether, the performance would have done admirably in the Malay Peninsula. The applause it gained was correctly estimated by an amateur critic, who informed his companion, as I passed him on the stairs, that "You can always fetch 'em if you make a jolly row." The Good Friday music was better; though even here the trombones, in giving out the Parsifal motive at the beginning, were allowed, and had no doubt been instructed, to force their power to a point of sinister coarseness which turned Parsifal into Klingsor at once. In the Siegfried Idyll the conductor at first worried his band more than he inspired them; but later on Wagner got the upper hand of both; and the result, if not thoroughly satisfactory, at least led to some happy moments. On the whole, though the London Symphony concerts have gained

149

ground absolutely, they have lost it relatively, owing to the fact that the orchestra's most immediate competitor this time has been no longer the Richter band, which, for excellent reasons, will always share its defects, but the Manchester men, whose recent exploits have been tremendous. In certainty of execution, and the rare combination of intimate knowledge of their repertory with unimpaired freshness of interest in it, they have distanced even the Crystal Palace orchestra. When they played Berlioz' difficult and complicated Fantastic Symphony they gave Hallé less trouble than Henschel would have with the overture to the Kalif of Bagdad. I do not see how Henschel can improve matters greatly as long as he has to be content with seasons of six concerts spread over three months.

What is wanted is a weekly orchestral concert at St James's Hall practically all the year round, conducted by Henschel from October to May, and thence to the end of the season by Richter. If the scheme does not pay at first, it should be taken over by the County Council, which could meet the loss by at once confiscating the entire property of the Duke of Westminster, as a judgment on him for signing a petition to prevent the schools of London being provided with pianos, on the ground of "extravagance." If this thrifty nobleman were worth his thousand a day to us he would long ago have put a Steinway grand into every Board School in London at his own expense.

Before quitting the subject of the Gerardy recital I should have chronicled the first appearance thereat of Mr Oudin, Sir Arthur Sullivan's Templar, as a concert singer. He revived Le Vallon, one of Gounod's best settings of Lamartine, and an old war-horse of Santley's, with success. His school is French; and he has the chief virtue of it, a charming mezza voce. But he has also its radical vice, a tremolo, which, though not very pronounced, is yet sufficiently so to occasionally obscure the pitch of his notes. With a little more humanity and variety of mood he would be a welcome figure on the platform. At present he seems unable to discard the Templar sufficiently to make himself at home there. As to Miss Kate Rolla, who also sang, she has two accomplishments: she can sing very well; and she can scream like a steam siren. When she screams she pleases herself: when she sings she pleases me. I recommend her to confine herself in future to pleasing me.

11 March 1891

THE Philharmonic Society, English to the backbone, never knows when it is beaten. It has repeatedly shewn itself capable of going on for years in a chronic state of ignominious defeat, without for a moment losing a sense of superiority which Napoleon at the height of his fortunes probably never enjoyed. At such times the critics always flatter it with smooth sayings; for otherwise they would have to attend the concerts, and take infinite pains to find out exactly what is wrong. Consequently no rally is ever made until the people who support the Philharmonic from mere habit die in such numbers that it becomes necessary either to recruit or to carry on the Society at an unbearable loss. Then the directors make good resolutions, and get a new conductor. They once, as all the world knows, got Wagner, who, with the strong common sense to which he then owed his reputation as an unpractical madman, told the directors that their programs were too long, and that no conductor could do better for them than make his choice between thoroughly rehearsing one or two things, leaving the rest to tumble through anyhow, and having everything only half prepared. This was as much as to say that the Philharmonic performances were not the very best and highest and most respectable in the world, an ignorant, ill-bred, presumptuous opinion, which at once stamped its holder as radically unfit for the position of Philharmonic conductor. Exit Wagner accordingly.

This is an old story; but it remains true to the present hour that whenever anything is well rehearsed for a Philharmonic concert, nothing else thereat is rehearsed at all.

For the last season or two we have seen certain composers—Grieg, Moszkowski, Benoit, etc.—all engaged to conduct their own compositions. At the rehearsals, they were of course accorded the first turn; and they naturally kept the band at their works until they had got the effects they wanted. Then there was the concerto player to be attended to: he or she, an artist of European reputation, was not going to be kept waiting for anybody. By the time composer and virtuoso were half satisfied, the men were hungry, impatient, due at other engagements: in short, the rehearsal was virtually over. Mr Mackenzie or Mr Cowen could at most approach the Society's illustrious guests with a polite request for just five minutes at the end to run through Beethoven's Ninth Symphony, or any other trifle that might have been announced. The effect of this was of course to make the unfortunate official conductor, in contrast with the composer who had appropriated all his opportunities of rehearsing, seem only half as competent and conscientious as he really was. But this was no ground for relieving him of the full blame. It was his business to insist on adequate artistic conditions, or, failing them, to resign. Besides, there was no alternative: it was useless to pitch into the Philharmonic directors, who pride themselves on keeping the outside public in its place, and not pampering it with concessions to clamor.

Under these circumstances it is not surprising that Sir Arthur Sullivan did not find it worth his while to retain the baton, and that Mr Mackenzie soon followed his example. Then came Mr Cowen, under whom matters came to such a point that Mr Edward Carpenter, having innocently paid hard cash to hear the Ninth Symphony done by the famous Philharmonic band, wrote to the papers indignantly describing the sort of value he had received. I, still thinking the Philharmonic worth a remonstrance, added a mild word or two; and I think the feeling got fairly afloat among those most concerned that Mr Cowen must either succumb to these attacks or else do away with the foundation for them.

Happily he seems to have chosen the latter course. The performance of Beethoven's C minor symphony on Thursday night was not the heartless, vapid, perfunctory affair it might have been if Mr Carpenter and the rest of us had pocketed our wrongs. A strenuous effort was made to rise to the occasion and sustain the reputation of the band; and the difference for the better was hardly to be described, so vast is the gulf between supercilious indifference and even the hastiest and least carefully concerted activity with a purpose in it. If Mr Cowen and the band keep on their mettle throughout the season, they may yet avert the periodic artistic crisis in the Society's affairs which seemed so imminent last year.

There is, however, another direction in which reform is necessary. On Thursday a new work was produced. It was an overture by Rubinstein, entitled Antony and Cleopatra, a great heaping-up of pompous and luxurious commonplaces into a pretentious tone picture—or rather tone oleograph. In purely mechanical bustle, in redundant platitudes out of Czerny's Études de la Vélocité, in shameless repetitions and complacent confident shallowness, it surpassed the padding of a Rossini overture. That might have been forgiven if Rubinstein had shewn in it the genius upon which Rossini presumed; but I doubt if anyone will have the hardihood to put forward such a claim on his behalf. Even if it had been thoroughly rehearsed, and smoothly and homogeneously executed, it would not have been worth the trouble. Still less was it worth while under the Philharmonic conditions, which tend to develop to the utmost that habit of relying on the adroitness of our players in making their way through new compositions at first or second sight without a breakdown, which is the bane of instrumental music in London. Were it not for the Crystal Palace band, it would be quite correct to say that we have no orchestra just because we have the cleverest players in the world.

We astonish foreign composers by the way we play their music at the first rehearsal. When they find out that we make this an excuse for doing everything with only two rehearsals, they generally thank their stars for the slower methods of the Continent. However, that is not my present point. I want to know why the Philharmonic Society nowadays deliberately devotes itself to the encouragement of cheap and showy music. The best novelty it has lately given us is Mancinelli's Venetian suite, a very pretty piece of promenade music, admirably adapted to the purpose of Dan Godfrey or Strauss, but out of place at concerts solemnized by the elevation of Beethoven's bust before the orchestra. I do not want to draw the line too high up, still less to drive the Society back on its worn-out Mendelssohn, Spohr, Sterndale Bennett repertory; but I do emphatically suggest that such unknown works as the first three scenes of Schumann's Faust are fitter for the Society's efforts than the mock heroics of Peter Benoit; that Berlioz wrote, besides the eternal Carnaval Romain, some overtures which we want to hear at least as much as Antony and Cleopatra; that dozens of English musicians can turn out as much Moszkowski ware as may be required; and that unperformed works by Bach, Haydn, Mozart, and Beethoven, of greater interest for Philharmonic audiences than the Venetian suite, are to be counted by the dozen. I am all for living in the present rather than in the past, as far as works on the same artistic plane are concerned; but between the treasures of the past and the trivialities of the present there should be no hesitation in a society like the Philharmonic.

Mr Manns, who is what the Philharmonic ought to be, and pretends to be, and is not, has produced a pianoforte concerto by Burmeister, a young Hamburger, now settled at Baltimore. The solo part was played by Madame Burmeister in a cheerful, wifely, willing way, but, as it seemed to me, quite inartistically. The work should be thoroughly revised and condensed, and then played again for us by a powerful Lisztian pianist with no domestic interests in the work to distort his or her artistic attitude towards it. It will then be possible to say with more confidence whether the concerto has any real stuff in it. At present it certainly has a great air of life and interest; but I failed to catch the content of all those strenuous climaxes; and the only judgments on it which I do not suspend are the unfavorable ones as to its want of conciseness and coherence in its present state. Madame Burmeister Petersen will, I hope, give us an opportunity of hearing what she can do apart from her husband's music. The rest of the concert was exceptionally interesting. Berlioz' Death of Ophelia and Funeral March of Hamlet, both perfect compositions of their kind, were finely executed; and the last act of Tannhäuser was given with an effect which cannot be imagined by those who have only seen it with the Covent Garden accessories. The orchestral features could not have been made more of, except at one point, the accompaniment to Venus' invitation, in which the wood wind produced nothing but a dry clucking, appropriate enough to Telramund's defiance in Lohengrin, but extremely unsuggestive of the voluptuous breathings of the Venusberg zephyrs. The chorus of younger pilgrims, too, did not swim along so tranquilly as it might have done; and Wolfram, after singing his opening lines very well, misplaced his voice in shifting to his upper register at the words "Da scheinest du," and, failing to recover himself, gave O du, mein holder Abendstern flat throughout. The rest was beyond cavil. Miss Thudichum, a very carefully trained singer, who shews herself more and more worthy of the pains taken with her, doubled the parts of Elizabeth and Venus; and Mr Edward Lloyd was the Tannhäuser.

I am not a very regular frequenter of the students' concerts at the Guildhall School of Music. They begin at the unreasonable hour of half-past six; and the surroundings always give me an uneasy sense of having been summoned before the Lord Mayor's Court for some misdemeanor. Nevertheless, I looked in at one last week, and found the huge room, as usual, crowded. There was the inevitable child violinist performing prodigies; there was the regulation young lady with the flexible voice, the high range, and the unawakened artistic sense, mechanically using the mad scene from Lucia as a stalking horse; there was the intelligent young gentleman cautiously playing the flute obbligato; and there was the harmless necessary assortment of students' original compositions, the pretty firstfruits of them that are Corporation Exhibitioners. I was unable to stay very long; and the most enjoyable thing I heard was a Mendelssohn prelude and fugue played by Miss Ethel Barnes, who shewed, before she played six bars, that she had been stimulated artistically as well as finger-trained mechanically. That prelude and fugue consoled me inexpressibly after Lucia; and as the next thing in the program was Il Segreto, I fled away into the night, lest a worse thing should befall, leaving Miss Ethel Barnes, as far as I was concerned, mistress of the situation.

18 March 1891

THE blizzard put back my arrangements on the 10th so far that I was late for Mr Somervell's Mass. When I arrived at the Bach Choir concert, Miss Eibenschütz and Mr Borwick were playing a masterly Bach concerto for two pianos, the more vivacious sections of which went capitally. The slow movement, unfortunately, was passed over as undemonstratively as possible, and went for nothing. Madame Schumann's novices do not know what to do with music of this kind; but they at least do not vulgarize it, as immature Lisztians are apt to do. On the whole I think I shall in future advise young pianoforte students to divide their apprenticeship between Madame Schumann and Sophie Menter, in order that they may lack neither the refinements of art nor "the joy of life." Those who stick to one school exclusively are apt to come out with slovenly habits of mind on the one hand, or ill-nourished hearts on the other.

The last two numbers at this Bach concert were curiously contrasted. One was an Offertorium and Tantum Ergo by Schubert, the other the Choral Fantasia. Beet-

hoven's genuinely religious music, without a shadow of fear
or mistrust on it from beginning to end, fit for happy and free
people to sing with the most buoyant conviction, came with
an extraordinarily refreshing effect after the hypochondriacal
tromboning with Schubert, in a perverse fit, devised to set
miserable sinners groveling. It would be too much to suspect the Bach Choir of any satiric intention in the arrangement of its program: in fact, I suspect it of thinking the
Tantum Ergo rather a fine piece of music. If that is so, I
will take the liberty of urging them to remember that it is
not the cowl that makes the monk, and that some of the most
frivolous, the most inane, and even the most wicked music
in the world is to be found in such forms as the oratorio, the
Mass, the anthem, or the like. Any musician can turn out to
order as much church music as you please, from a whole
service to a Christmas carol, just as a domestic engineer can
turn out a heating apparatus; but how is it likely to compare,
as religious music, with Mozart's Die Zauberflöte, for instance, which professes to be no more than a mere profane
Singspiel?

Among the pianoforte recitals which are helping to keep
an exceedingly dull season going are those of Miss Douste
at Steinway Hall, and of Max Pauer at Prince's Hall. Then
there is that excellent artist Miss Zimmermann, who gave a
recital last week; and Miss Janotha, whose concert on
Friday I was unable to attend. There is little to be said on
such occasions except to repeat old compliments; but they
are none the less important, although the Paderewskis and
the Sapellnikoffs get the lions' shares of notice. Naturally an
orgy gets talked of more than a plain meal; but the fact remains that orgies can be dispensed with for longer than
meals. Strongly as I sympathize with the gentleman who
said that he was prepared to do without the necessities of
life if the luxuries were guaranteed to him, I must warn the
inexperienced that they will poison themselves in rather
less than no time if they attempt to live on any such principle without a very high discrimination between spurious

and genuine luxuries. For instance, a man who should come to idolize Paderewski or Rubinstein, and to lose all appreciation of Max Pauer, would be in a parlous state.

This word discrimination reminds me that our plutocratic opera patrons have just bought their pig in a poke, by which vulgar observation I would convey that Mr Harris has sold out his pit and grand-tier boxes for the season without pledge or prospectus. So at least I am told by those who habitually regard themselves as well informed. And, in this instance, I do not doubt them in the least.

Nobody can recognize more fully than I do that if Mr Harris produces any new works, or in any way raises the artistic standard of the Covent Garden performances, he is actuated by no fear of the progressive instincts of his subscribers. All they ask is that the Italian Opera shall be fashionable. Even from the gallery the forward pressure is not very strong. All the arts are now experiencing the first effects of the wide diffusion of literate tastes caused by the operation of compulsory education in this country. Whole classes which formerly did not know what an opera was are now full of curiosity to see one; and as they have to begin at the beginning, they turn impresario's capital away from the satisfaction of the old opera-going class which has worn Italian Opera threadbare, to the primary education of naïfs who find Donizetti's finales abstruse, and his instrumentation strangely impressive. What does this point to? Is it to a struggle between two sections of the same audience as to which is to be bored to death—the adepts by Trovatore, or the inepts by Tristan? Clearly not: what we want is separate opera houses for elementary and advanced musicians, with a supplementary one for the display of diamonds, constructed so as to allow the public to promenade down the middle, in the style of the Burlington Arcade.

Differentiation is already in progress on these lines. The Savoy, Prince of Wales, and Lyric theatres provide for comic opera: and now we have the Royal English Opera for musical melodrama. Opera is thus provided with its Criter-

ion and its New Olympic. It has also got its Lyceum at
Covent Garden; though here, I admit, the analogy suffers
severely from the difference of about a century in the stage
of evolution reached by drama and opera. But on one vital
point it holds good. Both houses leave the most advanced
section of the public out in the cold. I go to see Irving play
Charles I; and my critical sense is highly gratified by his
now consummately cultivated artistic sense and perfect certainty of execution. I go to hear Jean de Reszke as the Prophet, or as Romeo, and am as keenly pleased, if not nearly so
completely satisfied, as by Irving. But now comes the difficulty. Charles I interests me so little as a drama that the
actor cannot, with all his art, make it affect me one-tenth as
strongly as a play of Ibsen's acted by novices who have not a
twentieth part of Irving's skill. And I would not go out of
London to hear the finest performance of Roméo et Juliette
that Europe can produce; whereas I have gone a long way
out of England to hear complete performances of Wagner's
works by quite stupendously unattractive singers. Now
since there is no regular theatre in London which provides
me with what I want, I am compelled to make the most
unjustifiable assaults on Manager Irving and Impresario
Harris in order to force them to attend to my wants for a
night or two at the expense of their contented patrons. If I
succeed, I know I shall get both gentlemen into no end of
trouble. The proper solution is to build another opera house
for the advanced party, where it can have the music dramas
it likes without ousting those who dont like them.

Of course, this would not settle the question for the
critics, who have to go to all the opera houses, and who, in
mere self-preservation, struggle desperately against any
movement that takes them out of their depth; but even this
might be settled by the newspapers appointing double sets
of critics. For example, Class A, the advanced critic, for
realistic novels, naturalist painters, Wagner and Ibsen; and
Class B, the bourgeois critic for Besantine novels, Royal
Academicians' pictures, the old Covent Garden repertory,

159

and the dramas of a gentleman whose name I shall save up until I have fresh occasion to get a letter written to the papers about me.

What is really stopping the way to a new opera house is the usual Utopian notion that nothing can be done without a capital of £100,000, and the patronage of eminent pluto-crats. Allow me to say, as a practical person, that a represen-tation of the Nibelungen tetralogy may cost anything from the hire of a barn by a knot of amateur enthusiasts, and a set of pasteboard placards indicating the scenery, up to any sum you like to spend on it. Mr Grein's example in the matter of the Independent Theatre is a highly instructive one. He first conciliated the demand for "something prac-tical" by putting before the public a complete working scheme for an endowed theatre, with a huge capital and the Prince of Wales as President. The impression produced was admirable: here was none of your cracked-brained imprac-ticable enthusiasts' dreams, but a sensible, well thought out, solid, business scheme on familiar lines, with money in it. Meanwhile, pending the subscription of the huge capital and the waking up of the Prince of Wales, Mr Grein tried what he could do under his own presidency with a handful of faddists and a matter of two-pound-ten or so. He took the nearest thing to a barn left in Tottenham Court Road, and organized a performance of one of Ibsen's greatest plays for the few people who cared about it. Result—barn too small; performance transferred gloriously to a real theatre, with Mr Augustus Harris surveying the proceedings in ineffable awe from a stage box; Ibsen's mortally wounded enemies filling London with their screams of anguish; and Mr Grein the most famous manager in Europe, bar M. Antoine of Paris, also of barn antecedents. And now, gentlemen of the Wagnerian persuasion, what are you going to do after this? Give another conversazione at the Royal Institute, no doubt. That is so like what Wagner himself did at Zurich, is it not?

25 *March* 1891

LOOKING back from Easter to Christmas, I pray, now it is all over, that it may be long before I again have to make such a tale of bricks without straw as during this most barren period. No doubt the early winter appeals *ad misericordiam* of Hallé and Henschel for audiences were discouraging to musical enterprise, and the frost was benumbing; but still, it ought to be impossible for a musical critic in London, even during a bombardment, to be compelled to fall back, as often as I have had to, upon him who finds mischief still for idle hands to do. This last week I have hardly heard a note of music, except the Crystal Palace concert, at which Isaÿe played, on Saturday. I am told that there was a Philharmonic concert on Thursday; but the directors thought it better not to mention it to me; and I, on my part, was unwilling to intrude at the risk of making the conductor nervous.

One of the good works done by the Royal College of Music has been the evangelization of Kensington, which I take to be the home of the submerged nine-tenths of the Art-affecting middle-class, by a guild of young fiddlers, ex-students of the College, and ready for anything in the way of chamber-music. The vigor and skill they shew always astonishes me. It may be that my early experience of amateur and apprenticed violinists, especially young women, was unfortunate; but I cannot help thinking that there has been an enormous improvement in them since my boyhood. At that time the sight of a fiddle-case in a drawing room filled me with terror: it boded all that was insufferable, infirm, and ridiculous in amateurism. But it was not alone the amateur that was to be dreaded. Even in good professional orchestras, a few bars of solo for the leader, the obbligato to Salve dimora! or the like, was an infliction which you bore sitting back, with your teeth set, and a grin of indulgent resignation on your drawn lips. I can remember thinking the violin a noxious instrument, and wondering why people

161

played it. My astonishment when somebody took me to hear Sivori was boundless: I perceived that the thing could be played after all, but concluded that it took a magician to do it.

As time went on, I became familiar with the feats of the virtuosi; but the orchestra leaders were the same as ever, except in so far as they got worse as they got older. Amateurism I kept clear of altogether, nothing doubting that it, too, was its old self. I suppose I grew belated and benighted by allowing an old conclusion to fossilize in this way. At all events, when, only a few years ago, I happened to hear a strong quintet played by five young Royal Collegians led by Miss Holiday, I was secretly amazed at the ease, the freedom, the boldness, the certainty of their execution. They did not seem in the least preoccupied by technical difficulties which would have kept players of their standing in former generations cramped and miserable from the first note to the last. The other day I heard some members of the same little band, now led by Miss Donkersley (it was at a concert given by that young lady at the Kensington Town Hall), play a couple of movements from a Mendelssohn quartet which I had heard at a Monday Popular Concert very shortly before. And I was sorry that I had not time to hear the quartet out; though at St James's Hall I could have left without remorse at any point. Between my Miss Holiday and Miss Donkersley experiences I had begun to understand better the marked effects of the reinforcement of our orchestras with young men whose off-handedness over Wagnerian scores takes away the breath of their elders; and I had even been at a concert where the virtuoso who obliged us with Beethoven's Concerto was far inferior, as a player, to the two men who sat at the leader's desk accompanying him —Hollaender and Seiffert, to wit. The progress has been immense; and, if it has left us more dissatisfied than ever, that is because our sense of artistic shortcoming has grown faster than the skill of the violinists, thereby guaranteeing further progress.

But now for the other side of the matter. All this refreshing boldness of execution was not as unknown everywhere as it was among lady amateurs before the era of Miss Donkersley and her fellow-students. Long before that time third-class travellers on the Underground Railway were subject to invasion by itinerant artists, who, fiddle and bow white from a monstrous excess of rosin, played the popular tunes of the moment with reckless speed, tolerable intonation, and piercing stridency of tone. In circuses, too, a pair of violin demons would enter the ring and go through all sorts of antics without intermitting a *moto perpetuo* of the liveliest character. These experts were better than the old-fashioned amateurs; but they were not so good as Sivori, or Sarasate, or Reményi, or Isaÿe. They had a quick left hand, and an ear for pitch; but when once a note was fairly in tune, they had no further concern about its quality, and were quite satisfied when their right hand was merely rasping and rubbing the bow up and down on the strings. Now, to be a great executant one must have not only an exquisitely delicate ear for quality of tone but a fine right hand trained to touch the strings with the bow (the really difficult instrument) with the marvellous legerdemain necessary to produce the tone one's ear demands.

The old masters—men like Baillot for instance—kept comparatively commonplace pupils for years trying to acquire this power of bowing by slow practice, leaving them in the end spirit-broken, timid, footling pedants, with irresolute touch, uncertain intonation, and thin tone, lacking the assurance of the itinerant third-class carriage troubadour on the one hand, and the special subtle mastery of which their instructor had been dreaming on the other. It was a case of Better being the enemy of Well. Nowadays, it appears, we let our students rasp themselves into familiarity and confidence, and then, having accomplished the first step of making them fiddlers, try to refine their tone and make them artists. It is undoubtedly a huge improvement on Baillot's plan of trying to make them artists before they

163

were fiddlers—a plan which never succeeded, except where Nature had done what Baillot omitted; but it has for the moment the disadvantage that our young fiddlers, comparing themselves with the old fogies who were dropped in their youth between the two stools, are apt to feel sufficiently glorious in their handicraftsman's smartness to lose sight of the step that lies beyond them.

And the modern orchestra, in which the violinist plays in unison with from sixteen to twenty others, no more encourages delicacy of tone in the individual player than choral singing encourages it in the individual singer. Therefore I warn this new generation, wonderfully handy as it is with the instrument which so puzzled its fathers, that much as I rejoice in its exploits, I intend to continue protesting very strongly against mere left-hand playing, especially at the opera, where the younger hands, when they are confronted with those "big guitar" accompaniments which are no longer "interesting," contemptuously refuse to try to make them beautiful—obviously because their ears are too hasty and their right hands too heavy and clumsy.

For the life of me I cannot see why the recent suggestion that the score of Parsifal may find a place on Signor Mancinelli's desk at Covent Garden should be scouted as "profane." I leave out of the question the old-fashioned objection, founded on the theory that all playhouses and singing-halls are abodes of sin. But when a gentleman writes to the papers to declare that "a performance of Parsifal, apart from the really religious surroundings of the Bayreuth Theatre, would almost amount to profanity," and, again, that "in the artificial glare of an English opera-house it would be a blasphemous mockery," I must take the liberty of describing to him the "really religious surroundings," since he admits that he has never seen them for himself. In front of the Bayreuth Theatre, then, on the right, there is a restaurant. On the left there is a still larger restaurant and a sweetstuff stall. At the back, a little way up the hill, there is a café. Between the café and the theatre there is a shed in

164

which "artificial glare" is manufactured for the inside of the theatre; and the sound of that great steam-engine throbs all over the Fichtelgebirge on still nights.

Between the acts the three restaurants are always full, not of devout Wagnerites (the Meister advocated vegetarianism), but of Spiers & Pondites, who do just what they will do at the Star and Garter when my Festspielhaus on Richmond Hill is finished. The little promenade in front of the theatre is crowded with globe-trotters, chiefly American and vagabond English, quite able to hold their own in point of vulgarity, frivolity, idle curiosity, and other perfectly harmless characteristics, with the crowd in the foyer at Covent Garden or the Paris Opéra. When they have seen every celebrity present pass and repass some twenty times, they become heavily bored, and are quite excited at seeing a small contingent from the orchestra, with the familiar German-band equipment of seedy overcoat and brass instrument, assemble under the portico and blare out a fragment of some motive from whatever music-drama is "on" that evening. This is the signal for entering the theatre, but nobody moves, as everyone knows that it is only the third blast that means business, when you do not happen to be at a distance—in which case, however, you hear nothing, unless you are dead to windward, with a strong gale blowing. Inside, the "honorable ladies" are requested by placard to remove their towering headgear; and not one of them is sufficiently impressed with the really religious surroundings to do so. Then the famous "Bayreuth hush" is secured by a volley of angry sh-sh-sh-es, started by the turning down of the lights; and the act begins. What sanctity there is in all this that is not equally attainable at Boulogne or Bayswater remains to be explained.

Mr Charles Dowdeswell's position on the subject is safer than that of his fellow-correspondent. He claims special sanctity, not for Bayreuth, but for Parsifal, and says (what is perfectly true) that the Bayreuth Festspielhaus is the only existing theatre in which justice can be done to the work.

But as to his practical conclusion—that for the immense majority here who cannot afford to go to Bayreuth it is better that they should never see any performance of Parsifal at all than see one even as good as the Covent Garden Meistersinger—no practical Wagnerite critic can endorse it. Let us build a Wagner Theatre, by all means, as soon as possible; but if, in the meantime, Mr Harris will produce even the second act of Parsifal—and he could quite easily do it—I, for one, will forgive him for La Favorita, and applaud his artistic enterprise to the skies the whole season through.

1 *April* 1891

THE world has suffered many things through Grieg's experiments in the grand style of composition; but assuredly the climax was reached on Saturday week, when his setting of three scenes from Björnson's Olav Trygvason was performed—wantonly performed—at the Crystal Palace. I have no idea of the age at which Grieg perpetrated this tissue of puerilities; but if he was a day over eighteen the exploit is beyond excuse. Possibly it would pass muster better in the theatre than it did at Sydenham; yet I cannot think that even the most innocent pit and gallery could be imposed on by the intonings of the sacrificer, with the weird interludes on the closed notes of the horns. But for these Simon Tappertit solemnities and turnip-ghost terrors we might all have caught the 4.55 train and saved half an hour.

A prominent feature in the instrumental treatment recalled to my mind the attempts I have made from time to time to sample the music halls. On one of these expeditions I heard somebody—Mr Herbert Campbell, I think—sing a ditty of which I remember nothing except that the refrain, delivered in a tone of the strongest expostulation, always began with the exclamation, "Oh, aint it awful!" And each time the trombone would indignantly echo, "Awful." At the other extreme of dramatic orchestration I have heard the cry of Donner echoed back from the clouds in Das

Rheingold, as he swings his hammer to fashion the rainbow bridge into Valhalla. That was also done by the trombones. Grieg makes the trombone echo his dreary Sacrificer again and again; and the effect always reminds you of Mr Herbert Campbell, and never of Donner.

Isaÿe's performance of Wieniawski's concerto in D, of a Bach fugue and prelude, and of Saint-Saëns's Rondo Capriccioso, gave a tolerably comprehensive display of his extraordinary accomplishments as a violinist. His terrific technique, his fondness for the intensely French Saint-Saëns, his self-assertiveness, his readiness to sacrifice higher artistic qualities to the speed of a dazzlingly impossible presto, his combination of a Latin finesse of execution with a German solidity of tone, and occasionally with a German obtuseness of intonation, all stamp his share of original sin as distinctively Belgian. That is not altogether a compliment: the nation which municipalized the Wiertz Museum has a good deal to apologize for in the way of art; but Isaÿe's individual force is of European volume: he is Sarasate's only serious rival among players of his own generation. We seem to be waking up but slowly to the idea that he is anyone in particular; but we will compensate him by making an idol of him years after he has lost all claim to that distinction. His selection of the Bach fugue may have been partly prompted by our habit of saying that nobody can play Bach but Joachim.

Isaÿe's power of polyphonic playing enables him to challenge any comparison on this score as far as technical mastery goes. For the rest, one need not commit the folly of making the one man a standard for the other, especially in view of the admirable performances with which Joachim has this year retrieved the one or two unlucky occasions on which he did himself some injustice in 1890 over Bach; but there is no harm in coupling the two names for the purpose of discouraging the people who are never satisfied until they have hall-marked somebody as the best player in the world. There is no such thing as the best player in the world, never was, and never will be, unless music falls so far out of cultivation that some one-eared person can claim the throne of the kingdom of the deaf. The rest of the program was of no special interest. Madame Emily Squire gave us one of those airs from La Clemenza di Tito, which anybody with the requisite range can sing in a fashion, but which can only be made interesting by an artist who has acquired all the essential qualities of the old classical style. The overture to Rienzi suited the martial vein in Mr Manns: he exulted in it much as he used to in the third movement of Raff's Lenore symphony, which, by the bye, is curiously neglected just now, considering that popular taste is passing through the very phase to which it ministers. Miss Dora Bright, who appeared on the following Saturday, is a pianist who writes her own concertos better than she plays them. She is dexterous and accurate, and a thorough musician to boot; but her talent has not the pianist's peculiar specialization. I do not know that she plays any better than I do, except in respect of her fingering scales properly, and hitting the right notes instead of the wrong ones. Her concerto is remarkable—apart from its undeniable prettiness —for its terse, business-like construction and its sustained animation. Somehow, there is an appalling soundness of the head and heart about our young English lady composers which prevents them from getting into the depths of tone poetry; but they certainly swim very engagingly on the surface.

The Good Friday performance of the Messiah at the Albert Hall reminds me that the Handel Festival will take place on the 22nd, 24th, and 26th of June, with the customary Messiah on the first day, Israel on the third, and a selection on the second. Mesdames Albani, Nordica, Belle Cole, Emily Squire; Miss Macintyre and Miss M'Kenzie; Messrs Lloyd, M'Guckin, Bridson, Brereton, and Santley will be seconded by four thousand choristers. Mr Manns will conduct; and the result will be regarded by some as "sublime," by others as an effective *reductio ad absurdum* of the principle of monstrosity in art. For my part, as I do not

wish to spoil sport, and had much rather see the Crystal
Palace Company doing this than merely not doing it, I shall
reserve my opinion until after the festival.

I have just received the first part of the Wagner Society's
translation of the Meister's prose works. It is well printed
and got up, and contains the much-quoted autobiographic
sketch which Heinrich Laube got from Wagner in 1843 for
his Elegant World's Times. Also the introduction and
beginning of Art and Revolution, which is one of the two
essays on art that everybody is expected to have read, the
other being Art and Religion. The translations, by Mr
Ashton Ellis, are excellent. The publishers are Messrs
Kegan Paul & Co.

Messrs Sampson Low send me a biography of Gounod
by Marie Anne de Bovet, the oddest imaginable mixture
of impertinence and information. She makes it impossible
for you to get a word in edgeways with her rapturous chatter
about the nature of genius, not to mention her explanations
to the effect that Planquette does not consider himself the
equal of Handel, and that those who prefer Les Cloches to
The Messiah are no judges; that the big drum does not
occupy so important a place in the orchestra as a Stradivarius;
that "it is well that Bach should have written the St. Matthew
Passion, and Beethoven the Ninth Symphony, though it
was not wrong for Mozart to have written Deh vieni alla
finestra or Gounod the lark duet in Roméo. I would not
stand ten minutes of this in private conversation from the
prettiest woman that ever walked; but I forgive Madame
de Bovet for the sake of the charming portrait of Gounod
which can be divined like a face in a cloud through her
irresponsible but spiritual prattle. For Gounod's music I
have never found any better words than heavenly and
angelic, in the simplest, childish sense. Imagine, then, my
delight on learning from Madame de Bovet that when
Gounod was studying in Vienna, he wrote on the margin of
one of his scores the words: "O heiliger Fra Angelico: wo
ist die Musik deiner Engelin!"

MUSIC IN LONDON 1890–94

ICAN only describe L'Enfant Prodigue, at the Prince of Wales, as touching. I was touched when I laughed no less than when I retired in tears at the end of the third act. But my emotion was not caused by the music. That is simply conventional French ballet music and *mélodrame*, elegantly fitted with all the latest harmonic refinements. And I must add that if the piece is going to have anything like the vogue here which it enjoyed at the Bouffes Parisiens, M. André Wormser had better lose no time in rescoring it for a full band. Accompaniments played by a pianist and eked out by a handful of wind-players and a string quartet are tolerated in Paris, where you will see Offenbach's operas treated in this way even at the Eden Theatre; but here such makeshifts stamp a performance as cheap and provincial, and that, too, on good artistic grounds.

The pianoforte is so convenient a substitute for an orchestra where no orchestra is to be had, that a good deal of money and trouble might be saved by employing it in all cases. But its monotonous repercussions and unalterably false equal-temperament tuning soon make it so tiresome that only a great artist, using a first-rate machine, and playing a varied program of music of great intrinsic interest, highly specialized for the peculiar qualities of the instrument, can induce audiences to sit out lengthy recitals. Even at the most modest suburban dance people crave for at least one fiddle to relieve the eternal strum of the piano. If M. Wormser thinks he has got over this difficulty in L'Enfant Prodigue, I can feelingly assure him that he is mistaken. Three-fourths of the pianoforte part have all the air of being a mere transcription from score; and if they had been played by Sapellnikoff on one of the best Steinways ever built, the transfer of at least those three-fourths to the orchestra would have been a gain. For the remaining fourth the piano can be retained if M. Wormser thinks that the one or two special effects it produces are worth the room it occupies. My own opinion is distinctly that they are not: indeed, I think I might safely venture upon an offer to replace them myself with orchestral effects without any loss of piquancy.

For the rest of this most entertaining dumb show I have nothing but praise. The service rendered by the music in making the drama intelligible is not great: there is only one point which would not be as intelligible to a deaf man as it was to me. That was the stipulation made by Phrynette that the Baron must marry her, a point which could easily be conveyed by pantomime, but which was more concisely and amusingly intimated by the introduction of the opening strain of Mendelssohn's wedding march in the orchestra. And nothing could be funnier or more felicitous than the humorous allusion to the same theme when the Baron is left alone. His shake of the head, accompanied by that mocking little scherzando, tells, better than the most elaborate panto-mime could without music, that he has not the smallest intention of keeping his promise.

I noticed during the sad last act that the domestic incidents repeated from the cheerful first act were now accompanied by the same music changed into the minor mode; but I cannot say that this device interested me much. I was even conscious of resenting it somewhat for obtruding its extreme staleness between me and the much more original and distinguished art of the actors. On the stage there was not a dull moment. If a cat had been present, I believe it would have purred with tickled satisfaction to see old Pierrot sitting there reading his newspaper, from the political article to the account of the latest duel, and from that to the newest impropriety. Madame Pierrot, too, was beyond praise: it will be a technical education to some of our own people to see how Courtés and Madame Schmidt keep the audience interested in the simplest domestic common-place. Pierrot's part is the one which requires the subtlest play; and Jane May is quite equal to the occasion: she has a quick sense of the character, and puts it into action with a high degree of stage skill. Francesca Zanfretta, a gorgeous brunette, produces the effect of a figure by Phillips introduced in a picture by Watteau. In spite of her eminently continental name, I cannot help suspecting her of being a particularly clever and jolly British columbine. She bounces through her part with much spirit and enjoyment; and though there is a conspicuous want of finesse in her play, and even of punctuality in her relations with the orchestra, I am not sure that she does not relieve and enliven the performance in a valuable way. Gouget, as the Baron, is as funny as possible; and yet he is artistic discretion itself.

In estimating the value of these eulogies, it must be remembered that although the satisfaction of seeing a simple thing consummately well done is most joyful and soothing after a long and worrying course of complex things imperfectly done, the simple success must not therefore be placed above the complex half success. A drama consisting of a series of emotions, so obvious in their provocation and so conventional in their sequence that they can be made intelligible to a general audience by pure phenomena is child's play compared to ordinary drama, or opera, although no actor can venture upon it without a degree of skill in pantomime which most speakers and singers think (erroneously) that they can afford to do without. This much being admitted, I may safely proceed to say that on the chance occasions when I descend from the opera house to the theatre I am often made to feel acutely that the play would be much more enjoyable if the dialogue were omitted. To me the popular dramatist always appears as a sympathetic, kindly, emotional creature, able to feel and to imagine in a pleasantly simple and familiar groove, but almost destitute of intellect, and therefore unable to think or to write. Whilst he is merely emotioning he is the best of good company for an easygoing hour of sentimental relaxation; but the moment he opens his mouth he becomes insufferable; you feel like the policeman in one of Wilkie Collins's novels, who, when the butler collared him, could

172

only say patiently, "You dont know how to do it in the least." If the *dramatis personæ* would only love and languish and storm and despair in dumb show and "do it beautifully," as Hedda Gabler enjoined upon her lover when he consented to shoot himself, then all the valuable parts of the play would be brought into full prominence, and all the rubbish eliminated. L'Enfant Prodigue proves triumphantly that this is quite practicable. Therefore, to those well-known dramatists of ours who have immense hearts but no brains worth mentioning—I cannot give names, as I never know one from the other, the drama not being my regular department—I most earnestly recommend the adoption of the dumb show form in future. Let them, as Hegel would have said, remain in the stage of consciousness without attempting to advance to that of scientific understanding. Or, as someone else actually has said—I forget who; but it was not Hegel—let them "cut the cackle, and come to the 'osses."

There is one point which, "in the present excited state of public feeling" (here I quote Mr Nupkins), may expose Mr Horace Sedger to severe animadversion for producing this wordless drama, and may even cause him to be threatened with a withdrawal of his licence or a prosecution under Lord Campbell's Act. Like the parable after which it is named, and like that charming novel Manon Lescaut, L'Enfant Prodigue is not, in the accepted sense, "moral." Many of our most sensitive critics must have blushed continuously through the second act; and the spectacle of a young man robbing his father, having his fling with the money, and re-filling his pocket by cheating at cards when that is spent, without once forfeiting our sympathies or coming to a bad end, is surely enough to provoke the virtuous indignation of any gentleman who deals in the article. Mr Sedger should really be more careful: comparatively puritanical dramatists, also of foreign origin, have quite recently made a most painful impression, without for a moment going so far as Michel Carré *fils* has gone in L'Enfant Prodigue.

173

MUSIC IN LONDON 1890–94

At the Crystal Palace on Saturday we had Dr Mackenzie's Dream of Jubal, or, rather, Jubal's dream of Dr Mackenzie, with Miss Nordica, Mr Iver McKay, Miss Hannah Jones, and Mr Vernon Taylor in the principal parts, and Mr Charles Fry as narrator. Jubal is our old friend the first-cousin of Tubal Cain, and the father of all such as handle the harp and pipe (it used to be the harp and organ in my day). Jubal, like Hermes, finds a natural lyre formed by a tortoiseshell, and at once begins, like any Englishman, to try his hand at picking out a tune. An angel is immediately sent to shew him what that sort of thing will inevitably lead to in the course of ages. Under the impression that the angel is proposing to give him a great treat, he allows himself to be transported to a cathedral, where they are singing a Gloria by the Principal of the Royal Academy of Music, concluding with a fugue on the words Cum sancto spiritu, with *stretti, point d'orgue,* and everything complete.

After this depressing glimpse into the future, Jubal becomes a prey to settled melancholy; but the angel relentlessly continues the torture, successively inflicting on him a solo and duet in the oratorio style, an ode, a battle-hymn, and a rustic ballad with chorus—all of quite stupendous factitiousness, and relieved only by a funeral march which has some rich and handsome, if not very novel, tone-coloring. Like poor Jubal, I was bored beyond all description; but I had the advantage of him, inasmuch as the composer could not put rapturous compliments into my mouth. If Dr Mackenzie had employed me to write either his libretto or his analytical program, instead of giving both jobs to the same brother critic, no doubt I should have been able to give a more polite account of his cantata. Unless some arrangement of this kind is made, or Dr Mackenzie becomes as a young student again, working at his composition instead of playing at it, I am afraid I shall always be a marplot when there is a new choral *magnum opus* in the wind.

AT Covent Garden there is nothing new before the curtain except a lining of mirror to the walls of the corridors; so that on diamond nights boxholders who are tired of being admired by the audience can go outside and admire themselves. When the season began on Monday last week with Giulia Ravogli in Orfeo, we were all in a state of high expectancy, thinking, not unnaturally, that if Gluck's masterpiece was so entrancing with that desperate fit-up of Lago's, what would it not be with the splendid staging of Harris? Even I had my hopes—why should I deny it?—though I had my doubts too, particularly after the mirror arrangement in the corridors. And I admit that if money could have made Orfeo an artistic success, an artistic success it would have been. But the fact that want of money failed to wreck the work last year with Signor Lago should have warned Mr Harris not to depend too much on his purse in dealing with Gluck. Unfortunately the warning was thrown away: Mr Harris has trebled the expenditure and spoiled the opera. It is true that Euridice's tomb, formerly a packing-case on end, with her name stencilled in the only direction it would fit in, is now a mediæval milestone, surprisingly old-established considering the recent interment. No longer in a desolate corner of Victoria Park, it stands now about two miles below Bingen on the Rhine, a spot all sunshine and pleasant hillside paths, in one of which Madame Bauermeister, tripping as she retired backwards from the boards, unintentionally sat down, and, somewhat stunned by the concussion, amazedly contemplated Orfeo, who surveyed her with speechless consternation.

The Elysian Fields have been shifted from the Bois de Boulogne, which at least looked infinitely spacious, to a villainous classical Monte Carlo, whither Orfeo comes straight out of the Mediterranean by a flight of stone steps, which land him amid an ill-arranged crowd of temples and columns. Not until the third act does the scene-painter, having exhausted the possibilities of making matters worse than last year, come to his senses and better them. As to the exploits of Madame Palladino and the ballet, I really cannot describe them adequately with any sort of reasonable good-nature. To combine such senseless noddings and trippings and kickings with Gluck's noble measures was a profanity from which Offenbach would have recoiled: it was indecent, not in Mr MacDougall's sense—though Madame Palladino was certainly not dressed with any special consideration for his feelings—but in the true artistic sense. I could not look at it; and I could not go out into the corridors because of the mirrors; so I furtively watched the hands of the lady next me, which, as it happened, were expressively artistic hands, until Giulia Ravolgi entered and shewed us the sort of move-ment that should be associated with such music. But even Giulia's pantomime, saturated with feeling as it still is, did not produce its former effect.

Last year the Elysian shades were shabby, certainly; but they all knew what they were there for; and Orfeo, in the focus of their breathless attention, made us forget their ridiculous makeshifts of costumes. This time the costumes are rich enough; but half the heroes are girls in tights with long ostrich feathers drooping from their helmets to their calves—girls who, like their colleagues of the ballet, stand listlessly where they have been told to stand, and trouble themselves no more about Orfeo's feelings than about mine. I do not propose to pursue the subject further than to note that Sofia Ravogli's voice is thicker and richer than it was, and to assure Mancinelli that he only makes matters worse by worrying the music; for the sources of the flagging and unsatisfactoriness which annoy him are not in the orchestra but on the stage. Mr Harris has the remedy in the hollow of his hand. If he does not care to fall back on the Lago Elysian Fields, he can order a new scene with a far remote horizon, in the style of Martin's Plains of Heaven. He can reserve Madame Palladino for modern romantic operas, and either prepare a classical ballet or else leave out the dancing alto-
176

gether. And he can banish from the stage the people who cannot be induced to take any interest in the action. Anything short of this will leave the opera what it is at present, the greatest disappointment of the season, so far.

Faust on the following night was a very different affair. Miss Eames, the newest American soprano, fully justified her engagement by her performance as Margaret. The middle of her voice is exceptionally satisfactory in volume and rich in quality, enabling her to make herself heard without effort in all sorts of quiet dramatic inflection. The low notes, as might be expected, are also very good; but the upper register, though bright, does not come so easily as the rest; and it was rather by a *tour de force* that she took the final trio right through the third repetition in B natural instead of using the old Opéra Comique abridgment. However, as it was a successful *tour de force*, we were all very grateful for it; for the abridgment spoils the finest passage in the whole opera. As an actress, Miss Eames is intelligent, ladylike, and somewhat cold and colorless. The best that can be said for her playing in the last two acts is, that she was able to devise quietly pathetic business to cover her deficiency in tragic conviction. As to Mlle Guercia, the Siebel, her sex bewrayed her: she was so intensely feminine in every line of her figure, every note of her voice, and every idea in her acting, that, without being at all a ridiculous or incapable artist, she presented us with quite the most comic Siebel on record. Perotti, with his *allures de danseuse* and his popular high notes, kept Goethe effectually at a distance; and the gentleman who took Devoyod's place as Valentine, though he did an admirable back-fall, was in all other respects quite as bad as anyone could be expected to be at such short notice.

Maurel's Mephistopheles cannot be dismissed with the mixture of contemptuous indulgence and conventional toleration with which one lets pass most of the acting at Covent Garden. He challenges criticism as a creative artist, not as a mere opera-singer. In doing so he at once rouses antagonisms from which his brother artists are quite exempt,

since his view of the characters he represents may conflict
with that of his critics—a risk obviously not run by eminent
baritones who have no views at all. His Mephistopheles is a
distinct individual character, exhaustively premeditated,
and put upon the stage with the utmost precision of execution. As to consistency, it is almost too consistent to be
natural. There is no sentimental trace of the fallen son of the
morning about it, much less any of the stage puerilities of
the pantomime demon (for example, take his original and
convincingly right play during the chorale as they break his
spell with the cross-hilted swords). It is the very embodiment
of that grim Gothic fancy of an obscene beast of prey with
the form and intellect of a man. The artistic means by which
this effect is produced—the mouse-colored costume, the
ashen face and beard, the loveless tigerish voice—could not
have been better chosen.

Yet I take some exception to the impersonation, especially in the last two acts, as lacking relief, both vocally and
dramatically. This could be best supplied by a touch of
humor, in which it is at present entirely deficient. In the
scene of the serenade and duel, Maurel is cumbrous and
heavy, dragging the serenade beyond all musical conscience,
and taking the whole scene as tragically as Faust himself,
instead of being the one person present to whom it is pure
sport. In the church, too, where Gounod has provided for
one of those changes of voice to which Maurel, in his
Lyceum lecture, attached so much importance, he sang the
pathetic, heart-searching Rammenta i lieti di, accompanied
by the organ alone, in the same strident tone as the menace
with which it concludes as the orchestra comes in at the
words Non odi qual clamor. The only really effective passage in this scene, which Miss Eames played lachrymosely
and without distinction, was his powerfully expressive play
at the chorus of worshippers.

The fact that, being seventy-five minutes late, I saw only
half of Giulia Ravogli's Carmen, tempts me to announce
publicly that it is a mistake to suppose that I am a sort of

178

boy-messenger, always in waiting at York Street, Covent Garden, to dash off to any concert or opera immediately on receipt of an invitation. But, after all, invitations are invitations; and those who send them have a right to choose their own time, without reference to my convenience, which points to at least a day's clear notice. However, I saw enough of Carmen, which went off brilliantly, to be able to testify that Randegger conducts it worse than ever; that Lubert, the latest Spanish tenor, is not so handsome as Valera, nor so fearfully afflicted with goat-bleat as Suane, and that his voice is of rather commoner quality than either of theirs, also that he is, like them, careful and intelligent about his stage business, rising even to energy as a melodramatic actor; that Celli, not knowing his part in Italian, and failing to get any help from prompter or conductor, sacrificed himself somewhat dreadfully as the Toreador; that Mlle Janson fitted into the cast very well as Frasquita (or was she Mercedes?); that Sofia Ravogli played Micaela exactly as she would have played Norma; and that Vaschetti as Zuniga, a small but important part, requiring some distinction of manner and finesse of play, especially in the entry in the tavern scene, maintained his reputation for brazen lungs and unalterable but good-humored incompetence. As to Giulia, I gravely doubt whether my opinion of her is worth the paper it is written on. If anybody else were to sing the florid passages in Bertoni's aria in Orfeo, or the lilt in the tavern scene of Carmen, as she sings them, how that person would catch it in this column! But in the presence of such a millionaire in artistic force as Giulia, Bertoni and Bizet lose their rights. So, I may add, does Prosper Merimée. His Carmen, with all her subtle charm, was only a gentleman's dream. Giulia's Carmen is real; and her reality reduced the catastrophe to absurdity. The idea of poor Lubert killing her was ridiculous: nobody believed that she was dead: she could have taken him up and thrown him at Randegger's head without exciting the least surprise, especially among those who are good judges of conducting. Indeed, the orchestra and the front row of the stalls, delightful as they are when this wonderful Ravogli is on the stage, are not altogether safe at such times. The face of Mr Antoine Matt, the well-known trombone-player, when he realized that the knife which Carmen had just plucked from Don Jose's hand, and sent whizzing down the stage with a twitch of her powerful hand, was coming straight at his jugular vein, expressed a curious alloy of artistic devotion with a rueful sense that she might just as easily have aimed a little higher and made her shot at a critic instead of imperilling a brother artist. On the whole, since there is no denying that Giulia's strength and reality made havoc with the flimsy and fanciful figment she was impersonating, anyone who likes may denounce her as the worst of all the Carmens. I shall merely add a heartfelt wish that her successors may all be as gloriously bad. As to the genius with which she puts into dramatic action not only what is contained in the part written for her own voice, but the contents of the orchestral score as well, I can only say that I wish our conductors had half her insight, or quarter of her courage, promptitude, and vigor in action.

I have only space left to record hurriedly that the Albéniz concerts are deservedly growing in favor, and that at the last one Tivadar Nachez advanced his status considerably by playing Bach's Partita in B minor and a chaconne by Corelli so well, that I could not help wondering what cynical estimate of our musical intelligence has hitherto induced him to waste so many opportunities by persisting in playing claptrap drawing room pieces, and playing them very badly too. Another series of three Saturday afternoon concerts which promises well has been begun by Willy Hess, the leader of the Manchester orchestra, and Hugo Becker, a 'cellist well worth hearing, as he proved by his performance last Saturday of Piatti's arrangement of an adagio and allegro by Boccherini.

I HAVE seen Faust again, and expect soon to be able to whistle all the tunes in his popular opera, having already made the most gratifying progress with the soldiers' chorus. The occasion of my second visit was the appearance of Maurel as Valentine, and his replacement as Mephistopheles by De Reszke—Brother Edouard of that ilk. I confess to a sort of paternal affection, inspiring inexhaustible indulgence, for Brother Edouard; and I believe this feeling is shared by the public. We all like to see him enjoying himself; and he never enjoys himself more thoroughly than in that outrageous crimson and scarlet costume, with two huge cock's feathers twirling in the Covent Garden draughts (exceptionally boreal this year), his face decorated with sardonic but anatomically impossible wrinkles, and a powerful limelight glowing on him through the reddest of red glasses. His firm conviction that he is curdling the blood of the audience with demonstrations of satanic malignity when he is in fact infecting them with his mountainous good humor; his faith in the diabolic mockery of a smile that would make the most timid child climb straight up on his knee and demand to be shewn how a watch opens when blown on; the exuberant agility with which he persuades himself that his solid two hundred and forty pounds of generously nourished flesh and blood are a mere vapor from the mists of the bottomless pit—all these sights are dear to the hearts of stalls and gallery alike.

And then his singing! Singing is not the word for it: he no longer sings: he bawls, revelling in the stunning sound with a prodigality which comes of knowing that he has so much voice to draw on that no extravagance can exhaust it. It is magnificent; but it is not Mephistopheles. The price we have to pay for it is the destruction of all dramatic illusion whilst he is on the stage; that is to say, during about three-quarters of the whole performance. To say the least, it is not cheap. It would be out of all reason if the singing were like

181

the acting. Fortunately, it is not; for the separation between
the musical and the intellectual is uncommonly marked in
the De Reszke family. In Edouard's case there is more than
separation: there is divorce. Not that I would imply for a
moment that our pet baritone has no intelligence. I have not
the slightest doubt that if he had to live by his brains, as I
have, he would find plenty of them—in an extremely rusty
condition, no doubt, but still of sufficient quantity and
quality. What I do say is that he has found his voice and his
musical instinct so entirely adequate to his modest needs,
that he never thinks about his work, and never makes any
point that is not a purely musical one.

The intellectual vacuity of his king in Lohengrin baffles
description: a deaf man would mistake the opera for Donizetti's Anna Bolena, so unlike anybody except Henry VIII
does he look as he stands there making the chandelier buzz
with O sommo Dio. The contrast between his huge apathy
and the restless cerebration of Maurel is almost ludicrous.
Even in the not exactly supersubtle part of Friar Lawrence,
of which, especially in the exquisite potion scene, he shews
the most perfect musical comprehension, he cannot divest
himself of a puzzleheaded air, as if he were far from sure
what was going to come of it all, and were depending rather
doubtfully on Brother Jack to see it safely through. Only as
Mephistopheles does he wake up, not to the dramatic requirements of the character, but to the opening for a rare
piece of sport as the devil in a red dress, with a serenade full
of laughs (in which, by the bye, it must be admitted that he
sings his rivals' heads off). Jean, whom it is hard to conceive
as the big brother, may be presumed to have his mind kept
active by domestic cares; for if the two brothers and Lassalle
still live together, it is evident that Jean must think for the
three. And yet it cannot be said that he overtasks his brain
on the stage. Except in a character like Romeo, which proceeds on the simplest romantic lines, he creates very little
dramatic illusion.

When I write my musical recollections, I shall probably

have to say that the parts I best remember his acting in are
Valentine and Don Giovanni. Good tenors are so scarce that
the world has always condoned any degree of imbecility
for the sake of an *ut de poitrine*, a necessity which has given
currency to the phrase *bête comme un tenor*. Now whether
Jean, in his anxiety to prove himself a real tenor after he had
compromised himself by starting as a baritone, resolved to
dissemble the intelligence which made him such a memorable Valentine, is more than I care to decide; but it is certain
that he has not fulfilled his early promise as an actor. He is
an enchanting Lohengrin; and his Walther von Stolzing,
though the very vaguest Franconian knight ever outlined
on the stage, makes Covent Garden better than Bayreuth on
Meistersinger evenings. But Wagner would have urged
Jean somewhat vehemently to make these heroes a little
more vivid, alert, and wilful, even at the cost of some of their
present nebulous grace.

The Tannhäuser on Saturday was a rather desperate
business. To begin with, Bevignani made his first bow amid
a gust of fiddle-rapping from the band, and proceeded at
once to give us a more than sufficing taste of his quality. He
treated the unfortunate opera exactly as the Chigwell
donkey-boys treat their steeds, literally *walloping* it from
one end of the course to the other. I have no doubt that the
more he walloped it, the more his unmusical admirers said:
"Ah, there you are, you see: fine conductor, Bevignani: no
mistake about his beat." And unquestionably there was not.
It was the neck-or-nothing beat of the man who, unable to
guide and control large combinations, crams on all possible
headway in order to rush them through, beginning too fast,
and ending in a breathless scramble. A choice example of
the results of this policy offered itself in the pitch of scurry
and confusion into which he had lashed the march in the
second act by the time the final section was reached. There
was no time to sing—no time to think. Would that there
had been no time to listen! It is deplorable to have to
complain of a well-intentioned and apparently quite self-

satisfied gentleman in this rude fashion; but the waste of enormously expensive artistic opportunities that goes on every season at Covent Garden for want of a conductor to utilize them is still more deplorable.

One can forgive Mancinelli a great deal on the score of his genuine enthusiasm in his work and his artistic feeling for orchestration; but his beat is fatally irresolute: it does not really lead; and the consequence is, that in such pieces as the prelude to Lohengrin, or the bridal march, the parts lose their consentaneousness, a blur of indecision spreads over the whole design, and at last one's memory wanders back almost regretfully to the pointed, steady, unwavering beat of Costa, who, unsympathetic, obsolete, and obstructive as he at last became, never allowed the threads of the orchestral loom to become tangled, and would have his band together on the fourth beat of the bar as well as on the first, whereas nowadays it is considered sufficient if, when the conductor swoops wildly down at the beginning of the bar, everybody who is ahead of that point goes back to it, and everybody who has not got so far skips forward to it. It is necessary to go often to the opera, and to listen attentively there, in order to realize how this gets on the nerves of an unfortunate critic after a time. It arises in the first instance with the singers, who, when they find that the complaisant conductor will follow them, no matter what they do, by pulling the band together at the first beat of every bar, become more and more careless, until at last melodies which are nothing if not symmetrical are delivered as shapeless declamations. Then the vice spreads until the habit of keeping accurate measure—a habit which is consistent with the most sentimental elasticity of *tempo*—is given up as unpractical; and matters go from bad to worse, until somebody with the musical conscience to feel about it as Mendelssohn, Wagner, Berlioz, and other masters have felt, gets angry enough to hit out without respect to persons. To that pass I am fast coming. With one conductor who can do nothing but wait, a second who can do nothing but wallop, and a

184

third who can do nothing at all, life at Covent Garden is getting unendurable.

Let me return for a moment to Tannhäuser, not to speak of Perotti, whom I propose to leave entirely to his own reflections, but to hail the re-entry of the rapturous Albani as Elizabeth, whom she played excellently, though her curious helplessness in using the middle of her voice is rather a grave set-off to her temperamental aptitude for Wagnerian parts. If Maurel was not at all like Wolfram von Eschenbach, he was at least very like Virgil, which did just as well. But he substituted the Maurel nuance for the Wagner nuance in O du mein holder Abendstern; and that certainly did not do as well. However, his Wolfram as a whole was an admirable performance, standing out from the rest by its intelligent artistic quality, like his Telramond, his Valentine, and, in short, everything he has done this season. Sofia Ravogli played Venus in an old-fashioned straight white robe, she being a brunette with a great wealth of black hair, which she allowed to hang straight down her back; so that we were able to compare the black and white in square pieces, much as we should on a draper's counter. It is true that by this method of dressing she gained an air of propriety which made Elizabeth look comparatively abandoned; but she spoiled the opera by turning the Venusberg into an anchorite's cave. With that beautiful hair made into a coronet in the Greek fashion, and a properly designed vestment of flame color, sea-green, orange, bronze, or anything but vestal white, were it even cream color, and her face toned to the right complexion, she would be a perfect Venus. As it is, she only abets the anti-Wagnerism of the stage manager, whose insanities must be seen to be believed. No words of mine can do justice to the Venus episode in the last act: I leave it to abler pens, and content myself with chronicling the appearance of several horses on the stage at the end of the first act in Rotten Row saddles and harness; whilst the hunting music, written for twelve horns, was played enthusiastically by the military band on cornets and saxhorns behind the scenes.

At Mr Manns's benefit concert next Saturday at the Crystal Palace, Isaÿe will play the Mendelssohn concerto; and the orchestral pieces will include Berlioz' Benvenuto Cellini overture, Schubert's B minor symphony (the unfinished one), and the prelude to Parsifal. Last Saturday Gerardy played, and played very well indeed. Miss Patterson should not have used Gli angui d' inferno merely as a stalking horse for her high F. I shall not pretend to blame her for the shocking interpolation of a shake and an extra F at the end, as no doubt that was the work of her teacher. But I hope the result convinced her that Mozart would have been a safer guide; and I must tell her frankly not to attempt the song in public again until she can sing a simple sequence of triplets smoothly and accurately. Rose Softly Blooming was much better: she was justified in trying her fortune with it, though it is by no means an easy song. The performance of Berlioz' Harold symphony was particularly fine, only needing about thirty extra strings in the last movement to make quite sound enough for the size of the concert room, a requirement with which the directors could not reasonably be expected to comply.

29 April 1891

AFTER a fortnight of Gluck, Gounod, Bizet, and Wagner, Covent Garden relapsed exhausted into the arms of La Traviata; and the audience promptly dwindled. Albani played Violetta on the occasion; and it is proper, if somewhat personal, to say that on her part too there has been a certain dwindling which does much to reconcile the imagination to her impersonations of operatic heroines. Not, of course, that she can by any conceivable stretch of fancy be accepted as a typical case of pulmonary consumption. But one has only to recall the eminent prima donnas who began their careers needing only a touch of blue under the eyes to make them look plausibly phthisical, and progressed with appalling rapidity to a condition in which no art of the maker-up could prevent them from looking insistently dropsical, to feel abundantly grateful to Albani for having so trained herself that nobody can say anything worse of her than that she is pleasingly plump. Indeed, in one way her figure is just the thing for La Traviata, as it does away with the painful impression which the last act produces whenever there is the faintest realism about it. Even in the agonies of death Albani robs the sick bed and the medicine bottles of half their terrors by her reassuring air of doing as well as can be expected. Still, I submit that though the representation is not painful, it is in the last degree ridiculous. In saying this I by no means endorse the verdict of those colleagues of mine who are declaring in all directions that the opera is antiquated, impossible, absurd, a relic of the old régime, and so on. Verdi's opera is one thing: the wilful folly of the Covent Garden parody of it is quite another. Take any drama ever written, and put it on a stage six times too large for its scenes, introducing the maddest incongruities of furniture, costume, and manners at every turn of it; and it will seem as nonsensical as La Traviata, even without the crowning burlesque of a robust, joyous, round-cheeked lady figuring as a moribund patient in decline. I have no doubt that when Mr Joseph Bennett is commissioned by Mr Harris to found a *libretto* for an opera by Signor Randegger on Hedda Gabler, and it is produced at Covent Garden with Hedda in modern costume, Tesman as a Dutch burgomaster after Rembrandt, Lövborg as a Louis XIII mousquetaire, Brack as the traditional notary, and Thea in black with a mantilla and a convulsive walk, Ibsen himself will be voted antiquated. The truth is that La Traviata, in spite of its conventionalities, is before its time at Covent Garden instead of behind it. It is a much more real and powerful work than Carmen, for instance, which everybody accepts as typically modern.

With this view of the capabilities of the opera, I read the promise of Maurel's appearance as Germont with some hope of witnessing a beginning of reform. Maurel is courageous in matters of costume: his Holbein dress as Valentine, his mouse-colored Mephistopheles, his stupendous helmet in Lohengrin, which reminded us all of the head-dress of the Indian in West's picture of the death of Wolfe, had proved him ready for any sacrifice of tradition to accuracy. I fully expected to see Germont enter fearlessly in frock-coat, tall hat, and primrose gloves with three black braids down the back. Judge of my disappointment when he marched forward in a magnificent Vandyke costume, without even an umbrella to save appearances. I knew then that he wanted, not to play Germont, but simply to sing Di provenza. However, to do him justice, he did not treat the part with utter frivolity. He came in rudely with his hat on; and when he found that Violetta had a noble soul, he took the hat off, like a gentleman, and put it on a chair. I instantly foresaw that Albani, when next overcome by emotion, would sit on it. So breathless became my anticipation that I could hardly attend to the intervening duet. At last she did sit on it; and never would that hat have graced Maurel's temples again if it had been historically accurate. This, then, I presume, is the explanation of the anachronism on Maurel's part. Albani must have refused to give up the business of sitting on Germont's hat, thereby forcing him to adopt one that would bend but not break under an exceptional pressure of circumstances. But the effect on Maurel was finally disastrous. In the fourth act his determination to take himself seriously faltered several times; and at last his tendency to laugh when he caught anybody's eye became patent. Montariol, the most amiable of tenors and swordsmen, did his best with Alfredo, and even brought down the house by an unexpected burst of vocal splendor in the third act.

La Traviata was followed up by Rigoletto on Wednesday; but my stall reached me too late for use. No doubt Maurel's Rigoletto is what it was last winter in Lago's time. It was then sufficiently powerful and interesting. The management, having thus produced two startling novelties, fell back for the further spring of getting out Le Prophète last

Monday. I see that Jean de Reszke has explained that he cannot master Siegfried in time for performance this season. It is a pity; for one would rather see him swinging the sledge-hammer and making the sparks fly in Mime's smithy, or conversing with the wood-bird in Fafnir's forest, or waking Brynhild on the fiery mountain, than shouting that detestable and dishonorable drinking song in the last act of the most conventional of the historical impostures of Scribe and Meyerbeer. He might at least play Tannhäuser once for us before the end of the season. The music must be pretty well known to him, whether he has studied it or not.

At Mr Mann's benefit at the Crystal Palace on Saturday, Isaÿe played the eternal but never quite unwelcome Mendelssohn concerto, which cut but a poor figure after the Parsifal prelude and the Benvenuto Cellini overture. The huge audience took Isaÿe rather coolly when he came upon the platform, as if most of them had never heard of him. But at the end of the concerto the applause burst out *con furore*; not without reason, for the performance was an astonishing one. Miss Adeline de Lara was hampered by a bad pianoforte. Broadwood is not the right maker for a touch like hers: probably Pleyel would suit her better. The particular Broadwood in question so resented her handling that it ruptured a hammer and stopped the performance. When, after much disconsolate contemplation of the interior of the instrument by everybody in the neighborhood, she consented to proceed with one note dumb, the maimed member extemporized a castanet and tambourine accompaniment by clattering and jingling among the strings. Altogether it was fortunate that the music was not of the slightest interest, being pure Rubinstein from beginning to end; so that Miss de Lara, in giving a convincing display of strength and dexterity, was doing all that she could have done in any case with such a composition. Madame Nordica sang Dich, theure Halle, from Tannhäuser, in a bright, bumptious, self-assertive, and otherwise quite unmeaning way that was as exactly as possible the opposite of how it ought to be sung; and a Mr E. O. Bane-

189

mann gave us an inappropriate air from Elijah without making any decisive effect, though his voice is of exceptionally fine quality, and his way of using it artistic and full of promise for its future. Mrs Hutchinson also sang; and there were two new orchestral pieces by J. F. Barrett; but the program was so long that I had to return to town immediately after hearing Isaÿe inhumanly accept an encore for his prodigious performance of Wieniawski's variation on Russian airs.

6 May 1891

ISAÿE'S concert last week was the most sensational we have had this season. His determination to cap feats impossible to other violinists by feats impossible to himself, and his enormous self-assertiveness (significantly associated with a marked personal resemblance to certain early portraits of the late Mr Bradlaugh), really broke up and destroyed the Beethoven concerto. Those cadenzas of his, monstrous excrescences on the movements, nailed on, not grafted in, have no form, being merely examples of madly difficult ways of playing the themes that have been reasonably and beautifully presented by Beethoven. One's comfort is, that since Isaÿe could hardly play them himself, nobody else is likely to be able to play them at all. Comparing him with Sarasate, there can be no doubt that at present the sum of pleasure to be had for one's money at a Sarasate concert is greater than at an Isaÿe concert, even if the excitement be less strenuous. Sarasate, however, is a fully-matured artist; and it is now evident that Isaÿe is not. His inscrutable age—guessed at as thirty, forty, and even fifty—turns out to be thirty-two, which is mere adolescence for a man of such prodigiously unmanageable temperament. His technical skill must have cost him prolonged and intense labor. Nature does not make anybody a present of a touch at once so fine and so vigorous, or of that power of playing with perfect smoothness chords in which other players—even very eminent ones—have to make an uncouth skip from string to string. But the very craving after the heroic and impossible (a highly Belgian craving) which nerved him to face this drudgery is now keeping him behind his chief rival. Sarasate never insists on his extraordinary feats: he treats his own skill as a matter of course—as part of his necessary equipment as a first-class workman—as something which only concerns the public through its musical result.

Joachim, whose cadenzas, by the bye, are much better than Isaÿe's, takes his place beside the conductor and his orchestral colleagues as the interpreter of Beethoven, whose supremacy he never obscures for a moment. But who can think of Beethoven, or even of music, whilst Isaÿe is Titanically emphasizing himself and his stupendous accomplishment, elbowing aside the conductor, eclipsing the little handful of an orchestra which he thinks sufficient for a concert in St James's Hall, and all but shewing Beethoven the door? The fact is, he has created himself so recently that he is not yet tired of the novelty of his own consummated self. As soon as he exhausts this theme, and devotes himself without a grudge to music, his position will be beyond all question. At present he is more interesting as a prodigy than delightful as an artist. I may add, with reference to the orchestra, that I was glad to have an opportunity of once more seeing Mr Cowen and several of the Philharmonic band at work together. Somehow, I never hear of a Philharmonic concert now until it is over. This troubles me somewhat; for though I never bear malice towards people who honestly admit that their performances will not bear criticism from my standard, I cannot help thinking that there must occasionally be a Philharmonic program which would pass muster with me.

At the vocal recital given by the Henschels at St James's Hall on Friday last, my equanimity was upset by an outrage perpetrated on me by the concert agent, the same being nothing less than my eviction from the corner seat to which The World has a prescriptive immemorial right, and the sandwiching of me into a place which I could not reach or leave without pushing past a row of people and making a public disturbance. I denounce the proceeding as a revolutionary one, and demand of that agent how he would like it himself if he had to go to thirty-three concerts every afternoon from Easter to Midsummer, and could not possibly avoid either arriving late or leaving early at every one of them. How would he like to feel as I do when I see the eyes of those young ladies who have been told the secret of where the celebrated critic sits, turning with awe and curiosity upon some imposter thrust into the seat which is morally mine? I hope that no personal consideration shall ever induce me to set down a word that is not scrupulously weighed in the balance of Justice; but if an agent deliberately goes out of his way to direct my attention to every fault in the performances he arranges, he has himself to thank for the consequences. I say now—and I defy anyone to contradict me—that Henschel's habit of singing out of tune is growing on him. In the duet Vedi che bella sera, he did not sing one solitary note from beginning to end that was not flat; and as Mrs Henschel, instead of singing equally flat to keep him in countenance, repudiated her wifely duty to gratify her artistic self-will (probably she had been misled by Ibsen's plays), and sang in tune throughout, the effect was far from delectable. This false intonation is not the result of a defective ear: it is a habit of which the ear becomes tolerant after a time. That is, be it understood, the ear of the person affected: the general ear retains its rectitude and protests. In some cases, it is true one gets used to it. Trebelli, for instance, had a way of leaning caressingly on the pitch of a note and depressing it the least bit in the world, so that she hardly ever sang absolutely in tune; but as the fault was too slight to be actually disagreeable, it passed as part of her individuality as an artist.

Albani is beginning to do the same thing; but she is carrying it too far, and will soon, unless she takes the trouble to readjust her intonation very carefully, be unable to sing piano in cantabile passages otherwise than quite painfully flat. Henschel is going Albani's way; for it is in sentimental, soft, sustained phrases that he comes to grief: in Crugantino's song and Loewe's setting of The Erl King there is nothing to complain of. The remedy lies ready to his hand. Mrs Henschel always sings in tune. Let him sing duets with her until the two voices blend without the slightest jar, when he may depend on it that he has recovered his musical integrity. If he neglects this he will find his popularity steadily falling off relatively to that of his wife—a state of things subversive of all domestic discipline.

Gerardy's last concert was an improvement on the previous one, at which, it may be remembered, I had to note a certain shortcoming from the perfection of his first public efforts here. This time he was himself again: there was not a trace of carelessness, weariness, or indifference at any point throughout the performance, except perhaps for a moment during the first section of a piece by Radoux, in which no living human being could have taken a very lively interest. The wonder is that a boy, who is not yet old enough to assert his right to choose his programs according to his temperament, should not let his attention lapse more frequently. As it is, the sustained artistic quality of his performances would be extraordinary in an adult. This concert also was the occasion of the first appearance of Eugène Holliday, whose style as a pianist is so foreign to that of Gerardy as a 'cellist that his appearance at the same recital made a positively unfavorable impression. He had his revenge, however, at his own concert on Saturday last, when, with a heroic program beginning with Beethoven's gigantic Opus 106, he held his audience throughout almost as if his master, Rubinstein, had come again.

After making my rounds for months past between the exponents of the Madame Schumann training on the one hand, and the Lisztian training on the other, going from Mr Borwick to Sapellnikoff, and from Miss Eibenschütz to Madame Menter, there is an immense satisfaction in this Rubinstein technique, which has the soundness and thoroughness of the one school and the artistic life and power of the other. In some matters—Chopin ballades, for example

—Holliday is too young to understand quite what he is about; and in no case is it safe to estimate his rank as an artist by the exploits for which he has been so lately crammed by a great master. But the fact that it has been possible so to cram him, proves extraordinary capacity, resolution, and endurance on his part. Even granting that his admirable playing of Tchaikowsky's Barcarolle was a feat of pure imitation, it is not to be doubted that he is fully sensible of the artistic nuances he reproduces. His occasional violence, which knocks some twenty-five pounds per recital off the value of the instrument he uses (a Broadwood), and his trick of striking the top note of a descending scale as if his little finger were the hammer of a rifle, make the milder Mendelssohnian amateur wince; but they are only exaggerations of a genuine executive power, and not the bluster of a weakling. He would do well, if he can afford it, or persuade the agents into the speculation, to give some further recitals, especially as his association with Gerardy was, through the difference of their artistic planes, something of a false start.

Boito's Mefistofele has been revived with success at the Opera; but I shall let that rest until next week.

13 May 1891

EVER since I was a boy I have been in search of a satisfactory performance of Don Giovanni; and I have at last come to see that Mozart's turn will hardly be in my time. I have had no lack of opportunities and disappointments; for the Don is never left long on the shelf, since it is so far unlike the masterpieces of Wagner, Berlioz, and Bach, that it cannot be done at all without arduous preparation. Any opera singer can pick up the notes and tumble through the concerted pieces with one eye on the conductor: any band can scrape through the orchestral parts at sight. Last year and the year before, it was tried in this fashion for a night at Covent Garden, with D'Andrade as Don Juan, and anybody who came handy in the other parts. This year it has been recognized that trifling with Mozart can be carried too far even for the credit of the Royal Italian Opera.

At the performance last Thursday, the first three acts of the four (twice too many) into which the work is divided at Covent Garden shewed signs of rehearsal. Even the last had not been altogether neglected. In the orchestra especially the improvement was marked. Not that anything very wonderful was accomplished in this department: the vigorous passages were handled in the usual timid, conventional way; and the statue music, still as impressive as it was before Wagner and Berlioz were born, was muddled through like a vote of thanks at the end of a very belated public meeting. But the overture was at least attentively played; and in some of the quieter and simpler numbers the exhalations of the magical atmosphere of the Mozartian orchestra were much less scanty and foggy than last year, when I could not, without risk of being laughed at, have assured a novice that in the subleties of dramatic instrumentation Mozart was the greatest master of them all. The cast was neither a very bad nor a very good one. Its weakest point was the Leporello of Isnardon. Lacking the necessary weight in the middle of his voice, as well as the personal force demanded by the character, he was quite unable to lead the final section of the great sextet, Mille torbidi pensieri, which, thus deprived of its stage significance, became a rather senseless piece of "absolute music." Again, in O statua gentilissima, he hardly seized a point from beginning to end.

Now if an artist has neither voice enough nor musical perception enough to interpret forcibly and intelligently such an obvious and simple dramatic transition as that which follows the incident of the statue nodding acceptance of the invitation to supper, he is not fit to meddle with Mozart. Isnardon certainly makes a considerable show of acting throughout the opera; but as he is only trying to be facetious—abstractly facetious, if I may say so—without the slightest feeling for his part, the effect is irritating and irrelevant. Such pieces of business as his pointing the words, Voi sapete quel che fa, by nudging Elvira with his elbow at the end of Madamina, almost make one's blood boil. Poor old Sganarelle-Leporello, with all his failings,was no Yellow-plush; he would not have presumed upon a familiarity of that character with Donna Elvira, even if she had been a much meeker and less distinguished person than Molière made her. There is one man in Mr Harris's company whose clear artistic duty it is to play Leporello; and he, unfortun-ately, is an arrant *fainéant*, whose identity I charitably hide under the designation of Brother Edouard, which, I need hardly add, is not that under which he appears in the bills. In Leporello he would have one of the greatest parts ever written, exactly suited to his range, and full of points which his musical intelligence would seize instinctively without unaccustomed mental exertion. And now that I have begun sketching a new cast, I may as well complete it. Dalla sua pace is not an easy song to sing; but if Jean de Reszke were to do it justice, the memory thereof would abide when all his Gounod successes were lapsed and lost.

With Giulia Ravogli as Zerlina, and the rest of the parts allotted much as at present, a tremendous house would be drawn. Nevertheless the tremendous house would be bored and kept late for its trains unless the representation were brought up to date by the following measures. Take a pot of paste, a scissors and some tissue paper, and start on the *recitativo secco* by entirely expunging the first two dialogues after the duel and before Ah, chi mi dice mai. Reduce all the rest to such sentences as are barely necessary to preserve the continuity of the action. Play the opera in two acts only. And use the time thus gained to restore not only the Don's song, Metà di voi, which Faure used to sing, but, above all, the last three movements of the second finale, thereby putting an end for ever to the sensational vulgarity of bring-ing down the curtain on the red fire and the ghost and the trapdoor. There are other suppressed pages of the score to be reconsidered—a capital song which gets Leporello off the stage after the sextet, a curiously old-fashioned tragic air, almost Handelian, for Elvira between Là ci darem and the quartet, and a comic duet for Zerlina and Leporello, one of the later Vienna interpolations, which, however, is a very dispensable piece of buffoonery.

To return to the actual Don Giovanni of Thursday last, I need say no more of Miss de Lussan, who does not grow more interesting as her voice loses freshness and sustaining power and her manner becomes perter and trickier, than that she is one of those Zerlinas who end Batti, batti, on the upper octave of the note written, as a sort of apology for having been unable to do anything else with the song. The effect of this suburban grace can be realized by anyone who will take the trouble to whistle Pop goes the Weasel with the last note displaced an octave.

I am sorry to add that alterations of Mozart's text were the order of the evening, every one of the singers lacking Mozart's exquisite sense of form and artistic dignity. Maurel, though he stopped short of reviving the traditional atrocity of going up to F sharp in the serenade, did worse things by dragging an F natural into the end of Finch' han del vino, and two unpardonable G's into the finale of the first ballroom scene, just before the final *stretto*, thereby anticipating and destroying the climax Odi il tuon from the sopranos. Madame Tavary still clings to that desolating run up and down the scale with which she contrives to make the conclusion of Non mi dir ridiculous; and Montariol, unable to evade Il mio tesoro by omitting it like Dalla sua pace, did strange things with it in his desperation. His Ottavio was altogether a melancholy performance, as he was put out of countenance from the beginning by being clothed in a seedy misfit which made him look lamentably down on his luck. Mr Harris would not dream of allowing such a costume to be seen on his stage in a modern opera; and I must really urge upon him that there are limits to the application even of the principle that anything is good enough for Mozart.

Maurel's Don Giovanni, though immeasurably better than any we have seen of late years, is not to be compared to his Rigoletto, his Iago, or, in short, to any of his melodramatic parts. Don Juan may be as handsome, as irresistible, as adroit, as unscrupulous, as brave as you please; but the one thing that is not to be tolerated is that he should consciously parade these qualities as if they were elaborate accomplishments instead of his natural parts. And this is exactly where Maurel failed. He gave us a description of Don Juan rather than an impersonation of him. The confident smile, the heroic gesture, the splendid dress, even the intentionally seductive vocal inflection which made such a success of Là ci darem in spite of Miss de Lussan's coquettish inanity, were all more or less artificial. A Don Juan who is continually aiming at being Don Juan may excite our admiration by the skill with which he does it; but he cannot convince us that he is the real man. I remember seeing Jean de Reszke play the part when he had less than a tenth of Maurel's present skill and experience; and yet I think Mozart would have found the younger man the more sympathetic interpreter.

It seems ungrateful to find fault with an artist who rescues a great rôle from the hands of such ignoble exponents as the common or Covent Garden Dons who swagger feebly through it like emancipated billiard-markers; but it would hardly be a compliment to Maurel to praise him for so cheap a superiority. And, indeed, there is no fault-finding in the matter. It is a question of temperament. When all is said, the fundamental impossibility remains that Maurel's artistic vein is not Mozartian. One or two points of detail may be mentioned. He was best in the love-making scenes and worst in those with Leporello, whom he treated with a familiarity which was rather that of Robert Macaire with Jacques Strop than of a gentleman with his valet. The scene of the exposure in the ballroom he played rather callously. Nothing in the score is clearer than that Don Juan is discomfited, confused, and at a loss from the moment in which they denounce him until seeing that there is nothing for it but to fight his way out, he ceases to utter hasty exclamations of dismay, and recovers himself at the words Ma non manca in me cor-

aggio. Maurel dehumanized and melodramatized the scene
by missing this entirely, and maintaining a defiant and self-
possessed bearing throughout.

And again, on the entry of the statue, which Don Juan,
however stable his nerve may be imagined to have been, can
hardly have witnessed without at least a dash of surprise
and curiosity, Maurel behaved very much as if his uncle
had dropped in unexpectedly in the middle of a bachelor's
supper-party. The result was that the scene went for nothing,
though it is beyond all comparison the most wonderful of
the wonders of dramatic music. But if the audience is ever to
be cured of the habit of treating it as a sort of voluntary to
play them out, it must be very carefully studied by the artist
playing Don Juan, upon whose pantomime the whole action
of the scene depends, since the statue can only stand with a
stony air of weighing several tons, whilst the orchestra makes
him as awful as the conductor will allow it. Since Maurel let
this scene slip completely through his fingers, I do not see
how he can be classed with the great Don Juans (if there
ever were any great ones). The problem of how to receive a
call from a public statue does not seem to have struck him as
worth solving.

The Elvira (Madame Rolla), whose B flat at the end of
her aria was perhaps the most excusable of all the inexcusable interpolations, was as good as gold, not indulging once
in a scream, and relying altogether on pure vocal tone of remarkable softness. In Mi tradi she succeeded in being more
pleasing than any Elvira I can remember except Di Murska,
who understood the full value of the part and played it in-
comparably, like the great artist she was. Madame Rolla
does not act with the force of Nilsson; and in the quartet she
failed to bring off the effect at the end, where Elvira gets
louder and angrier whilst the wretched Don gets more and
more agitated by the dread of her making a scene; but I think
Maurel was a little unequal to the occasion here too. On the
whole, Madame Rolla, whose voice reminds one somewhat
of Marimon's, is a useful addition to the company. Mr

Harris had better now turn his attention to achieving a really serious performance of Le Nozze di Figaro.

20 *May* 1891

EVERY schoolboy, as Mr Churton Collins would say, remembers Macaulay's story of how Voltaire received Congreve's snobbish application to be regarded as a gentleman, and not as a writer for the theatre. "If you were merely a gentleman," said Voltaire, "I should not have bothered to come and see you." Yet here is Mr Walter Pollock, writing one of those curious valentines which are recited at benefits and on other effusive occasions, complimenting Sims Reeves on being a gentleman. There are thousands of gentlemen in England, and there is only one Sims Reeves. And yet Sims Reeves is told to his face that he is a gentleman. Only one worse outrage could have been perpetrated; and that was to have called him a real gentleman, or person who gives a tip of a sovereign when a common gentleman only gives five shillings. My own opinion is that Sims Reeves is no more a gentleman than I am; for I have seen him appear at an afternoon concert in a black velvet coat, lavender trousers, a canary-colored tie, and primrose gloves—an exceptional and therefore essentially ungentlemanly costume. And no gentleman that I have ever met would be capable of singing as Sims Reeves sings. However, Mr Pollock no doubt meant well. Unable, as a merely literary man, to appreciate his hero's singing, he paid him a conventional compliment to shew his general goodwill, and threw in a literary allusion to Edgar and Captain Macheath by way of local color.

Whether the great farewell of Monday week will prove a last farewell is a point on which I prefer not to hazard an opinion. Certain it is, that though Sims Reeves at seventy has lost his powers of endurance so far that he cannot now count upon getting safely through a trying song like Blumenthal's Message, yet in such Handelian airs as Total Eclipse, in which the instrumental interludes give plenty of time for rest after each strain, he can still leave the next best tenor in England an immeasurable distance behind. Indeed, he does this even in the songs to which he is no longer fully equal; and the general recognition of his pre-eminence is a powerful support to the critic whose counsels of perfection are cavilled at as righteous overmuch.

For if I were to advise a young man to do what Sims Reeves has done I should apparently be advising him to ruin himself. Rejecting all the coarser, baser, more exciting elements in popular singing for the sake of a pure artistic integrity which only a few appreciate fully, and which many rebel against and scoff at as mere feebleness and affectation; throwing not only your concert engagements, but coveted positions at the opera and the Handel Festivals to the winds whenever their conditions prevent you from doing your very best; allowing rivals to pass you and seize your golden opportunities as if you had eternity at your disposal: these would seem to be infallible methods of securing discredit, failure, and bankruptcy. Fortunately there is Sims Reeves to prove that they land an artist at the head of his profession. Doubtless they require enormous artistic conviction, courage, and self-respect; but they have left at least one man better off than the methods of vulgar ambition have left any of his rivals.

The concert came off very happily in every respect. Some of us may have begun by feeling a little anxious as to how much was left of Christine Nilsson; but we were soon relieved on that score. Her figure is ampler than of yore; and her eyes are aided by glasses fixed to the end of an exasperating tortoiseshell pole. The features, too, are perhaps more matronly by a line or so than they were twenty years ago; and it cannot reasonably be asserted that her extreme upper notes are as fresh and free as those, for example, of Miss Eames. But Nilsson is Nilsson still, for better for worse. I do not say that she is not a little more dignified than in the old days, when no law, human or divine, restrained her from doing anything that she wished to do, just as the whim took her. Mine eyes have seen her, as Leonora in Il Trovatore, after listening with a critical air to Ah si, ben mio sung by a tenor who must have been a veteran when she was in her cradle, slap the patriarch on the back with a hearty bravo at the end.

At the Albert Hall she refrained from slapping Sims Reeves on the back; and her curtsies on entering were of a splendid, courtly, regal kind; but before she had got through ten bars of the Jewel Song she was gesticulating nearly as vigorously as ever she did on the stage; and when encore followed encore, she pulled off her gloves and sat down at the pianoforte in her old way to give us that same old Swedish ballad of which no critic knows the name, and every critic of a certain age knows the tune. And when that was encored too, she sang a ditty in which she whooped, and laughed, and screamed like any *gamin*. She had previously re-established her old right to do as she pleased by her sing-ing of The Erl King; and oh! the relief of hearing that song sung again by one whose sense of it was as perfect musically as dramatically. If Paderewski and Stavenhagen, who are fond of putting Liszt's transcription on the piano and pounding the life out of it, would only listen to her once as she winds her way into every turn of the melody with exactly the right dramatic inflection, how much guilt might they not escape in the future? Unfortunately it is only mere composers, like Mozart or Wagner, who are not ashamed to learn from women and singers; no great pianist could so compromise himself.

When it was clear that Nilsson's reappearance was a huge success, curiosity shifted to Irving's chance of making himself heard in that immense amphitheatre, crowded from floor to ceiling. He settled the question by proving, in his first half-dozen words, that he was no less a master of fine vocal tone than any of the singers who preceded him; and the speech was nearly as well heard as the songs. Still, highly cultivated as Irving's voice is, the normal pitch at which he has accustomed himself to speak is artificially low for him, and his method of production is a little too "throaty." It was necessary to listen attentively in his case, whereas when Sims Reeves himself made a speech later in the evening, he was, very unexpectedly, heard with quite startling ease and distinctness. It was a final and remarkable triumph of perfect vocal art. On the rest of the program it is not necessary to enlarge. Mr Manns conducted the band: Arditi, Kuhe, and Ganz were also down as "conductors" in the Miscellaneous Concert sense, and were assisted in that ornamental function by a Mr Maunder, who accompanied Sims Reeves very well.

Janotha played Mendelssohn's G minor concerto at a stupendous pace, but with all her characteristic reserve of sentiment. When I first heard Janotha play I was enchanted: here, I thought, was a truly noble and delicate talent: the best part of Madame Schumann would live again in this pupil of hers. But somehow it was not to be. She was proud, exacting, perhaps shy: at any rate, when her playing lost its freshness it did not gain the warmth and sympathy of the mature artist. She never would give herself away to the public, though she would play always with the utmost skill and refinement. Now the public year's for more generous treatment; and feels that though Janotha has preserved her dignity and her individuality, she has turned out a somewhat stonyhearted daughter of Music. It is not to Art and to the people that she devotes herself so scrupulously every time she sits down to play; and on behalf of Art and the people, I feel justly jealous.

One word more on this farewell program. Why does Madame Antoinette Sterling play so persistently on the fourth string, so to speak? Nobody could sing We're a' noddin' better than she if she chose; but she clings to her pathetic stop so fondly that she will not give the right accent of joy, relief, and half-hysterical laughter to the refrain. The result is that before the third verse is reached the song has become monotonous and maundering; and I, for one, become rather impatient of hearing any more of it.

203

Isaÿe's recital last week was a greater success than his orchestral concert. He was much more in the vein, and shewed unexpected power and insight as an interpreter of chamber music. His treatment of the Beethoven concerto on the previous occasion had left an impression that in this department of his art he was inferior to Joachim; but after his masterly reading of the sonatas by Raff and Beethoven at the recital—not to mention the Bach pieces—there can no longer be any doubt that the leadership of the quartet at the Popular Concerts will be safe in his hands for another generation. He played one Bach prelude decidedly too fast; and he threw a bunch of thistles to the donkeys at the end of the recital in the shape of an atrocious show piece of his own composition; but for the rest he played magnificently in every respect; and one could only wonder that the reputation of such a genius should spread so slowly as to leave the seats as loosely packed as they were.

After Isaÿe, we all hurried across the street to Prince's Hall to hear a concert given by the Bach Choir at the eccentric hour of half-past five. Unaccompanied part singing was the staple of the entertainment; and I can frankly and unreservedly say that I would not desire to hear a more abominable noise than was offered to us under pretext of Bach's Singet dem Herren and some motets by Brahms. I will not deny that there was a sort of broken thread of vocal tone running through the sound-fabric; but for the most part it was a horrible tissue of puffing and blowing and wheezing and groaning and buzzing and hissing and gargling and shrieking and spluttering and grunting and generally making every sort of noise that is incidental to bad singing, severe exertion, and mortal fear of losing one's place. It was really worse than the influenza. Most fortunately there were some pieces which the choir knew well and took quietly, notably a motet by Palestrina—whose music seems to me as fresh and beautiful today as it can ever have been—and some old English madrigals. These were done as well as could be expected from a choir with an average age of at least fifty-five. There certainly used to be no such lack of young people in it. Can it be that there are members who are such cowardly deserters in the hour of need, as to object to appear on the platform at a public concert? If so, they should at once be threatened with ignominious expulsion. If not, then the sooner Mr Stanford begins to recruit vigorously for young blood the better. It is reassuring to see that the great Mass in B minor is to be performed again next winter.

Isaÿe seems to have stimulated a number of gentlemen who can fiddle a bit to try their luck at concert-giving. I have attended two orchestral concerts given by Herr Waldemar Meyer, who is quite the most easygoing *virtuoso* I can remember. He plays anything you please—Brahms, Bach, Beethoven, Mendelssohn—with apparent facility and satisfaction. Such feats are not commonplace; but Herr Meyer contrives to make them appear so. Mr Haddock, an ambitious orchestral player from Leeds, as I understand, has also considerable powers of manipulating his instrument; but I cannot say that I caught anything in his conception and quality of execution sufficiently exceptional to warrant me, as yet, in admitting his claim to the same eminence as a soloist which he is entitled to in the orchestra. Finally, I have heard Max Reichel, who has the good fortune to be supported by a very clever and original singer, Madame Swiatlowsky, a sort of Russian Antoinette Sterling, though with a certain variety and fire peculiar to herself, and with some charming *virtuoso* tricks of *mezza voce*, etc.

The Opera has been mercifully repeating itself. Montariol has retired from the rôle of Ottavio in Don Giovanni, his place being taken by the useful Ravelli, who must feel some mild exultation in the inability of the Royal Italian Opera to get on without him.

27 *May* 1891

LAST week will stand as one of the most memorable under Mr Harris's management. On Tuesday, Manon, or The Triumph of Van Dyck; on Wednesday, The Sleeper Awakened, or Jean de Reszke on his Mettle; and on Thursday, The Voice of the Sluggard, with Brother Edouard as Leporello. And now, who was it that named Van Dyck as the man for Covent Garden at a time when the experimental evenings at that house were reserved for Signor Rawner *et hoc genus omne*? Who prophesied the effect on Brother Jean, and cast Brother Edouard for Leporello? Well, no matter who; but if his counsels are not henceforth treated with respect, there is no such thing as gratitude in the world.

I cannot remember a more complete and unqualified operatic success than that of Van Dyck as Des Grieux. To begin with, the man himself is irresistible. If any lady has been disqualified by her sex from fully appreciating the charm of Ada Rehan's smile, let her go and see it on Van Dyck's virile face. If any dramatic critic has failed to imagine how a man with Garrick's figure could be a model of active dignity, let him hasten to Covent Garden; for Van Dyck is Garrick to the life. Those who were at Bayreuth when he played Parsifal will need no description of the charm of his youth and strength, his rapid, impulsive, spontaneous movements, his enormous unaffectedness and *bonhomie*, and withal his perfectly serious and dignified comprehension of his position as an artist.

On Tuesday the house found out his merits with surprising quickness. There was a small *claque*; but as it had not been retained for him, his entry in the first act was received with dead silence. Before five minutes had passed, the admirable discipline which usually prevails in the gallery was disturbed by ebullitions of applause. At the end of the act Van Dyck was in the position of a lyric Cæsar, having come, and sung, and conquered. I own that I waited for the

206

second act with some apprehension as to the effect of that charming air which Des Grieux sings to Manon at the dinner-table, when, regardless of the toothsome appearance of a Vienna roll four feet long, they literally dine off love. It seemed only too likely that a Belgian tenor would resort to the conventional artificial French *mezza voce*, and thus spoil the pathos of the air for English ears. I am happy to say that I reckoned without Van Dyck's genius. Nothing could be more unstudiedly original and natural in conception, more skilful and artistic in execution, than his performance of this number, which brought down the house as domestically as if it had been Sally in our Alley sung by Mr Edward Lloyd at a ballad concert. As to the scena in the second part of the third act, with the explosion of ringing high notes at the end, its success was a foregone conclusion.

But far more conclusive than any isolated achievements of this kind were the sustained excellence of the impersonation as a whole, the bright intelligence, the variety, the fine musical sensibility, the invigorating and thoroughly male character of even the tenderest and most playful episodes of his infatuation for Manon, and the utter absence of that detestable blight of bravado and flunkey-like attitudinizing which has spread to Covent Garden from the Paris Grand Opéra. To have such an artist in London without hearing him in Siegfried, which he was surely born to play, is not to be suffered without protest. The present project of allowing him to confine himself to Manon and Faust is a wanton belittlement of an opportunity which is all too narrow at best.

I have said that there was a small *claque* in the house; and this reminds me of Miss Sybil Saunderson, who received of flowers six baskets or thereabouts. There can be no objection to Mr Harris varying the scheme of grand opera at his theatre by engaging Miss Saunderson; but why not Chaumont at once? Long ago I suggested that an experiment in this direction might be tried by engaging Coquelin for Leporello; and not long since, Mr Irving, in a speech before the curtain, hinted pretty plainly that he would not be indis-

posed to consider an offer for the part of Mephistopheles at
Covent Garden if business became unprofitable at the
Lyceum. They do this sort of thing systematically in Den-
mark with satisfactory artistic results. Why not here? Miss
Saunderson does not sing so well as Coquelin—very few
people do—but she could hold her own with Mr Irving,
having a pretty talent for imitating French singing of the
Opéra Comique *genre*.

Of the other parts little need be said. The quartet in the
second act will go better another time if MM. Ceste and
Dufriche will kindly recollect that in singing concerted
music it is necessary to listen sympathetically to the singers
with whose notes their own are intended to form chords.
Their present plan of standing at opposite corners of the
stage and—I do not like to call it howling; and I positively
refuse to call it singing—say, delivering their parts in a
spirit of unbridled competition, has the effect of extinguish-
ing Miss Saunderson, of making it impossible for Van Dyck
to save the situation, of spoiling the quartet, and consequently of making themselves highly obnoxious to the public. Dufriche seemed to enjoy his part, playing it not badly,
if somewhat roughly; and Isnardon was good as Des Grieux
senior. The opera fell quite flat when Van Dyck was off the
stage. It is clever, lively, ingenious, and strongly supported
by its relationship to one of the most charming stories ever
written (I had almost as soon omit The Vicar of Wakefield
or The Pilgrim's Progress from my bookshelf as Manon
Lescaut); but it made less effect as a whole than at Drury
Lane with Carl Rosa. It is too flimsy and too local in its
style to make a permanent place for itself on the English
stage.

Les Huguenots on the following night drew an immense house, the cast being an exceptionally attractive one.
As to Jean de Reszke, he was hardly recognizable. Even the
invariable golden beard was gone, replaced by a much
sterner and darker arrangement. Had Van Dyck been
dressed at the wing, ready to go on and take his place at the
208

slightest sign of indifference, he could not have worked harder at his part. The very attitudes of fifteen years ago came back to him: there was no more irresolute mooning about the stage and thinking better of each languid impulse to do something: he acted with passion and sang with his utmost eloquence and tenderness. Any great brilliancy of vocal effect was put out of the question by the audacious transpositions to which he resorted in order to bring the highest notes of the part within his range; but he was all the better able to handle his music sympathetically, the chief sufferers from the transpositions being the unfortunate bassos, who, in the *stretto* of the duel septet, were growling in their boots in the most uncomfortable way. On the whole, Brother Jean, though Van Dyck has torn away the enchanted veil from his lack of solidity and variety, rallied magnificently against his terrible rival: the gallery was cheering him enthusiastically as I left the theatre.

Brother Edouard, in a faultless Lincoln & Bennett hat, distinguished himself, as usual, in the duet with Valentine, but was otherwise a mere makeshift in the absence of a true *basso profondo*, finishing his chorale by singing the canto fermo in unison with the trumpet part, instead of going down into the depths plumbed by Meyerbeer. The general effect of his voice in Marcel's music is like that of a bass clarinet part played on a saxhorn, the characteristic tone-color aimed at being quite misrepresented. San Bris, and not Marcel, is Brother Edouard's affair in Les Huguenots. Nevers was easy work for Maurel, who forced the management to make a first step in the long-called-for reconsideration of the mutilations of the score, by restoring the colloquy with the servant and the bravura which follow the Piff-Paff song. The present Covent Garden version of the opera is the result of a music-butchery perpetrated half a century ago in order to bring the performance within reasonable limits of time. In accordance with the taste of that Rossinian period, the whistleable tunes were retained, and the dramatic music sacrificed.

209

Now that the public takes a lively interest in picturesque
descriptive music, and that the whistleable tunes have in
some instances survived their popularity, the score needs to
be recut, so as to bring the acting version up to date, and to
take full advantage of the time that was gained some years
ago when the rags and tatters of the fifth act were given up
as a bad job. The first thing to do is to gain more time by
making further cuts—to give up the awkward and absurd
repetitions of the Piff-Paff and of the Rataplan, and to do
away with the silly ballet of bathers in the second act, and
indeed (saving your presence, divine Giulia) with that very
superfluous afterthought, the page's No, no, no, no, no, no.
Then the restoration just effected by Maurel in the first
scene could be followed by that of the concerted piece L'Av-
ventura è Stravagante, and of the really brutal cut of the unaccompanied episode in the scene of the oath-taking before
the Queen, whilst the impetuous finale could be given in its
entirety. In the Pré-aux-Clercs scene, the exciting climax to
the duel, in which Maurevert brings a troop of Catholics to
the aid of San Bris, and Marcel knocks at the door of the
inn and summons the Huguenot soldiers to the rescue with
his Lutheran chorale—the omission of all which at present
makes the upshot of the duel septet lame and ridiculous—
could easily be added. The opera would not then take longer
to play than at present; and it would be greatly freshened
and strengthened.

To return to Wednesday night, Albani is the only Valentine of whom it can be said that she does not miss a point in
the part. If her intonation had been true throughout, which
it hardly was, her praise would be unqualified. Mravina, the
new Russian soprano, has a voice of such exceptional range
and flexibility that she was able to execute all the shakes and
roulades of Marguerite with a facility which I do not take to
be altogether the result of hard work, because there were
suspicious lapses into a comparatively familiar and commonplace manner between whiles. However, as her natural
musical gifts are great, and she, moreover, an intelligent and

sympathetic person, she is unquestionably a happy acquisition of Mr Harris's. She has, by the bye, that very rare accomplishment, a true shake. The superficiality of Giulia Ravogli's vocal training is brought out rather glaringly by the music of Urbano; but her acting is irresistible, aided as it is by that elation which every energetic woman feels when relieved for a moment from the fetters of feminine costume. Lassalle was the San Bris; but the part is not one in which he distinguishes himself specially: his opportunity did not come until Saturday, when he was better than ever as Hans Sachs in Die Meistersinger, in which Albani also was excellent, and Jean de Reszke was wide awake and in earnest for the first time as Walther von Stolzing—the performance, on the whole, being the most deeply enjoyable of the season.

Several other matters must stand over for another week, notably Carl Armbruster's concert in commemoration of Wagner's birthday, which took place at Lord Dysart's (Ham House, close to the site proposed by me for the English Wagner Theatre).

3 June 1891

THE Richter concerts opened on Monday week with a program the like of which for thrilling novelty has not been heard in London for a long time. The Seventh Symphony, the Parsifal and Meistersinger preludes, the Ride of the Valkyries: these, with a suite by Bach, were the pledges of the progressive and enterprising spirit that chafes in its protuberant prison-house beneath the great conductor's waistcoat. Seriously—for the finer shades of musical humor are hardly safe with the English public—Richter has no right to stuff a program with the most hackneyed items in his repertory in order to save the trouble of rehearsing. I do not, of course, mean to say that the Seventh Symphony and the rest should be discarded because they have been performed several times already. But I do mean most emphatically that their execution should be elaborated and perfected every time the public is asked to put its hand in its pocket afresh to hear them. Nothing can be artistically meaner than to trade on the ignorance of those who think that the name of Richter is a guarantee for unimprovable perfection. As a matter of fact, the orchestra is by no means what it ought to be; and it has been getting worse instead of better for some years past.

Let me take an instance or two—always worth a ton of general statement. Every Bayreuth pilgrim is by this time familiar with that wonderful throbbing, fluttering, winnowing cloud of sound which the violins make as the Grail descends in Parsifal. That is to say, the violins ought to make it; but without the most patient and critical preparation they make nothing but a muddle in which the scoffer will justly refuse to recognize anything but a confusion of groups of three notes with groups of four. Now, as prices are high at Richter's concerts, and there is no reason whatever why cheap work should be tolerated there, we are, I consider, entitled to call upon his band either to master this effect or let Parsifal alone. On Monday week they did neither; and the enthusiasm created by the performance of the prelude was due entirely to the extraordinary beauty of that large portion of the work which presents no special difficulties of execution. Why it was immediately followed by the Walkürenritt is more than I can explain. Whether Richter, in a frenzy of contempt for the London musical public, resolved to shew that it had no sense of artistic congruity to be shocked, or whether he took just the opposite view, and thought he would indulge himself with a Mephistophelian joke at its expense, is more than I can guess; but certain it is that the last divine strains of Parsifal were still in our ears when the wild gallop of the Valkyries was upon us with a heathenish riot. And I can unreservedly assure Richter that a more villainous performance of it never was heard before in St James's Hall. To offer us such an orgy of scraping, screeching, banging, and barking as a tone-picture of the daughters of Wotan was an outrage to Wagner. Surely Richter does not conceive Ortlinde, Waltraute, and the rest of them as a parcel of screaming, delirious viragoes, without grace, strength, majesty, or regard for their steeds. For that is the sort of Valkyrie Ride suggested to me by fiddles rasped as if they were whirling grindstones, and trombones overblown until they sound like cracked cornets. Such treatment degrades Wagner to the level of Wiertz, and makes novices guess that Walkürenritt must be German for "cruelty to animals," which The Meister abhorred with Shelleyan intensity.

I have often enough done justice to Richter's genius as an interpreter both of tone poetry and of absolute music to claim exemption from all suspicion of ill-will towards himself or his school; and I suffer too often from the vapidity of orchestras which, for all their polish, fail miserably whenever sustained tone is needed, to undervalue the example set by the Richter band with its magnificent *sostenuto*. But when it comes to depending on the reputation of the band and the conductor to dispense with careful preparation, and to snatch popular victories with exciting pieces like the Walkürenritt by dint of what I can only describe as instrumental ruffianism, then it is time for every critic whose former praise meant anything but acquiescence in the fashion of admiring Richter, to warn him that unless he promptly takes steps to bring the standard of quality of execution in his orchestra up to that set by the Crystal Palace orchestra, and the standard of exhaustive preparation up to that set by the wonderful performances of Berlioz' works achieved here last winter by the Manchester band, he will lose his old pre-eminence in the estimation of all those who really know the difference between thorough work and scamped work in performing orchestral music of the highest class.

The Wagner birthday concert at Ham House was in many respects a huge improvement on Bayreuth. Twickenham Ferry is an excellent substitute for the Channel or the German Ocean; and the reduction of my travelling expenses from £7 to £8 to 1s. 5½d., and of the time wasted in locomotion from forty hours to one, was highly acceptable. As to comparisons between the country about Richmond and the Fichtelgebirge, or Richmond Park and the Hofgarten, or the view from Richmond Hill and that from the Hohe Warte, it would be ungenerous to Germany to press them. On the other hand, I freely admit that not even the expedient of sending the cornet-player out into the garden before the second part of the concert, to blow the sword motive from The Niblung's Ring, quite made up for the absence of the Wagner Theatre and Parsifal. Lord Dysart did what a man could: he annihilated the very memory of the Theatre Restaurant by a marquee in which I took my sober Wagnerian meal of brown bread and lemonade next to disciples who were trying reckless experiments with *sauerkraut* and rum custard; and he received us in a house and grounds almost as fit for the purpose of the afternoon as our own place at Hampton Court. Still, a house is a house, and a theatre is a theatre, and I strongly urge Lord Dysart to secede from the useless London branch of the German Wagner Society, and form a really important English society with the object of building a Wagner Theatre within ten minutes' walk of his own door.

The concert was not so good as it might have been had the singers been able or willing to avail themselves to the fullest extent of the very favorable conditions for delicate and expressive vocal art presented by a room in which the weakest singer could have been heard without the slightest effort. Unfortunately, most of them seemed rather bent on making a noise; and as the band was equally anxious to avoid doing so, the result was that the orchestral part of the concert was better than the vocal part. Under these circumstances I could not help thinking it rather cool of Mr Henschel to publicly rebuke a momentary roughness in the orchestra by making them recommence the prelude to Wolfram's Blick' ich umher, and then to sing it in the strident and savagely self-assertive accents of Klingsor, instead of in the elevated and spiritual style of the poet

Wolfram. If I had been that orchestra, I should have stopped Mr Henschel and made *him* begin again. Maurel, a southern Frenchman who puts forward no claim to any special sympathy with Wagner, would never have inflicted such a misreading on us.

If Mr Henschel had not atoned somewhat by a comparatively reasonable performance of Wahn, wahn, it would be impossible to pay him the smallest compliment on his share in the afternoon's proceedings. The only excuse for him is that he is a German—I have long since come to the conclusion that the German nation labors under a congenital incapacity to understand the musical side of the universal Wagner. Even Miss Pauline Cramer, whose sympathy with his sentiment makes her a genuine enthusiast, and often leads her to find the right musical expression unconsciously, has failed to see that unless a singer patiently builds up for herself an eloquent, rich, easy middle to her voice, and can attack her high notes in all sorts of ways, quietly or vigorously as the case may demand, half the music of a Wagner part will be lost, and the other half will be apt to produce the general effect of a series of screams. Miss Cramer is so much in earnest, and has such excellent natural gifts—especially a voice which has all the brightness which German voices so commonly lack—that there is no reason why she should not treble her present resources as a lyric and dramatic artist. Her singing of the final scene from the Götterdämmerung was by no means bad; but it was deficient in variety, and cost her more effort than it need have done.

The only orchestral piece performed was the Siegfried Idyll, which has seldom been heard under more suitable conditions (Wagner wrote it, not for public performance, but to serenade his wife with). It went very well, except for a few moments in the middle section, when Mr Armbruster, who has the faults as well as the qualities of an intellect of the most restless and discursive kind, hurried along with mechanical regularity whilst he thought out some remote scientific question, which fortunately did not occupy him very long. On the whole, it was a pleasant half-holiday; and if Lord Dysart would like to give another concert on my birthday, which is due in a month or two, I shall not discourage the project.

Van Dyck was unlucky enough to have a baddish cold on Saturday when he appeared as Faust. He had to take the highest notes in the second and third acts in a cautious falsetto, and to work more or less uphill all the evening; but he, nevertheless, was by far the best Faust I have ever seen, making him the central figure in the opera, instead of the sentimental walking gentleman to whom we are accustomed. Little as there is in the part as treated by Gounod, it is surprising to find how far that little can be made to go by an artist of genuine power and abundant vitality. Van Dyck quite startled the house with the reality and intensity of his appeal for renewed youth in the first scene—a point at which no tenor has ever before carried the slightest conviction to me. From this to the final trio, to which he gave a tremendous impetus, the interest of his impersonation never flagged. Édouard de Reszke, who has met his match at last in the duet at the end of the first act, played Mephistopheles with fratricidal relish and vigor. In the middle of the garden scene he was so tickled by a monstrous sunflower which Mr Harris had placed among the extremely miscellaneous *flora* in Margaret's flower-bed, that he very nearly accomplished the feat known as "queering the pitch" of the quartet by plucking the giant vegetable and replanting it in the dress of Madame Bauermeister, before whose diminutive figure it flourished like an umbrella during the rest of the scene. It is to be hoped that this jape will not become traditional. Lassalle was announced to play Valentine; but it soon appeared that he only wished to prevent anyone else from playing it, as he omitted Dio possente, and would not even pretend to act in the death scene, which accordingly fell flat. A Mlle Passama, who appeared as Siebel, was almost as feminine and tearfully tragic in the part as Mlle

Guercia. Miss Eames, as Margaret, improved on her old success. The opera is to be repeated tonight (Wednesday) with a newcomer, Plançon, as Mephistopheles.

Some incredibly stupid and unmusical people are setting a fashion of treating the beginning of the great trio in the prison scene as a signal to troop out of the house. I suggest to Mr Harris that, though the law on the subject is not defined, it might be worth while to take their names and summon them for "brawling." Even if the interpretation could not be sustained, the shock would probably bring them to their senses.

10 June 1891

WITH Isaÿe, Sarasate, and Paderewski all at work together among us, the atmosphere of musical hero worship becomes overwhelming. Yet the audiences have not been so large this year as last. In Isaÿe's case, this is perhaps due to the fact that the public does not yet realize that he is one of the greatest violinists in the world, since it depends so largely for its information upon that inoffensive, considerate, say-nothing-to-nobody sort of criticism which offers Isaÿe and Sarasate exactly the same polite congratulations which it offered the day before to Herr Waldemar Meyer. Isaÿe at his second recital came triumphantly through the highest test a violinist can face— a Mozart sonata. He also brought forward a sonata by Gabriel Fauré, the *maître de chapelle* of the Madeleine; but this, however it might have sounded before Mozart, made no effect after.

Sarasate came on the following Saturday, not so fresh as during his last visit. He is never as good in the summer as after the autumn, when he has just had a rest. After Isaÿe the thinness of his tone and his exclusive attention to the absolutely musical side of his classical repertory, which he carries to the extremity of appearing to be perfectly in-different whether he is playing Mackenzie or Beethoven, make themselves felt more strongly than on former occa-

sions when he was not brought into immediate comparison
with his great rival; but, on the other hand, his extraordinary
smoothness and certainty of execution, and the fine quietude
with which he performs miraculous technical feats, are no
less thrown into high relief. At his recital on Wednesday
last, in a cadenza which formed part of an encore piece, he,
without turning a hair, did some things—notably a scale
passage against a shake sustained above, and a chromatic
run in sixths—with a speed, a delicacy of touch, and an
exquisite precision of intonation that would have astonished
Tartini's devil.

Mr Cusins gave his annual concert on Monday week;
and an excellent concert it was of its kind, with the Ravoglis,
Maurel, and Sauret lending a hand. I mention it just in this
place because there is a point—a very delicate point—which
must be put frankly to Sarasate and Mr Cusins. Mr Cusins,
as all the world knows, conducts at Sarasate's orchestral
concerts. I venture to ask the twain, are they quite the men
for one another in this relationship? Sarasate, whatever his
failings may be, is an extraordinarily good violinist. Mr
Cusins, with a host of excellent qualities, is an extraordinarily bad conductor. The result is that Mr Cusins
spoils Sarasate's concerto-playing, and Sarasate exposes Mr
Cusins to public execration. Why should they persist in this
reciprocity of injury? As one who has not the option of
staying away from the concerts, I must press this question
somewhat urgently.

At the same time I cannot blind myself to the fact that
though Sarasate can hardly hit on a less suitable conductor,
he may easily get one who is not sufficiently better to make it
worth while to face the friction of making the change. As a
solution of the difficulty, I suggest that he should offer the
bâton to the faithful Cor De Las, who is such an excellent
accompanist that he would probably be able at least to keep
the band with the soloist in the quick movements of the
concertos; whilst if, in attempting a Beethoven overture—
say the Coriolan, which was in the program at the first
218

concert—he should lose his way through the score, the band could do for him what it now does in extreme cases with Mr Cusins: that is, look the other way, or, as I am told the fashionable expression now is, wink the other eye.

After Sarasate's concert came Paderewski's. He gave two concertos—one too many—Beethoven in E flat and Schumann. It was hard on us, and harder on Schumann. I am by no means naturally predisposed to admire Paderewski's style. His master, Leschetitzky, seems to me to have done more to dehumanize pianoforte-playing than any other leading teacher in Europe. When I hear pianists with fingers turned into steel hammers, deliberately murdering Beethoven by putting all sorts of accelerandos and crescendos into his noblest and most steadfast passages, I promptly put them down without further inquiry as pupils of Leschetitzky.

Paderewski's excessive hardness of touch, which tells even when he is playing with the most exquisite lightness, and which must be referred to his master rather than to himself, would limit him seriously if his exceptional comprehensiveness as a musician did not enable him to seize about ten points of treatment in a composition for every one that comes within the range of the ordinary pianist. He plays the Schumann concerto, for instance, so intelligently that if I were told that he was the composer, and did not know to the contrary, I could easily believe it, although I should be surprised at any composer having submitted to such an arduous technical training as he has evidently undergone. In spite of Leschetitzky, then, the concert, though a tiring one from its inordinate length, was real and interesting throughout.

Paderewski treated the orchestra better than they treated him; for he played with an unfailing sense of the relation of the solo part to the rest, whereas they, in their one great opportunity—the first allegro of the Beethoven concerto—played roughly and hastily, a misfortune for which the chief blame must lie upon Mr Henschel, who handled this beautiful movement with a want of tenderness which was at times almost brutal. It is a pity that so able and modern-spirited a musician as he should repeatedly provoke remonstrances of this sort from critics who would much rather help than hinder his influence as a conductor and musical *entrepreneur*. As to Paderewski himself, I have only one demurrer to put in. I maintain that the great octave passage which occupies twenty bars or so of the middle section of that first movement, should be given in an unwavering fortissimo until the point when it breaks up and melts like a cloud. Paderewski made a marked crescendo in all the ascending passages, and thereby reduced the whole trait to a mere commonplace. Save for this Leschetitzkyism, I unreservedly congratulate him on his concert.

Among other pianists whom I have recently heard are Mr Frank Howgrave and Señor de Silka. Mr Howgrave's fluency of execution is so prodigious that it produces an irresistibly comic effect. Why it should have deserted him in the Prometheus variations by Beethoven, of which he made rather a mess, I do not know, since the sly velocity with which it carried him through Bach's chromatic fantasia brought out a facetiousness which has, I suppose, been latent in the composition all these years. He played a piece by Schumann really well; but somehow his face and air, which are those of a born comedian, lead me to doubt whether his future will lie in the more serious walks of pianism. Señor de Silka has done much to consolidate his technique since last year. A further spell of really hard work will place him beyond all risk of relapsing into a mere brilliant drawing room player—a danger of which he is not yet quite clear. On Thursday last he began by playing a couple of pieces by Scarlatti, and Schumann's symphonic studies, with considerable technical vigor, and with a certain distinction of style which is as yet rather negative than positive: that is, it is due rather to the vulgarities from which he refrains than to any refinements which he introduces. In the middle of the program he placed Beethoven's andante in F, and a couple of pieces by Chopin. Here he was decidedly weak. He was not altogether on the wrong tack in his quiet handling of the Chopin polonaise; but when it came to Ballade in A flat, the introduction to which is surely as eloquent as human speech could be, he entirely failed to interpret it, and, in fact, played the whole ballade in one piece as a trivial gallop. The rest of the program was eked out by his drawing room repertory, in which he shewed an appropriate charm of musical manner; but if he allows himself for a moment to overestimate the value of work of this sort, or of the applause which it gains from that section of the audience which is impressed by the rumors that he is "a real nobleman," the result will be the spoiling of a very promising player.

At the Albéniz concert on Thursday evening I looked in for a few minutes, and caught the concert-giver napping over the A flat polonaise of Chopin, which he really played shockingly—I do not know why. Herr Johann Kruse, the violinist, has improved since he played the Beethoven concerto at a London symphony concert; but he was not completely successful in the Bach piece which he gave when encored for a Tartini sonata. On the previous day a concert was given by Herr Carl Fuchs, a young 'cellist well known in Manchester. He is a pupil of the Russian Davidoff, and is an unpretentious but excellent player, a trifle modest in tone compared with the greatest masters of the instrument, but by no means a buzzing bore, as 'cellists are rather apt to be. The second Richter concert was a great improvement on the first, although the program was knocked all to pieces by the influenza. Having bid "Conscience avaunt" the Monday before, Richter was himself again on this occasion.

17 June 1891

THE most important event in the musical world since my last article, from my point of view, has been the influenza catching me, or, as my friends preposterously insist on putting it, my catching the influenza.

Fortunately for me, many cases of critics and singers disabled by it had occurred under my eyes within a few weeks;
so that by scrupulously doing the very reverse of what they
did in the way of treatment, I managed to come through
without missing a single engagement. I abstained from
medical advice and ammoniated quinine; I treated the fever
by enjoying the morning air at an open window in an entirely unprotected condition for a prolonged period before
finishing up with a cold bath; I stimulated myself by transitions from the overwhelming heat of the crowded St James's
Hall to the chill coolness of Regent Street at night; I wore
my lightest attire; I kept out of bed as much as possible, and
held on to railings and lamp-posts when the temptation to
seek a brief repose at full length in the streets became almost
irresistible, as it did once or twice on the day when the fever
was at its height; I fed myself resolutely (though not on the
corpses of slain animals), and took no alcohol in any form.
The result was that I routed the enemy in a series of pitched
battles, in which I was assailed successively with delirium,
with weakness and fever, with pains in various portions of
my person, including a specially ingenious one in the eye-
balls, and, finally, with a vulgar and abominable cold in the
head, which pursued me with unabated rage for forty-eight
hours before it lost heart. Had I drugged the fiend, coddled
him, inebriated him, and lavished doctors' fees on him, no
doubt I should have left The World musicless for three
weeks at least. As it was, I did more work in the five days
during which the combat lasted than in the five days before
that. Singers will now know how to deal with their foe. It is
always worth while to fly in the face of that unvenerable
survival of witchcraft which calls itself medical science. To
recover triumphantly under such circumstances becomes a
point of honor.

On my way to hear Mireille in French at Covent Garden,
on Wednesday last week, a rascal offered me for a shilling
a book of the opera. But I was too old a bird to be caught in
that way. I recognized at a glance the yellow cover of the old

Davidson libretto, with the Italian words and the superseded four-act arrangement of bygone Maplesonian days. I
did not give the fellow in charge, for he was miserably poor,
and perhaps had no very clear idea of the differences between the new and the old Mireille. Instead, I went my way
into the theatre, and there purchased, from Mr Harris's
official representative, an authorized libretto for eighteenpence. I hardly expect to be believed when I add that when
I got to my stall and proceeded to investigate my purchase,
it turned out to be that identical obsolete Italian Davidson-
ian libretto, disguised with a blue cover. As an art critic I
know nothing about the City, and have never troubled myself as to the worth of the rumors that have reached me concerning the authenticity of the Lord Mayor's sermons. But
as to the value of the Sheriff's librettos I have now formed a
very strong opinion, which is at the service of the next Royal
Commission upon the morals of the Corporation.

Why Mireille was performed I do not know. It is about
as suited to Covent Garden as L'Enfant Prodigue is. Still
more inscrutable is the casting of Miss Eames for the title
part, the requirements of which are great range and great
flexibility, enabling the singer to shake on high D at her
ease. Miss Eames, even with her chief numbers transposed
and cut to pieces, only got through, and that in a sufficiently
commonplace manner, by the skin of her teeth—if she will
pardon the expression. As to any attempt she made to place
before us the ideal Mireille, I can only say that she never in
her life was more emphatically that very attractive and ladylike person Miss Eames of the Royal Italian Opera—well
educated, and with no nonsense about her, as Mr Sparkler
would have been the first to admit. As it is on Mireille that
the whole play depends, it is hardly necessary to add that
every attempt to give the scenes an air of conviction soon
broke down. Isnardon, Miranda, Madame Passama, and
the rest were willing enough; and Ceste, who took Maurel's
place as Ourrias, was, if anything, rather too willing; but
Mireille's propriety and her black silk dress were too much

for them: they flagged, and finally gave it up as a bad job. Lubert alone came off with honor: he redeemed the performance from utter flatness by his unaffected and earnest playing as Vincent. The duets in which he took part, with the farandole and the overture, were the only numbers in which the least whiff of the characteristic atmosphere of the piece got across the footlights. On the whole, unless Mravina or Melba is prepared to take Miss Eames's place in the cast, the opera had better go back to the shelf. I am indebted, by the bye, to Mr Fisher Unwin for sending me, just in time for the performance, a neat new edition of Miss Preston's translation of Frédéric Mistral's Mireio, which I quite intend to read some day.

The orchestral concert given by the students of the Royal College of Music last week was a vast improvement on the preceding one. Mr Henry Holmes, who has taken Mr Stanford's place as conductor, gets quite a different class of work from his young battalions, who are probably individually better solo players than the members of the best professional orchestra Beethoven ever saw in his life. After hearing Mr Stanford last season driving them mechanically through a Berlioz score of which they had not mastered a single bar, it was pleasant to see Mr Holmes, as the head of a happy family of musicians, leading them through Cherubini's Les Abencerrages overture with all the fine taste and genuine musical feeling which distinguished him when he was almost the only English violinist whose praises could be sounded without the tongue in the cheek. They responded to him with affectionate goodwill, and achieved a really excellent performance. All that the instrumental department at the Royal College seems to want now to bring it into line with its Continental rivals is a more vivid artistic life—a fresh charge of electricity. Mr Sutcliffe, for instance, played the Beethoven violin concerto very creditably, but still in a humdrum, sleepy way that would have filled a pupil of the Brussels Conservatoire with disrespectful amusement.

As to the vocal department, it seems as hopeless as ever. Of the two young ladies who sang—both announced as holders of scholarships—one was as ignorant of the artistic use of her voice as it is possible for any naturally musical person to be in a civilized country; and the other, though she had evidently had plenty of warnings and cautions from some musician of considerable taste, seemed to have had no positive instruction worth mentioning. In fact, any second-rate elocutionist could teach both young ladies all they know about the production of their voices. Considering how every innocent young provincial with a voice will henceforth turn to the Royal College and its scholarships as the one trust-worthy chance of getting that voice artistically trained, I would suggest that a board with the inscription *Lasciate ogni speranza*, etc., be placed over the doors of the singing rooms at the College, and a policeman stationed to explain it to novices from the country.

Mr Harris took advantage of his miscellaneous concert at the Albert Hall on Saturday to get another shilling from me for a book which gave the Italian version of a portion of Lohengrin which Van Dyck did not sing. What he did sing he sang in German. The smithy music from Siegfried was merely described as Schmiedelieder, without any words at all; and what that very innocent audience, consisting largely of people with conscientious objections to the theatre, must have thought of it, baffles my imagination. Half a crown going bang in one week for useless literature is more than I can afford. At the same time it was mildly amusing to know that the audience which recalled Van Dyck three times to the platform after the Lohengrin number, supposed him to have been saying something to which both his manner of declamation and the music were outrageously inappropriate. An arrangment which struck me as especially shabby was the admission of the public to the seats provided for the members of the chorus, who were consequently crowded in a ridiculous fashion on the platform for the Meistersinger selection, and then bundled off. That, I submit, is not the

225

way in which the Royal Italian Opera should treat its artists; and I shall now mention what I might otherwise have passed over—that the shilling book did not contain a third of what the chorus actually gave us, so that the chorale with which Hans Sachs is greeted passed as the trade song of the tailors. The only artist with whom I was not familiar was a M. Plançon, a *basso cantante* of considerable ability, as far as I could judge from his singing of Au bruit des lourds marteaux.

At the Richter concert last week we had all the Fidelio overtures, except that in E, one after another. The result was that the first on the list, Leonora No. 2, was magnificently played, whereas the others, by comparison, produced the effect of very carefully executed taskwork. The more artistically alive a band is, the less it can face two heavy Beethoven overtures in immediate succession. Still, the contrast between the two works was interesting. In No. 2 (I am using the customary numbering) the subjects are instrumented with a freshness and charm which is wanting in the more serious and penetrating No. 3; but the imperfect grip, the irrelevant prettiness, and, above all, the long *quasi*-academic working out in the middle, are insufferable when once No. 3 is thoroughly known; and, in my opinion, the work should be presented definitely as a first and *unsuccessful* attempt at No. 3, and not as an independent composition. The distinction made between the two by Richter was most masterly. Any of our ordinary time-beaters would have taken the allegro in both at exactly the same speed, because the subjects are identical. Richter, in No. 2, was easy, gracious, slow, almost caressing. In No. 3, starting at a much higher speed, he was decisive, strenuous, full of serious business, with no time or disposition for dallying with the charms emphasized in the scoring of No. 2.

An equally admirable example of genuine conducting was the performance of Mozart's symphony in D—the one which begins with a couple of springs up two octaves by the
226

violins. Perhaps this was why it got above the heads of most of the audience; but the knowing few were duly appreciative. The typical Richter frequenter is hardly up to the mark in absolute music, being more at home with tone-poetry and program music. The rest of the concert was occupied by Mr Lloyd, who sang Tannhäuser's account of the pilgrimage to Rome, and Siegfried's bellows and anvil music, very tunefully and smoothly, without, however, for a moment relinquishing his original character of Edward Lloyd. Max Heinrich was the Wolfram, and Mr Nichols the Mime of the evening.

24 June 1891

THE admirers of Brahms had a succulent treat at the Richter concert last week. His German Requiem was done from end to end, and done quite well enough to bring out all its qualities. What those qualities are could have been guessed by a deaf man from the mountainous tedium of the unfortunate audience, who yet listened with a perverse belief that Brahms is a great composer, and the performance of this masterpiece of his an infinitely solemn and important function. I am afraid that this delusion was not confined to those who, having found by experience that good music bores them, have rashly concluded that all music that bores them must be good. It raged also among the learned musicians, who know what a *point d'orgue* is, and are delighted to be able to explain what is happening when Brahms sets a pedal pipe booming and a drum thumping the dominant of the key for ten minutes at a stretch, whilst the other instruments and the voices plough along through every practicable progression in or near the key, up hill from syncopation to syncopation, and down dale from suspension to suspension in an elaborately modernized manner that only makes the whole operation seem more desperately old-fashioned and empty.

Brahms seems to have been impressed by the fact that Beethoven produced remarkable effects by persisting with

227

his pedal points long after Mozart would have resolved
them, and to have convinced himself by an obvious logical
process that it must be possible to produce still more remarkable results by outdoing Beethoven in persistency.
And so indeed it is, as Bach proved before Mozart was born.
Only somehow it has not come off in Brahms' hands, though
he has prolonged and persisted to the verge of human
endurance. Yet, as I say, the academic gentlemen like it,
and seem pleased even by those endless repetitions, which
are only the "rosalias" of the old Italian masses in a heavy
and pretentious disguise. I can only say, with due respect,
that I disagree with the academic gentlemen.

The fact is, there is nothing a genuine musician regards
with more jealousy than an attempt to pass off the forms of
music for music itself, especially those forms which have
received a sort of consecration from their use by great composers in the past. Unfortunately, such impostures are sure
of support from the sort of people—pretty numerous in this
country as far as art is concerned—who think that it is the
cowl that makes the monk. Any conspiracy between a
musician and a literary man to set Wardour Street Jacobean
English to Wardour Street Handelian counterpoint will
find ready victims in this class, which may be seen at any
festival impartially applauding the music of Handel and
the profane interpolations of any opera singer who has
learned by experience how to turn its ignorant hero-worship
to account.

Sometimes, of course, we have, for the sake of some
respected professor, to put up with performances of honest
pieces of pedantry like the oratorios of Kiel of Berlin, or
Macfarren, not to mention names of the living. But I altogether demur to making concessions of this kind to Brahms.
It will only end in his doing it again; for his extraordinary
mechanical power of turning out the most ponderous description of music positively by tons, and the stupendous
seriousness with which he takes this gift, are unrestrained
by any consciousness on his part of the commonplaceness of
228

his ideas, which makes his tone poetry all but worthless, or of the lack of constructive capacity which makes his "absolute music" incoherent. He is quite capable of writing half a dozen more Requiems, all as insufferable as this one, if we hail him as "the most prominent living representative of the classical school," as some enthusiastic simpleton did the other day on the strength of a couple of motets which were inferior in every essential characteristic of the classical school to the best bits of part-writing in Sir Arthur Sullivan's comic operas.

These are not gracious things to say of a composer who has written so many really pretty trifles; but self-defence is the first law of Nature; and though I am at this moment lying broiling on the sands at Broadstairs, at peace with all mankind, and indulgently disposed even towards Brahms, I can say no less when I think of that dreary Requiem, and of the imminent danger of its being repeated next season.

After this it may seem rather unhandsome to describe Sgambati, who gave a concert of his own compositions at Princes' Hall last week, as the Brahms of Italy. But I mean to be complimentary, nevertheless; for Brahms, after all, is not without his merits. Besides, Sgambati's friends do not make considerate criticism impossible by claiming that he is another Beethoven; nor does he vie with the codfish in fecundity. Again, he has a certain Italian clearness and reasonableness which saves him from the oppressiveness of the German. On Thursday last, with Sauret and Piatti in his quartet, and Mrs Henschel and Franceschetti to sing his songs, he had no reason to complain of the way in which his work was handled. One incident in the concert raised a point of etiquette, which was decided wrongly, as usual, by the audience. When distinguished persons attend concerts in their private capacity, discreet persons do not make public demonstrations of recognition. When the distinguished persons happen to be fifty minutes late, one would think that the least tactful mortal would perceive the advisability of not emphasizing their arrival.

However, there are always a number of people at every concert who, the moment they catch sight of a royal face, spring up as if they saw a chance of being knighted on the spot. This being so, and incurably so, would it not be better to manage these entrances so as to avoid ridiculous scenes in which half the room—the blundering half—rises in the middle of a song, and the vocalist has to stop, curtsy, and begin all over again?

In that part of the Richter concert which was not devoted to Brahms there was a performance of the Tannhäuser overture which ought to have been phonographed as a model of correct and eloquent phrasing in the Pilgrims' March, and of consentaneous execution in the shakes and tremolandos of the Venusberg music. Such a model is badly wanted, now that this composition has taken the place in popular favor accorded, in ages which already seem remote, to the overture to William Tell, with the result that our orchestras play it offhand whenever there is a scratch program to be made up. Need I add, that playing it offhand means playing it all at sixes and sevens, as they do, with great applause, at Covent Garden for instance. Mr Barton McGuckin, who, being a native of these islands, has the pleasure of spending his spare evenings at that theatre listening to the performances of leading foreign tenors, of whom three out of five are much inferior to him, had a chance in the first scene of Tannhäuser to shew that it is not *faute de mieux* that we have to accept Perotti in the part on the stage. Mrs Moore Lawson, an American singer, who uses with excellent taste and skill the solitary stop with which her organ is provided, was the Venus. This must have displeased the president of the London branch of the Wagner Society, who has, I hear, protested against the employment of any but German singers at the Richter concerts. Why, I do not know, for I have not noticed that Germans sing Wagner's music better than outer barbarians. Perhaps Lord Dysart would rather hear Gudehus as Walther von Stolzing than the Pole, De Reszke, Vogl as Parsifal than the Belgian Van Dyck, or Theodor Reichmann as Hans Sachs than the Frenchman, Lassalle. If so, I can assure him that his bargain would be a very bad one indeed on the musical side. As I by no means wish to imply that German singers are necessarily worse than others, perhaps I should in fairness compare on the other side such a group of German *prime donne* as Sucher, Malten, and Materna with—well, no matter with whom, for my conclusion would be the same—namely, that since the true Wagnerism is to sing the Meister's works always in a tongue understanded of the people, Richter's preference for English singers and English texts is not only good artistic policy, but orthodox also, in opposition to the rank heresy of Lord Dysart. In fact, I am not sure that the Bayreuth Church does not bind Richter himself to take out letters of naturalization here.

The Handel Festival is in full swing. I hope to have something to say about it next week, and, in the meantime, cordially recommend the Wednesday selection to lovers of Handel, of whom I hope there are still a few left.

1 *July* 1891

FUNDAMENTALLY my view of the Handel Festival is that of a convinced and ardent admirer of Handel. My favorite oratorio is The Messiah, with which I have spent many of the hours which others give to Shakespear, or Scott, or Dickens. But for all this primary bias in favor of Handel, my business is still to be that of the critic, who, invited to pronounce an opinion on the merits of a performance by four thousand executants, must judge these abnormal conditions by their effect on the work as open-mindedly as if there were only four hundred, or forty, or four. And I am bound to add that he who, so judging, delivers a single and unqualified verdict on the Festival, stultifies himself. The very same conditions which make one choral number majestic, imposing, even sublime, make another heavy, mechanical, meaningless. For instance, no host could be too mighty for the Hallelujah Chorus, or See

231

the Conquering Hero. In them every individual chorister knows without study or instruction what he has to do and how he has to feel. The impulse to sing spreads even to the audience; and those who are old hands at choral singing do not always restrain it.

I saw more than one of my neighbors joining in the Hallelujah on the first day; and if my feelings at that moment had permitted me to make a properly controlled artistic effort, I think I should have been no more able to remain silent than Santley was. Under the circumstances, however, I followed the example of Albani, who, knowing that she had to save her voice for I know that my Redeemer liveth, kept a vocal score tightly on her mouth the whole time, and looked over it with the expression of a child confronted with some intolerably tempting sweetmeat which it knows it must not touch.

But The Messiah is not all Hallelujah. Compare such a moment as I have just described with the experience of listening to the fiercely tumultuous He trusted in God, with its alternations of sullen mockery with high-pitched derision, and its savage shouts of Let him deliver him if he delight in him, jogging along at about half the proper speed, with an expression of the deepest respect and propriety, as if a large body of the leading citizens, headed by the mayor, were presenting a surpassingly dull address to somebody. There may be, in the way of the proper presentation of such a chorus as this, something of the difficulty which confronted Wagner at the rehearsals of Tannhäuser in Paris in 1861, when he asked the ballet master to make his forces attack the Bacchanal in a bacchanalian way. "I understand perfectly what you mean," said the functionary; "but only to a whole ballet of *premiers sujets* dare I breathe such suggestions."

No doubt Mr Manns's three thousand five hundred choristers might better his instructions so heartily as to go considerably beyond the utmost licence of art if he told them that unless they sang that chorus like a howling bloodthirsty mob, the utter loneliness of Thy rebuke hath broken his heart, and Behold and see, must be lost, and with it the whole force of the tragic climax of the oratorio. Besides which, there is the physical difficulty, which only a skilled and powerful orator could fully surmount, of giving instruction of that kind to such a host. But I see no reason why matters should not be vastly improved if Mr Manns would adopt throughout the bolder policy as to speed which was forced on him after four on Selection day by the silent urgency of the clock, and persisted in to some extent—always with convincing effect—in Israel. Increased speed, however, is not all that is wanted. To get rid completely of the insufferable lumbering which is the curse of English Handelian choral singing, a spirited reform in style is needed.

For instance, Handel, in his vigorous moods, is fond of launching the whole mass of voices into florid passages of great brilliancy and impetuosity. In one of the most splendid choruses in The Messiah, For He shall purify the sons of Levi, the syllable "fy" comes out in a single trait consisting of no less than thirty-two semiquavers. That trait should be sung with one impulse from end to end without an instant's hesitation. How is it actually done in England? Just as if the thirty-two semiquavers were eight bars of crotchets taken *alla breve* in a not very lively tempo. The effect, of course, is to make the chorus so dull that all the reputation of Handel is needed to persuade Englishmen that they ought to enjoy it, whilst Frenchmen go away from our festivals confirmed in their scepticism as to our pet musical classic. When I had been listening for some minutes on Wednesday to the festival choristers trudging with ludicrous gravity through what they called Tellit Outa Mongthe Hea-ea Then, I could not help wishing that Santley, who roused them to boundless enthusiasm by his singing of Why do the nations, had given them a taste of their own quality by delivering those chains of triplets on the words "rage" and "counsel," as quavers in twelve-eight time in the tempo of the pastoral symphony. The celestial Lift up your heads, O ye gates, lost

233

half its triumphant exultation from this heaviness of gait.

Again, in the beginning of For unto us, the tenors and basses told each other the news in a prosaic, methodical way which made the chorus quite comic until the thundering Wonderful, Counsellor, one of Handel's mightiest strokes, was reached; and even here the effect was disappointing, because the chorus, having held nothing in reserve, could make no climax. The orchestra needed at that point about twenty more of the biggest of big drums. Another lost opportunity was the pathetically grand conclusion of All we like sheep. Nothing in the whole work needs to be sung with more intense expression than But the Lord hath laid on Him the iniquity of us all. Unless it sounds as if the singers were touched to their very hearts, they had better not sing it at all. On that Monday it came as mechanically as if the four entries of the voices had been produced by drawing four stops in an organ. This was the greater pity, because it must be conceded to our young Handel-sceptics that the preceding musical portraiture of the sheep going astray has no great claims on their reverence.

I am aware that many people who feel the shortcomings of our choral style bear with it under the impression, first, that the English people are naturally too slow and shy in their musical ways, and, second, that bravura vocalization and impetuous speed are not possible or safe with large choruses. To this I reply, first, that the natural fault of the English when they are singing with genuine feeling is not slowness, but rowdiness, as the neighbors of the Salvation Army know; second, that it would undoubtedly be as risky to venture far in the bravura direction with a very small chorus as to attempt the Walküre fire-music or Liszt's Mazeppa in an ordinary theatre orchestra with its little handful of strings. But both these compositions are safe with sixteen first and sixteen second violins, because, though notes are dropped and mistakes made, they are not all made simultaneously, and the result is that at any given instant an overwhelming majority of the violins are right. For the same reason, I do not see why nine hundred basses, even if they were the stiffest and slowest in the world, could not be safely sent at full speed in the *bravura* style through Handel's easy diatonic semiquaver traits, as safely as our violinists are now sent through Wagner's demisemiquavers.

So much for the compatibility of speed with accuracy. As to safety, I need only appeal to the results achieved by Mr Manns on Friday, when he got away from The Messiah, which is too sentimental for him, to Israel, which is far more congenial to his temperament. The only choral number in this which was quite unsatisfactory was I will exalt Him; and here the shortcoming was made unavoidable by the peculiar style of the chorus, since it—like And with His stripes in The Messiah—requires a beauty of execution which would suffice for a mass by Palestrina, and which is out of the question under Handel Festival conditions. The other choruses were spirited and forcible—some of them magnificent. He gave them hailstones, But the waters overwhelmed, and The horse and his rider were tremendous: one felt after them that the festival had justified its existence beyond all cavil.

If these criticisms are to bear any fruit in raising the festival performances of The Messiah to a typical artistic perfection—a result which I believe to be quite possible, and certainly well worth striving for—they must be weighed, not by Mr Manns or the Crystal Palace authorities, but by the local conductors throughout the country, who coach their contingents in the work, and send them up with preconceived ideas as to its execution which Mr Manns is powerless to change or even greatly to modify. Every contingent trained by a mere organist, to whom The Messiah is but a part of the drudgery of his professional routine, is simply a nuisance on the Handel orchestra. And every contingent trained by an artist who ranks the work among his treasures, and part of whose artistic ambition it is to hear at last in England a really adequate performance of it, is, as Judas Maccabæus says, "a thousand men."

Space hardly permits of a more particular account of the details of the performances. The successes of the orchestra were the Berenice minuet, cleverly reserved by Mr Best so as to give the seventy-two 'cellos a rare opportunity, and the Bourée from the Water Music, in which the tenor-register of the bassoons came out very prettily. The accompaniments used in the Messiah were Mozart's, including, besides the usual reinforcements of the brass parts, even that beautiful variation on The people that walked in darkness, which has no more business at the Festival than Liszt's Don Juan fantasia would have at a performance of that opera. The solo singers shewed a considerable growth of artistic self-respect as well as of respect for Handel. Even Albani, who at her first appearance at a Festival took appalling liberties, was this time comparatively faithful to the text. She does not shine as a Handelian singer; but except in I know that my Redeemer liveth, and in an air from Rodelinda, both of which were badly sung, she disarmed criticism if she did not exactly satisfy it. Santley was the hero of the occasion, as far as the applause went; and I am not sure that his admirers were not in the right; for, in spite of his curious want of sang-froid, and his shots at perfectly safe notes, none of the other voices were quite so sound, so even, so unspoiled, and so telling. Lloyd's greatest successes were gained on Selection day, in a solo from one of the Chandos anthems, and in Love in her eyes, which he sang delightfully. The contralto part in The Messiah was made a success by dint of resolute exertion and clear diction; but when Miss Marion McKenzie reaches Santley's age, she will not find herself able to depend so largely as she does now on physical force. On the last day the principal singers were at their worst. Lloyd was obviously out of sorts, and fought hard but vainly against having to repeat The enemy said. Nevertheless, he fully sustained his reputation, and, with the assistance of Madame Belle Cole, made some amends for the duet between Madame Nordica and Miss Macintyre, which I was about to put down as the worst thing in the

Festival, when something in Nordica's expression magnetic-ally conveyed to me that I had better wait to hear the two gentlemen sing The Lord is a man of war before I rushed to any conclusions. And I must confess that Messrs Bridson and Brereton gallantly rescued the two ladies from me. Nordica, having had plenty of opportunities of distinguishing herself previously, was able to afford this reverse of fortune; but Miss Macintyre had to depend on Thou didst blow to retrieve herself, which I hope she will not mind my saying that she entirely failed to do. A Handelian singer really must not drop notes to take breath, like an Irish lilter. On Selection day, Mr Barton McGuckin would have had a very distinguished success with Waft her, angels, if he had refrained from that old-fashioned bid for applause with a prolonged high note, which spoiled the ending. His Love sounds the alarm was excellent.

Of the chorus the tenors were the best among the men, though they collapsed unaccountably during the first part on the Wednesday. The basses were for the most part baritones, the low notes in Israel being comparatively ineffective. The altos were superb: nothing better could have been desired. On the other hand, the sopranos, for their numbers, had but little tone, and that of the most commonplace kind. Mr Manns was at his best on the last day; and I have no quarrel with him except as to an *allargando* which he made at the words, "There was not one feeble person among their tribes," which should, I maintain, proceed with swift, determined, unslackened step to the very last bar.

8 July 1891

ON thinking it over I am inclined to conclude that Mr D'Oyly Carte did not quite accurately measure the vacancy made at the Savoy by the withdrawal of his dramatic poet and his tone poet. His wish to continue on the old lines as closely as possible is obvious; but instead of trying to find another Gilbert and another Sullivan, he has tried to find another Mikado, which, I admit, is exactly what nobody wanted, one Mikado being enough for any reasonable generation. Perhaps Mr Carte may have found that another Gilbert does not exist. That may very well be the case; for Mr Gilbert, at his best, was a much cleverer man than most of the playwrights of his day: he could always see beneath the surface of things; and if he could only have seen through them, he might have made his mark as a serious dramatist instead of having, as a satirist, to depend for the piquancy of his ridicule on the general assumption of the validity of the very things he ridiculed. The theme of The Pirates of Penzance is essentially the same as that of Ibsen's Wild Duck; but we all understood that the joke of the pirate being "the slave of duty" lay in the utter absurdity and topsyturviness of such a proposition, whereas when we read The Wild Duck we see that the exhibition of the same sort of slave there as a mischievous fool is no joke at all, but a grimly serious attack on our notion that we need stick at nothing in the cause of duty.

Nevertheless, there was a substratum of earnest in Mr Gilbert's joking which shewed that he was not exactly the sort of writer whom Mr Carte could have replaced by merely going into the Strand in the usual managerial way and hailing the first librettist he met there. Now, in the case of the musician, matters were on a very different footing. Sir Arthur Sullivan made his reputation as a composer of comic operas by a consummate *savoir faire* which was partly, no doubt, a personal and social talent, but which had been cultivated musically by a thorough technical training in the elegant and fastidious school of Mendelssohn, and by twenty years' work in composing for the drawing room, the church, the festival, and the concert room. In 1875, when he composed Trial by Jury, no manager would have dreamt of approaching him with a commission for an Offenbachian opera: he was pre-eminently a sentimental and ecclesiastical composer, whose name suggested Guinevere and Thou'rt passing hence, Nearer, my God, to Thee, and Onward Christian soldiers, In Memoriam and the additional accom-

paniments to Handel's Jephtha. When he plunged into the
banalities and trivialities of Savoy opera he carried his old
training with him. He taught the public to understand
orchestral fun; but his instrumental jokes, which he never
carried too far, were always in good taste; and his workmanship was unfailingly skilful and refined, even when the
material was of the cheapest.

Why, under these circumstances, Mr Carte should have
looked to Mr Solomon to replace Sir Arthur is a problem
which reason cannot solve. The right man, Mr Villiers Stanford, was ready to his hand—for I presume that the composer of the Irish symphony would not disdain to follow in
the footsteps of Mozart any more than Sir Arthur did. He
has the technical training and the culture which stood Sullivan in such good stead; and there must be still alive in him
something of the young Irishman of genius who wrote those
spirited Cavalier tunes, not to mention some numbers from
The Veiled Prophet, before he was forced back into the dismal routine of manufacturing impossible trash like The Revenge for provincial festival purposes, and into conducting,
which is so little his affair that when I lately described his
Bach choir work in my unliterary way from the point of view
of a person whose business it is to use his ears, the only champion who ventured to say a word in his defence did not dare
to sign it. But I do not want to force Mr Stanford on Mr
Carte. I might have cited Mr Cowen with equal point. He,
also, is no more fitted to be a conductor than the majority of
brilliant and popular writers are to be editors. My interest in
getting both gentlemen back to their proper work, which I
take to be intelligent and vivacious dramatic composition, is
that it would then become a pleasure to criticize them, instead of, as it generally is at present, a disagreeable duty.

All this may seem rather hard on poor Mr Solomon, the
composer upon whom Mr Carte's choice has actually fallen.
But then Mr Solomon has been very hard on me. He has
given me the worst headache I ever had in a theatre by an instrumental score which is more wearisome than the conver-

sation of an inveterate punster, and more noisy than the *melodrame* which accompanies the knockabout business in a music-hall. Mr Carte had better remove the bassoon, the piccolo, the cymbals, the triangle, and the drums, both *timpani* and *tamburo*, from the theatre; for Mr Solomon is clearly not to be trusted with them. If Sir Arthur Sullivan used these instruments in an artistically comic way once in a thousand bars or so, is that any reason why Mr Solomon should use them in an inartistically comic way nine hundred and ninety-nine times in the same period? Besides, Sir Arthur only did it to point an allusion. Mr Solomon does it, allusion or no allusion, out of a mere schoolboyish itching to lark with the instruments. When he has an allusion to excuse him, he does not make it with anything like the neatness which he shewed once or twice in his Penelope. Sometimes he simply stops the opera whilst the band plays a fragment from some familiar work, and then calmly resumes. This is how he manages the phrase from the Hallelujah Chorus which follows the reference to the Salvation Army, a jape which is open to the double objection that the warriors of the Salvation Army never sing the Hallelujah Chorus, and that Mr Solomon ought to have more regard for his own music than to remind people of Handel's whilst it is proceeding. In the end this topical sort of orchestration becomes distracting, worrying, even exasperating. I do not insist on this to disparage Mr Solomon's incessant inventive activity, or to drive him back into routine instrumentation. But I certainly do wish to recall him to the necessity of exercising that activity under strictly artistic conditions, the first of these being that the score shall be at least agreeable to the ear, if it is too much to ask that it shall be beautiful.

Nothing in The Nautch Girl sustains the orchestral traditions of comic opera—the delicacy and humor of Auber, the inimitable effervescence of Offenbach, or the musicianly smoothness and charm of Sullivan and Cellier, all of whom felt that the function of the orchestra was primarily to make music, and only secondarily to make fun. If Mr Solomon ever had that feeling, he has allowed it to become blunted; and for want of its guidance he has now landed himself in mere horse-play, and brought the artistic standard at our leading comic opera house down with a run. The remedy for him is by no means to acquire the polite but unprogressive technique of our Mendelssohn scholars, which, though it would carry him a safe distance, would then stop him dead, but simply to cultivate the sense of beauty in music until it becomes an infallible monitor as to the point at which those twitches on the piccolo, and grunts on the bassoon, and slams on the drum cease to amuse, and become offensive disfigurements of the tone-fabric instead of eccentric ornaments upon it.

Of the opera as an artistic whole I cannot very well speak, because it hardly *is* an artistic whole. The book was evidently selected for the sake of its resemblance to The Mikado, of which it might almost be called a paraphrase if it were not that the secession of Mr Grossmith and his replacement by Mr Wyatt has necessitated the substitution of a second edition of the Duke of Plaza Toro for the Lord High Executioner. The managerial argument evidently was that since The Mikado had been so unlike externally to any previous Savoy opera, the way to secure a repetition of its success was to produce the most slavish possible imitation of the best known previous Savoy opera. Managers always reason in this way. The result on the first night was that when the rather characterless equivalents of the Mikado opening chorus, and of A wandering minstrel I, and of the three girls' trio had been sung, there were signs of the settling down of an ominous dullness, which was only dispelled by the appearance of Mr Rutland Barrington, who changed the fortunes of the evening, and, in fact, saved the opera. At this point, too, the dialogue brightened a good deal; and thenceforth, though there was a plentiful lack of freshness, there was liveliness enough and to spare. Miss Snyders, the only member of the cast whose accomplishments are not too well known to need description, owed her success chiefly to a truly Circassian beauty; for, though she has sufficient taste and address to do her business very presentably, she is not as yet specially interesting as a singer or actress. As usual at the Savoy, the piece has been well rehearsed; the *mise-en-scène* is of exceptional excellence; and Mr Charles Harris, the stage-manager, was received with a cordiality which, I hope, convinced him that he has lost nothing by getting rid of the ballets of infants and the interminable processions in which he formerly delighted. As to the music, it is, to say the least, not distinguished; but it is obvious, lively, and easily caught up by the amateur strummer. Those who rejoiced in An everyday young man will be enchanted with Vive la liberté; and if here and there a number is a little too stale and vulgar for even such words as It was all my eye, on the other hand the mosquito song, and one or two others in the same vein, are by no means graceless.

It will not escape observation that the utmost that can be said for The Nautch Girl amounts to no more than can be said for any piece at the Lyric or the Prince of Wales. In other words, the Savoy has lost its speciality. This, I think, is a misfortune; and if Mr Carte wishes to remedy it, and cannot discover two new geniuses, he had better make up his mind at once to give a commission to Mr Grundy for his next libretto, and to Mr Stanford or Mr Cowen for his next score.

15 July 1891

THERE is nothing that we do in this country more thoroughly and artistically than our authorized denials of statements which everybody knows to be true. From the honorable gentleman in the House of Commons who asks a question about some notorious job, down to the poorest wretch who protests against being worked for seventeen hours a day, we all receive the same crushing denial, the same dignified rebuke for giving currency to silly and vulgar gossip, the same pledges of the highest credit and the best authority that the statement made is absolutely

without foundation. And within three weeks everyone concerned, including the unimpeachably respectable deniers,
openly admit that the statement was perfectly true, and that
they knew it to be perfectly true all along, and, in fact, denied
it on that account.

These observations are suggested to me by recent events
at the Opera. When the State performance was first announced, M. Henri Rochefort said, in effect, to the French
members of the company, "Do, if you dare." The exact form
which the threat took was an assurance to the French public
that no French artist would sing a note for the ravisher of
Alsace and Lorraine. Our national genius for authorized
denial saw its opportunity at once, and seized it. These
French artists, it was solemnly declared, were, like the
Kaiser, England's guests; and as gentlemen they would
know their duty to their hostess and to their distinguished
fellow-guest. The report of their refusal to sing was entirely
false: not one of them had refused: all were indignant at the
monstrous suggestion that they could so forget themselves.
M. Rochefort being thus snubbed, shut up, and put to
public shame, the next event was the publication of the program for the evening, with the parts of Telramund, Capulet,
San Bris, and Nevers, which have been played throughout the season by Maurel, Dufriche, and Lassalle, transferred to Messieurs Alec Marsh, Edouard de Reszke, and
Franceschetti, and the promised act from Die Meistersinger
omitted, evidently because Lassalle could not be replaced as
Hans Sachs: in short, with the authoritatively denied report confirmed in every essential particular. Doubtless it
would have been highly un-English to have faced the obvious truth in the first instance; but it certainly would have
been simpler to have admitted frankly that the French artists could not afford to run the risk of offending M. Rochefort and the section of the French public represented by him,
instead of leaving it to be inferred that they are either Re-
publicans haughtily refusing to take part in a monarchical
pageant, or else patriots on whose hearts the names of Alsace

and Lorraine are indelibly graven. The moral of the whole affair for future distinguished visitors is, Go to the Royal English Opera rather than to the Royal French-Italian-Austrian-Spanish-German-Jewish-Polish Opera; and these unpleasantnesses will not arise.

Lest I should myself become the innocent cause of an international misunderstanding, let me hasten to explain that my abstention from acceptance of Mr Harris's invitation on this occasion had no political significance. I have always understood that one of the advantages of not being an Emperor is that you need not go to ceremonies of this kind unless you like; and I availed myself of my privilege. That is all—absolutely all. Those scraps of Wagner, Meyerbeer, and Gounod may have been delightful novelties to the Kaiser: to the critic they were the oldest of old stories; and the critic consequently stayed away, and had a pleasant unprofessional evening.

Meanwhile, the Opera has been pursuing its accustomed routine. The repeated postponements of Otello were accounted for by the regrettable illness of Jean de Reszke, who gave a touching proof of his prostrate condition by playing Don Jose instead, and, I must say, playing it very well. Lassalle was admirable as Escamillo; and if Ravogli's only too powerful Carmen had been substituted for Miss de Lussan's, which has now been seen often enough for one season, the evening would have been quite a memorable one. Melba did not strengthen the cast as much as she might have done: she was Melba, of course; but she was not Michaela. In the smaller details the performance was slipshod and perfunctory. Melba, De Reszke, Lassalle, and Miranda sang in French; Ciampi and the chorus sang in Italian; and Miss de Lussan sang in whatever language seemed to have the best of it for the moment. The night before this, Fidelio was produced; and the brisk sale of librettos betrayed the mournful fact, unspeakably disgraceful to London, that Beethoven's one opera—and how great an opera!—was new to the audience. It cannot be said that the work received any great instalment of the justice for which it has waited so long; for Tavary, though she deserves unstinted credit for the earnestness and the very considerable ability which she shewed, has not the dramatic genius (nothing less than genius will do) for the part of Leonora. Devoyod as Pizarro was confused and incompetent; whilst Mr Alec Marsh, who sang well enough as the Minister, comported himself with uncalled-for-irascibility. On the other hand, Ravelli was exceptionally good as Florestan; and Plançon made an excellent Rocco. Madame Bauermeister, probably the most indispensable member of Mr Harris's company, and by no means the least efficient, was Marcellina. The performance of the overtures was disturbed by an unusually copious influx of young barbarians celebrating their first appearance among civilized people at a musical performance by treating themselves to boxes on the pit tier. They chattered and laughed and enjoyed themselves generally, with an unconsciousness which would have been delightful to contemplate if Beethoven had not had prior claims to our attention. I may remark in passing that the extent to which private boxes encourage this sort of misconduct, even among disciplined people, appears to me to form a strong argument for their entire abolition. Always toward the end of the season, when the boxes are frequently let to strangers, Covent Garden suffers more and more from visitors who have never learnt how to behave themselves in an opera-house, and who are excited by the novelty of their situation. Things were particularly bad on this Fidelio night. Not only were there two pit tier parties who were behaving quite outrageously, but there was a gentleman next me with a huge stick, with which he beat time mercilessly on his own ankles, whilst a man behind me supported him in the less subtle rhythms by knocking with his boots against the back of my stall. Add to this that Randegger, to whose achievements as a Beethoven conductor I shall not attempt to do justice, hammered his desk freely with his stick—perhaps to relieve his feelings after a slight altercation with the bassoon which graced the conclusion of the first act—and you will understand the difficulties under which I endeavored to taste the full flavor of Fidelio. Still, with all these drawbacks, I could not help noticing that the work was far better understood in the orchestra, and a little better even on the stage, than it used to be.

Marta, which was revived for Mravina, is an opera which one hardly knows what to do with. The first two acts make such a capital piece of naïve story-telling, and the rest is so hopelessly dull and artificial, that every experienced critic now knows that the man who is pleased and indulgent in the middle of the performance will be bored and disenchanted at the end. If I were Mr Harris, I think I should boldly transfer Plunket's beer song from the third act to the Richmond fair scene, and bring Tristan to the rescue after Dormi pure with an overwhelming force of courtiers, finishing the performance there and then with the concerted piece from the end of the third act. The evening could be filled up with that one act opera of Mascagni's which we were led to expect this season. Mravina's beautiful unspoiled voice was just the thing for The Last Rose; and Giulia Ravogli and Edouard de Reszke (the only Plunket I ever saw without a huge hat strapped upon his back) enjoyed themselves at their ease, and pleased us all immensely. Ravelli, as Lionel, was less happy; the part is too high and exacting to be successfully attacked in the robust style which he depends on.

Otello reached its third postponement on Saturday night; and the public, having had proof on the State night and on the previous Saturday that Brother Jean can sing if he chooses, reached the conclusion that its desire to see Maurel again as Iago is not taken in good part by our sensitive tenor.

Though the season is not to be compared to last year's for musical activity, and is now, of course, waning precipitously, concerts still occur pretty frequently. Paderewski's recitals, which ended on Saturday, have been crowded in spite of the heat. He has shewn himself proof against hero worship, never relaxing the steadiest concentration on his business as an artist, so that however you may differ with him occasionally, you have nothing to reproach him with. At one of his recitals he played four of Mendelssohn's Songs without Words, which have dropped out of the stock pianoforte repertory lately, ostensibly because they are too easy for our young lions, but really, I suspect, because they are too difficult. If you want to find out the weak places in a player's technique, just wait until he has dazzled you with a Chopin polonaise, or a Liszt rhapsody, or Schumann's symphonic studies; and then ask him to play you ten bars of Mozart or Mendelssohn. At the same time I must confess that it was Chopin, in the B minor sonata, who found out the limits of Paderewski's skill on Saturday last. Another Pole, Stojowski, has given one recital at Princes' Hall. He can play, and that very cleverly; but he did not leave the impression that his musical ability is irresistibly specialized for the pianoforte. Schönberger's recital was welcome because he avoided the stereotyped program, omitting Chopin, playing a Weber sonata, and giving Haydn, Mozart, and Mendelssohn a turn. He plays with remarkable elegance and brilliancy; but in simple passages, where elegance and brilliancy are of little use, he appears diffident and uneasy. At such moments his technique becomes his worst enemy, because he seems to have so much more faith in it than in himself that when it drops out of action he loses confidence. If this is really so, his apprehensions are uncalled for, since his musical feeling, as far as he ventures to give it free play, never betrays him. In his appearances with Isaÿe and other artists throughout the season he has distinguished himself greatly. Simonetti is a young Italian violinist of whom I have formed no adequate judgment, as I arrived at his concert when the room was crowded to suffocation, and had to content myself with hearing a few bars through the doorway. I can only say that the few bars impressed me favorably by their clean, refined execution and sympathetic tone.

22 *July* 1891

ICONFESS to having witnessed with a certain satisfaction the curious demonstrations which enlivened the first performance of Otello at Covent Garden. The first sign of tumult was a disposition to insist on applauding Maurel in season and out of season, even to the extent of causing ridiculous interruptions to the performance. The second was an almost equally strong disposition to disparage—I had almost said to hoot—Jean de Reszke, who was defended by vehement counter-demonstrations, in leading which Lassalle, standing in a box next the stage on the grand tier, was the most conspicuous figure. Fortunately, the majority in an English audience generally declines to concern itself in green-room politics; and at Covent Garden the majority is so huge that it is not possible to make much of a scene there. By the end of the second act matters relapsed into the usual routine, greatly, I should imagine, to the relief of Maurel. However, partial as the demonstration was, it was far too general to be the work of a claque; and I recommend it to the most serious consideration of Brother Jean. It is to his petulant laziness, and to nothing else, that we owe the frightful waste of artistic resources at Covent Garden on stale repetitions of worn-out operas night after night, when we might have been listening to Siegfried and Otello, not to mention half a dozen other works which are familiar in every second-rate German town, and of which we know nothing in London. The height of his ambition would be attained, as far as one can judge, if he were permitted to maintain his status as leading tenor at the Royal Italian Opera by a single performance of Romeo every year, leaving the rest of the work to be done by Perotti, Montariol, and Ravelli. And yet, at the beginning of this season, he had the—shall I say the ingenuousness?—to favor an interviewer with some observations about his devotion to Art. Can he wonder at the frequenters of the Opera shewing a little temper in the matter at last?

248

His acting as Otello was about equally remarkable for its amateurish ineptitudes and for its manifestations of the natural histrionic powers which he has so studiously neglected for the last fifteen years. Though he overcame his genius for being late so far as to get on the stage punctually for his first utterance in the storm, it reconquered him when he entered to interrupt the fight between Cassio and Montano; and in his sudden appearance at the masked door in Desdemona's bedroom, which depended for its effect on being timed exactly to a certain chord, he was a good half bar behindhand. His reluctance to determined physical action came out chiefly in his onslaught on Iago, which he managed in such a way as to make the audience feel how extremely obliging it was of Maurel to fall. And at the end of the third act, in simulating the epileptic fit in which Otello's fury culminates, he moved the gods to laughter by lying down with a much too obvious solicitude for his own comfort.

On the whole it may be said that throughout the first two acts his diffidence and irresolution again and again got the better of his more vigorous and passionate impulses. This was intensified no doubt by nervousness; but it was partly due also to his halting between a half-hearted attempt at the savage style of Tamagno and the quieter, more refined manner natural to himself. In the third act, when the atmosphere of the house had become friendly, he began to treat the part more in his own fashion, and at last got really into it, playing for the first time with sustained conviction instead of merely with fitful bursts of self-assertion. Indeed, but for that gingerly fall at the end, this third act would have been an unqualified success for him. As it was, it shewed, like his Don Jose and other post-Van Dyck performances, that when the rivalry of younger men and the decay of his old superficial charm with advancing years force him to make the most of all his powers, he may yet gain more as an actor than he will lose as a singer.

His Otello will never be like Tamagno's; but he need

not regret that, as the same thing might have been said of Salvini. The Italian tenor's shrill screaming voice and fierce temper were tremendously effective here and there; but the nobler side of the Moor, which Salvini brought out with such admirable artistic quietude and self-containment, and which De Reszke shews a considerable, though only half cultivated, power of indicating in the same way, was left untouched by Tamagno, who on this and other accounts is the very last man a wise tenor would attempt to imitate.

There is less to be said as to the other principals. It is no compliment to Albani to declare that she was better than Madame Cattaneo, as she could hardly have been worse. Like De Reszke, she redeemed herself in the latter half of the opera. Her intonation improved; and her acting had the sincerity which so honorably distinguishes her from most of her rivals, and which so often leads her straight to the right vocal treatment of purely dramatic music. If she will only forgo that absurd little stage run with which she embraces Otello in the first act, she will have nothing to reproach herself with as far as her playing of the part is concerned. Maurel, tired out as to voice, dropping all the G's, and unable to make the pianissimo nuances tell at anything softer than a tolerably vigorous *mezzo forte*, was yet able to repeat his old success as Iago. His playing is as striking and picturesque as ever; but I have come to think that it requires a touch of realism here and there to relieve its somewhat mechanical grace and effectiveness. The excessive descriptiveness which is the fault in his method, and even in his conception of the actor's function, resulting in a tendency to be illustrative rather than impersonative, occasionally leads him to forget the natural consequences of the actions he represents on the stage.

For instance, when Otello half throttles Iago, it is a little disillusioning to see the victim rise from a faultless attitude, and declaim Divina grazia, difendimi, with his throat in perfect order. Nothing is easier to produce than the *voce soffocata;* and there are not many operatic passages in which

250

it is more appropriate than here. Apart from these matters of detail, the chief objection to Maurel's Iago is that it is not Iago at all, but rather the Cæsar Borgia of romance. As far as it is human, it is a portrait of a distinguished officer, one who would not be passed over for Cassio when he was expecting his step. I am aware that this view of him falls in with the current impression in artistic circles that Iago was a very fine fellow. But in circles wherein men have to take one another seriously, there will not be much difference of opinion as to the fact that Iago must have been an ingrained blackguard and consequently an (if I may use a slightly Germanic adjective) obviously - to - everyone - but - himself - unpromotable person.

A certain bluffness and frankness, with that habit of looking you straight in the face which is the surest sign of a born liar, male or female, appear to me to be indispensable to "honest Iago"; and it is the absence of these, with the statuesque attitudes, the lofty carriage of the head, and the delicate play of the hands and wrists, that makes the figure created by Maurel irreconcilable with my notion of the essentially vulgar ancient who sang comic songs to Cassio and drank him, so to speak, under the table. There is too much of Lucifer, the fallen angel, about it—and this, be it remarked, by no means through the fault of Verdi, who has in several places given a quite Shakespearean tone to the part by *nuances* which Maurel refuses to execute, a striking instance being the famous Ecco il leon at the end of the fourth act, when Iago spurns the insensible body of the prostrate Otello.

Nobody, it seems to me, can escape the meaning of the descent to the rattling shake on the middle F which Verdi has written. It expresses to perfection the base envious exultation of the ass's kick at the helpless lion, and suggests nothing of the Satanic scorn with which Maurel, omitting the ugly shake, leaves the stage. His performance is to be admired rather as a powerfully executed fantasy of his own than as the Iago either of Verdi of Shakespear. If his suc-

cessors in the part try to imitate him, their wisdom will be
even less than their originality.

It remains to get through the most melancholy part of
my task—the criticism of the staging of the opera. I need
hardly say that what money could secure in the way of
scenery and dresses has been secured, and that amply. But
money alone does not go very far in the first act of Otello,
which stands or falls by the naturalness of the delightful
scene where the storm subsides, the thunder dies out of the
air, and there begins that merry scene round the bonfire
which is perhaps Verdi's freshest and prettiest piece of descriptive music. Its total failure at Covent Garden was a
foregone conclusion. I should be sorry to assail any such
hard-worked body as the Covent Garden chorus with so un-
graceful an epithet as pigheaded; but really if they could
have seen themselves standing just clear of the pale flame of
that miserable penn'orth of methylated spirit, staring at
Mancinelli, and bawling without a ray of feeling for what
they were supposed to be doing, they would not venture to
defend themselves against any extremity of abuse. The
scene was so effectually extinguished in consequence, that
those who had seen the Scala people at the Lyceum were to
be heard in all directions during the interval naïvely declaring that they found the first act very dull now that the
novelty of the work had worn off. The final outrage of the
stage-manager (if there is really any such functionary at
Covent Garden) was the turning on in the sky of a most outrageous constellation, intended, I think, for the Great Bear,
and consisting of gas lamps of the first magnitude and of
aggressive yellowness. I remember believing implicitly in
the reality of everything I saw on the stage at my first pantomime; but even then I do not think I should have been
taken in by such incredible heavenly bodies as these. They
achieved a sort of *succès de rire* by winking at the most rapturous part of the duet which De Reszke and Albani were
carrying on below in happy ignorance of the facetiousness
of the firmament; but, though I could not help laughing, I

strongly recommend Mr Harris to send down to Greenwich for an expert to superintend this part of the opera before he repeats it.

It cannot be said, unfortunately, that the tediousness stopped after the first act, although the stage-manager's opportunities ceased then. The tact, steadiness, and—when needed—the authority with which Faccio brought Otello through at the Lyceum without letting it flag for a second was beyond the powers of the amiable and enthusiastic Mancinelli. He shewed his usual feeling for the orchestral points; but, on the other hand, he let things drag terribly, particularly in the third act, by waiting for singers who were waiting for him, and often choosing unnecessarily slow *tempi* to start with. In the second act he astonished Maurel by taking the applause at the end of the Credo as an encore —an unheard-of artistic mistake; and, shortly afterwards, he astonished De Reszke still more by doing exactly the reverse after the Ora per sempre addio, sante memorie. On the whole, if he could have borrowed a little of Bevignani's disposition to whack an opera along, without also acquiring his characteristic imperviousness, Otello would have been over sooner, and the audience would have gone home with a better opinion of the work.

29 July 1891

THE announcement that Maurel had at the last moment found it impossible to undertake the principal part in Mr de Lara's Light of Asia, and the consequent withdrawal of that work, were the final disappointments of the opera season; and one may perhaps be excused for mildly suggesting that Maurel might have made up his mind on the subject a little earlier, instead of keeping innocent critics, who might have been recuperating in the country, waiting vainly in town to witness his début as Buddha. However, it did not matter to me: I should have been in town in any case; and I am willing to believe that Maurel was justified in concluding that the task of making the work

253

a success was too delicate to be achieved under the rough-
and-ready conditions which prevail at Covent Garden. Still,
if Mr de Lara was ready to face that risk, the collapse of the
project is rather hard on him. I am not, by temperament,
one of Mr de Lara's special devotees: his music appears to
me to be one-sided; and a little of its one side goes a long
way with me. But, for all that, I look with some indignation
on the tendency among the Philistines to regard him as fair
game for a sort of criticism which means, if it means anything, that an artist, as such, has no right to live in this country. We no longer literally heave half-bricks at strangers; but
we certainly do chivy artists occasionally for no other mortal
reason than that they are artists. I do not deny that musicians,
when they are very young men, make themselves ridiculous,
as other very young men do, through mere ignorance of the
art of life. It is easy to find excuses for laughing at beginners
in any profession; but we do not laugh fairly all round: we
let the overweening young curate, or doctor, or lawyer off
very easily in comparison with the overweening young artist,
thereby implying that the nature of his profession is an ag-
gravating circumstance. This does not hurt the bold, adroit,
and witty spirits if they can handle the pen or use their
tongues publicly: all they have to do is to turn the attacks
into advertisements, and live on their notoriety until the
maturing of their powers enables them to build solidly on
that foundation. But the inarticulate musician has to live it
down as best he can. It is therefore important that it should
be dropped as soon as he does live it down, if only for the
sake of the scoffers; for there is a point in this popular sport
of artist-baiting at which the quarry outgrows the hunters.
If criticism is to pursue a man to the death, it must carefully
calculate the time at which such epithets as callow, immature, conceited, and the like, must be exchanged for old-
fashioned, obsolete, exploded, and played-out. In London
the upstart fades so quickly into the superfluous veteran
(from the abusive point of view) that one has to keep exceedingly wide awake lest the laugh should suddenly change

sides. No doubt Mr Isidore de Lara, some fifteen or twenty years ago, had about him a certain quantity of the nonsense proper to his age, emphasized by a style sufficiently pronounced to rouse the artist-hunting instinct in the Philistines. Whenever, in the due course of his struggle for recognition as a singer and composer, he did those things which (artistically speaking) he ought not to have done, and left undone those things which he ought to have done, he was generally pretty promptly and publicly informed that there was no health in him. Even the youngest critics wrote of him with all the freedom of men old enough to be his father. This was all very well in its day; but I submit that Mr de Lara has now grown up, and had better either be treated seriously, or else frankly burnt alive as a warning to young gentlemen who dislike city work. I have, I hope, an open mind in the matter; but I doubt whether it would be wise to burn him. He appears to me to stand out with no small distinction from the ruck of our catchpenny ballad manufacturers and barren professors of the art of doing what has been done before and need not be done again. His popularity with a certain section of London society is a perfectly legitimate popularity, arising from the fact that his music exactly expresses the poetic sentiment of that section, and is therefore felt in it to be genuinely inspired and not merely put together for the royalty market. Of course, if you happen to have a violent antipathy to both section and sentiment, the very genuineness of the inspiration may make his music all the more nauseous to you. But to put forward your antipathy for what he expresses as a proof of his incapacity to express it is ridiculous: the fact of the music rousing that antipathy shews conclusively that the music is alive. And it cannot reasonably be contended that its workmanship is deficient in quality. For my part, if Mr de Lara were to leave his Light of Asia in its original form, and try his hand at a new opera in which he would freely express in music those sides of life which appeal to his humor, intellect, and observation, instead of confining himself to a few threadbare

255

disguises of lovesickness, I have no doubt that the result would be awaited with a degree of interest which will certainly never be aroused by the favorite heroes of the writers who appear to think that they are under no obligation to treat him with common politeness, much less to criticize him rationally.

Mlle Teleki, whose début at the opera on the last night but two of the season had been so long deferred that it was obviously made at last only to give the lady the Covent Garden hall-mark, is undeniably clever and attractive. When a young artist is tall, handsome, and unaffected, with fine eyes, black hair, a well-proportioned head, a nose, mouth, and teeth that can be admired both separately and collectively, a good voice, and plenty of musical aptitude, one is not surprised to hear that she is a favorite with the Hamburg public, or any other public. I watched her with pleasure during two acts of the ridiculous spectacle which they describe as Verdi's La Traviata in the Covent Garden bills; and then, as the performance was hackneyed, the cast bad (Maurel being out of it), and my mind sufficiently made up, I withdrew, and so cannot testify as to the degree of success the new prima donna met with in the later scenes. Nor was I present at the performance of Otello on Saturday, when Miss Eames and Dufriche appeared instead of Albani and Maurel as Desdemona and Iago.

One of the results of the Military Exhibition of 1890, the musical department of which was taken good care of by Colonel Shaw-Hellier, has just appeared in the shape of a guinea volume, containing a descriptive catalogue of the instruments exhibited, illustrated with heliogravures. In producing these, by the bye, the photographer, for the sake of a pretty picture, has occasionally scorned all technical classification. However, as the references are clear enough, and the plates very effective, the work is none the worse. As far as I know, there is no reference book available in any musical library which could supply the place of this catalogue. In order to get at the information it gives concerning modern wind instruments, I have sometimes had to hunt through inventors' pamphlets, "methods" written for bandsmen by bandsmen in a style unrivalled for confused illiteracy and set up by music printers in the ineptest of typography, instrument-makers' catalogues of surpassing mendacity, and standard works on "modern instrumentation" containing statements which must have been already obsolescent when Nebuchadnezzar engaged his orchestra.

The difficulty about producing really comprehensive and exhaustive treatises on the subject is that they are not of sufficiently general interest to circulate to the extent needed to make them remunerative to publishers. It took a whole Military Exhibition to make this catalogue possible; and if I were not, as a critic, bound to pretend that there is nothing musical in heaven or on earth that I did not know all along, I should not mind confessing that my knowledge was materially enlarged both by this exhibition and "The Inventions" of 1885. In one or two places, notably in Mr Blaikley's essay on pitch, with its valuable and somewhat astonishing table of variations caused by changes of temperature in concert rooms, the catalogue is written rather from the point of view of the instrument-maker and military bandmaster than from that of the musician who has to keep the interests of the dramatic singer always in sight; and there is a slight survival of the regulation treatises in the old-fashioned passage about "the growing tendency to replace the trumpet in the orchestra by the cornet." This way of putting it is absurdly out of date, the fact being that the cornet *has* completely superseded the trumpet, and that what is now happening is an attempt to re-introduce the trumpet in the shape of the new straight clarino with two valves on which Kosleck played in Bach's B minor Mass so brilliantly and successfully at the bi-centenary performance in the Albert Hall in 1885, and which has since been taken up by Mr Morrow.

I cannot find this instrument, which struck me as a very important one, in the catalogue: neither is there any mention of the bass trumpet, for which Wagner has written a part in Die Walküre, usually played on an alto trombone at the Richter concerts. It is in such omissions as these (if I am not complaining only of my own oversights) that the military limitations of the Kneller Hall purview of instrumental music make themselves felt; but they are not typical omissions: Colonel Shaw-Hellier and Captain Day have gone to work in a most catholic spirit, and are evidently guiltless of having purposely excluded any wind instrument on the ground of its not having come into use in military bands.

An excellent little book for Bayreuth pilgrims is Smolian's Themes of Tannhäuser, which has just been translated by Mr Ashton Ellis and published by Chappell for a shilling. I am afraid one or two of its interpretations will considerably startle those admirers of the Tannhäuser overture who have innocently accepted most of its details as mere phrases of absolute music; but Herr Smolian's analysis certainly carries conviction. In looking over it I have been somewhat taken aback by the number of points which had escaped me in a work with which I have an acquaintance of some twenty years' standing. *The* commentary on Tannhäuser, however, must always be Wagner's own instructions for its performance, a translation of which is now running through The Meister.

A very important work for Wagnerites is Glasenapp's new Wagner Encyclopedia, recently published by Fritsch of Leipzig. I bought the two volumes at David Nutt's in the Strand for—I forget the exact price; but it made a huge hole in a sovereign. It is not so impossibly thorough as it has been declared by one or two critics (who must, I think, have had complimentary copies); for, after all, the only genuine Wagner Encyclopedia is a complete collection of his works; but still it gives the most striking verdicts of the greatest art critic of the century. It is a pity that an English translation is not available; for our notions of Wagner are still a jumble of superstitions: hardly anywhere do you meet with recognition of the vigorous common sense, the clearsighted practicalness, the unfailing grip of the vital and permanent ele-

258

ments in art as distinguished from its fashions, its aberrations, its flights down no-thoroughfares of all sorts, which made him master of the situation in the teeth of all Europe.

5 August 1891

EUROPE, it is to be hoped, will understand that Sir Augustus Harris has not been knighted in public recognition of the claims of Music on the English nation. I forget who it was that paid the Order of the Garter the tribute of acknowledging that there was no nonsense about merit connected with it; but Sir Augustus must have been reminded of that epigram when he received the accolade, not for his services to Art, but for happening to be Sheriff when the Emperor of Germany happened to pay a visit to the City of London, as if it were not easier to find a dozen Sheriffs than one capable operatic manager. There is, however, some satisfaction in the circumstance that the interest created by our impresario's elevation is due entirely to his connection with music and the drama. Before it occurred, I was the only person in London who, in private conversation, invariably spoke respectfully of him as "Mr Harris." Everybody else spoke of him as "Gus." I do not know what warrant they had for the familiarity; but that they did so is beyond all question. Now, had he been merely a Sheriff all his life, nobody would ever have known his first name, nor cared a straw whether he was knighted or not. Nor should I have to go into the question of whether he deserved the compliment after his achievements last season.

On the whole, I am inclined to answer that question in the negative. I admit that he has not grudged prodigious sums of money; and in view of his alleged intention to modify his plans next season in the direction of fewer performances it seems probable that he has not recovered as much of that expenditure as he expected; but it partly serves him right, because neither he nor the public got value for what he spent. He made an initial mistake in engaging five leading tenors and no stage manager. For want of a stage manager Orfeo was murdered. For want of a stage manager the first act of Otello was laid waste. For want of a stage manager Tannhäuser was made a laughing-stock to every German who went to see it, except in the one or two passages which Albani stage-managed. For want of a stage manager, the first scene in Boito's Mefistofele remains so absurd that it is to be hoped that when Edouard de Reszke appears at one of the holes in a ragged cloth, and sends a hearty "Ave, Signor," in the direction of another hole, the audience do not know whom he is supposed to be addressing. For want of a stage manager, no man in Les Huguenots knows whether he is a Catholic or a Protestant; and conversations which are pure nonsense except on the supposition that the parties cannot distinguish one another's features in the gloom are conducted in broad moonlight and gaslight. I have been told that the moon in Die Meistersinger has to be superintended by Jean de Reszke in person; but for the truth of this I cannot vouch. As for the prison doors that will not shut, and the ordinary door that will not open, I do not complain of that: it is the stage way of such apertures. One gets at last to quite look forward to Valentine attempting a dashing exit through an impracticable door into his house opposite the cathedral, and recoiling, flattened and taken aback, to disappear ignominiously through the solid wall at the next entrance. I would not now accept any house as being that in which Rigoletto so jealously immured his daughter, unless the garden door were swinging invitingly open before every onset of the draughts, more numerous than the currents of the ocean, which ventilate the Covent Garden stage, and the courses of which have so often been pointed out to me by the horizontal flames of the guttering candles in the first act of La Traviata.

It must be understood that by a stage manager I do not mean merely a person who arranged the few matters which cannot either be neglected or left to arrange themselves as best they may. I mean rather the man who arranges the stage so as to produce the illusion aimed at by the dramatic poet and musician. Such a one, for instance, would begin his preparation for Mefistofele by reminding the scene-painter of Mesdag's Sunrise in the Museum in Amsterdam, and coaxing him to substitute some great cloud region like that for the dingy cloth with the two holes in it which lames the imagination in spite of Boito's music. He would give some touch of nature to that garden of Margaret's, where, beneath the shade of tall trees, a discordantly gaudy flower-bed blazes in an outrageous glare that never was on sea or land; for, if he could not adapt the light to the scenery, he could at least try to adapt the scenery to the light. He would bring his common sense to bear on La Traviata, his intelligence on Les Huguenots, his reading on Tannhäuser, and his imagination on all the operas. And withal, instead of putting Sir Augustus Harris to any additional expense, he would make fifteen shillings go further than a pound goes now. That is what really offends my economic instincts in the business— that so much money should be wasted. I was able to forgive the shabbiness of Signor Lago's Orfeo, because money was scarce there; but the splendors of the Harrisian Orfeo were infuriating, because the effect was reduced more than the cost was increased.

Whether, if a stage manager who was a real artist were placed in command of the Covent Garden stage, anyone there would pay much attention to him, is another matter. In any case, he would need to be seconded by an impresario of great authority, who would make up his casts without fear or favor in the interests of the public alone. Perhaps Sir Augustus's newly-won spurs may strike awe next season into his company; but, so far, the contingent from the Paris Opéra seem to rule the roost. Jean de Reszke and Lassalle, who might, with Ravogli, have made Carmen one of the chief successes of the season, and that, too, without any considerable strain upon them, condescended to play in it just once. Jean was especially trying. He shirked Siegfried; he shirked Tannhäuser; he would obviously have shirked Raoul if he had not been startled into alarmed activity by the success of Van Dyck; and he put off Otello to the last moment.

Yet nobody dared to remonstrate, as far as one can see. The impresario's hand was wanted on other occasions as well. Les Huguenots should have been recast with Plançon as Marcel, Edouard de Reszke as San Bris, and Lassalle omitted; and in Fidelio the part of Pizarro should never have been left to Devoyod.

It is true that we were spared a second resurrection of La Favorita to please Mlle Richard; but the performances of Lucia solely to shew off Madame Melba's singing, and of La Traviata to gratify Madame Albani's weakness for the part of the consumptive Violetta, were probably nearly as hard on the public as they undoubtedly were on the critics. On the other hand, Il Trovatore, which has been inflicted on us season after season with hopeless casts, was dropped this time, apparently because Lago's experiment had shewed that Giulia Ravogli's Azucena would have made it interesting. Her Carmen, which was a very remarkable performance, was supported by artists who, in this opera at least, were not worth hearing, and was then withdrawn to make way for the hackneyed and trivial Carmen of Miss de Lussan, who learns nothing and forgets nothing. Maurel's Mephistopheles, a striking and well thought-out impersonation, far superior to that of his predecessor Faure, was given up to make room for Edouard de Reszke, who, with the utmost good humor, makes the whole drama ridiculous.

It is only fair to say, however, that Brother Edouard did his share of the season's work manfully, seconding Van Dyck with a will, coming to the rescue of Don Giovanni, achieving a success no less artistic than personal as Mefistofele (Boito's), and throwing in Plunket in Martha with the best grace in the world. But this was evidently due to his complaisance, and not to the authority of the management. Still, it is hardly conceivable that Mr Harris (as he was then) was content to see his huge expenses squandered so often upon stale performances by the second-rate singers of his company, whilst his most popular artists were, so to speak, eating their heads off; or that he would have permitted it if he could have helped it. There is, in short, no discipline at the Opera.

The reason, I suggest, is that the Opera does not pay as an ordinary theatre pays. The manager has to spend more than he can hope to receive in payments for admission; and the deficiency, plus his profits, must be made up by rich guarantors who require an opera-box in the season just as they require a carriage or any other part of their social equipment. They, therefore, have to grant the subvention which, in Paris or Berlin, is granted by the State. It is this system of private subvention that breaks the manager's back, as far as discipline is concerned. His artists are able to go behind him and make friends with the mammon of unrighteousness in the persons of the guarantors; and he soon finds that he cannot afford to offend his idolized tenor, his fashionable soprano, or his pet baritone, without also offending his most influential guarantors, which he, of course, cannot afford to do. Probably the stories that circulate in the foyer between the acts as to casts vetoed by enamored and jealous lady patrons who object to their idols making even stage love to song-stresses whom they are suspected of admiring, are all false; but the fact that they might quite possibly be true is as strong an objection to the system as if they actually were true.

The complete remedy is a social rather than an operatic problem; but it is worth pointing out that if the subvention came from public instead of from private sources, the manager could deal far more boldly with those of his artists who are favorites in the drawing room, and far more fairly with those who are favorites only on the stage, than he dares at present, whilst the interests of the public would be materially reinforced.

I purposely refrain from saying anything about the praise-worthy points in the past season. The critic who is grateful is lost. Sir Augustus has given us Otello and revived Fidelio. Instead of thanking him, I ask why he has not given us Siegfried. When he gives us Siegfried (which he can do by engaging Van Dyck for it), I shall complain of the neglect of

Die Walküre. Let him add that also to his obsolete repertory, and I shall speak contemptuously of an opera-house where Tristan is unknown. After that, I can fall back on Das Rheingold, Götterdämmerung, and Parsifal; but by that time, at the present rate of progress, I shall be celebrating my hundred and fiftieth birthday. If even then I say that I am satisfied, let there be an end of me at once; for I shall be of no further use as a critic.

The very last concert of the season was a little affair at Collards' Rooms the other day, at which a few artists gave their services to help a lady who has been unfortunately disabled. There was the usual middle-aged lady who sang rather well, and the usual somewhat younger lady who sang very badly, and the usual youngest lady of all who sang the Donizetti cavatina which her master had been drilling her in for the past two years. A fortnight ago I would have scorned such a concert with the utmost arrogance: on this occasion I was glad to have something to do in the laziest hour of an idle afternoon. The entertainment, luckily, was considerably strengthened by Seiffert, who lent a powerful helping hand with his violin, and by Mlle de Llana, who played Thomé's Serenade d'Harlequin better than we deserved, considering our very feeble numbers. On referring to my program, by the bye, I find that Mlle de Llana is no longer Mlle de Llana, but Madame Seiffert.

16 *September* 1891

NOT Bayreuth, but Paulus, is the cause of this momentary lifting up of my voice amid the silence of the dead season. As a matter of fact I have not been to Bayreuth. Those who remember how earnestly I warned my readers to secure tickets in good time will not be surprised to hear that I spoke as a man taught by his own incorrigible remissness in the past. When at the eleventh hour, being wholly unprovided, I found that there was not a ticket to be had in Europe—that there were two hundred and fifty names down for returned tickets for every performance, and that the average of returns was not above twenty-five, I became quite mad to go. But in a day or so, resigning myself to the inevitable, I came to the conclusion that Bayreuth was an overrated place, and made arrangements for an excursion of a different sort. No sooner had I done this than the difficulty about tickets vanished: Carl Armbruster offered to manage it for me: Van Dyck offered to manage it for me: Messrs Chappell actually did manage it for me: Europe, in short, had realized the gravity of the situation, and Bayreuth was at my feet. But it was too late: the other arrangements stood inexorably in the way; and I now had to refuse. Nobody will be surprised to learn that the proffered seats were no sooner sorrowfully disposed of to mere ordinary Wagnerians, than circumstances again modified my arrangements so as to remove all obstacles to my going. I braced myself up once more to face that forty hours' rush from Holborn to Bavaria, with its eight hours' *malaise* between Queenborough and Flushing, less deadly in its after effects than a railway journey from Calais or even Ostend to Brussels; its inevitable inspection of the latest improvements in the Cologne cathedral, in which every inch of new steeple adds an ell of insignificance and vulgarity to the whole structure; its endless joggle along the Left Rhine Railway, with the engine depositing a ring of soot between one's neck and collar, and the impermanent way disintegrating into whirlwinds of dust; its two or three hours' wait after midnight at Würzburg for the Bamberg train, or else the push on to Nuremberg, there to pay a mark for every penn'orth of sleep you have time for; and the final entry into Bayreuth within four hours of the trumpet call to the theatre, hoping desperately that the novelty of the place and the stimulus of Wagnerian enthusiasm will enable you to keep awake during the first performance. I had run it so close that no easier stages were practicable. But I was spared after all: the tickets were gone this time in earnest. At least the Committee thought so, and telegraphed "Impossible," though it afterwards turned out that they were wrong, as they usually are about everything except lodgings. Howbeit, I took their word for it; and now the Bayreuthites may boast as outrageously as they please about the Tannhäuser: I shall never be able to contradict them. But since it is clear that the Wagner Theatre was filled at every performance by people many of whom must have spent at least twenty pounds in getting there, it seems to me that it is time, from a mere business point of view, to begin building the Wagner Theatre on Richmond Hill. Unfortunately the noble president of the London branch of the Wagner Society, who might be expected to move in the matter, is preoccupied by the question of his seignorial rights over Ham Common. Perhaps he is going to build the Wagner Theatre there. If not, it will be interesting to see whether it will occur to any of the commoners to impeach before the Wagner Society its London president's fidelity to the principles of the illustrious exile of '48.

However that may be, I have not been out of England, and have indeed heard no good music lately except a brass band of shoemakers, conducted by a compositor, playing for pure love of their art on the racecourse at Northampton one Sunday afternoon, and playing very well indeed. They gave us a Gloria of Haydn's with a delicacy of execution and a solemn reverence for the old master which were extraordinarily refreshing after the stale professional routine playing of the London concert platforms. It was like seeing a withering flower put into water. This has been, so far, the only musical episode in my wanderings, which are chiefly devoted to *viva voce* criticisms delivered gratuitously to the man in the street who cannot afford to buy The World. It is a salutary thing after the worry and hurry of a London season to abandon one's typewriter, fly beyond the reach of the endless deliveries of the metropolitan postal service, and deliver one's soul face to face with one's fellow-man under the open sky. To take a trap through a countryside, driving from one village green to another, and criticizing by the oratorical instead of the literary method, rejuvenates me rarely after three months on the treadmill whose well-worn steps are
266

St James's Hall, Prince's Hall, Steinway Hall, and Covent Garden. With good company to keep you merry during the home journey in the dark, there is no pleasanter way of spending a day, except perhaps lying on one's back on a hillside doing absolutely nothing, a luxury which requires an unconscionable deal of preliminary hard work to give it a really fine flavor. Oral criticism in the streets of a manufacturing town at night is not quite so romantically pastoral; but on a fine evening in such a place, there are much duller diversions than hiring an itinerant shooting gallery or the like, strikingly illuminated with a supply of naphtha flares, from some gipsy showman; assembling a crowd under the false pretence of being a cheap Jack; and then firing off your weekly article at them by word of mouth. You can then see for yourself how many people yawn and drop your column before they have half finished it. You can even test its pecuniary estimation by sending or taking round your hat, as, upon sufficient occasion, I have often done. Or, if there is no necessity for that, you can mark the degree of emphasis with which the drunken man who persists in interrupting you is finally seized and hurled into the outer darkness. I cannot but think that criticism would be greatly improved if our leading critics were to rub off the illusions and unrealities of London literary life occasionally in this fashion. They are probably restrained solely by a vague impression that something would happen to them if they followed my example—musty eggs, dead cats, the police, social ostracism, and what not? Now it is no doubt true that if they were to bore the public to its face with the platitudes they sometimes inflict on them under cover of anonymous journalism, it is impossible to say to what lengths popular indignation might go. And it might be as well for even those who have opinions of their own, and are not over-sensitive to the very solid reasons which exist for hiding them, to clothe them in vernacular English and not in the literary jargon which is considered good enough for print. But with something to say and a reasonably human way of saying it (and without both why

should anyone be a critic at all?) a man may take his criticisms
into the market place with every prospect of an astonishing
width of toleration, and considerable benefit to his lungs.

Thus you can roam about for a while at little cost, receiv-
ing much—nay, sometimes overmuch—gratuitous entertainment from hospitable enthusiasts, and sampling provincial art by an occasional visit to the theatre, where the latest
London success in the way of farcical comedy will generally
be found going the rounds in an edifyingly bowdlerized condition. Or you can stop for a few hours at a cathedral town,
and see how the dean and chapter have covered the outside
of the greatest of our art treasures with figures ordered whole-
sale from this or that eminent firm of stonemasons; filled exquisite windows with stained glass resembling transparent
linoleum; and blocked up the inside with paltry elaborations
of the commonest tombstone-makers' ware to the memory
of their own sons and nephews killed in some of our unright-
eous little market-making colonial wars. One is not surprised
to find that these cenotaphs have to be fenced in with iron
railings to prevent visitors who know the value of the out-
raged building from summarily removing them with pick-
axes. When I halted on the way from Stafford to Northampton on Saturday week, I could not help asking myself
whether it was any great gain to have escaped Cologne only
to come to Lichfield.

But from all such reflections I was recalled by the overwhelming artistic importance of the event in London to
which I have alluded. Paulus was (and is) at the Trocadero,
singing L'Amant de la Tour Eiffel, Le Père la Victoire, and
so on. I could not catch the whole meaning of his songs; but
as I could catch no meaning at all in the English songs of
the evening, perhaps there was not much meaning to catch.
He has a certain personal force, has Paulus, and so stands
out brilliantly among the twinklings of aborted artistic impulse which make up the music-hall firmament. It may be
said of him, as Marx said of Mill, that his eminence is due
to the flatness of the surrounding country. Still, his talent
268

and industry as a comedian would in England soon transfer him to the comic opera houses; his singing conveys the impression that he could refine upon it a good deal before an audience which could be trusted to appreciate the improvement; and he whistles much better than Mrs Alice Shaw. The rest of the program left me more convinced than ever of the need for free trade in dramatic art. Those items which were the direct product of the law for the protection of theatres seemed to bore the audience almost as much as they bored me—were enough, indeed, to drive a man to make himself uncritically drunk in self-defence. Some ballad singing of the ordinary concert type, by Mr Christian and Miss Yeamans, was much relished; but why the lady should have sung Millard's Waiting in a limelight, gesticulating in the manner of a fourth-rate German prima donna struggling with Ocean, thou mighty monster, is more than I can undertake to account for, especially as the audience shewed a lively sense of the absurdity of the proceeding.

The success of L'Enfant Prodigue had its inevitable sequel in the production of Yvette at the Avenue Theatre last Saturday. Yvette was not a success in Paris; and it will not be a success here. L'Enfant Prodigue had drollery, domestic pathos, and the charm of novelty. Yvette has nothing but a pretty and refined musical setting by André Gedalge, whose labor has been entirely wasted. For the sake of Mlle Milly Dathenes and the rest, I wish it were possible to be less blunt; for they play as well as it is possible to play under the circumstances; but they cannot save a piece which is so utterly void of interesting ideas that I cannot help suspecting that Michel Carré designed it originally as a libretto for a grand opera by Gounod.

As there seems no prospect of any revival of musical business before the Birmingham Festival next month, I propose to drop round to Venice until then.

I CANNOT say that I am unmixedly grateful to the Birmingham Festival people. They brought me all the way from Venice by a polite assurance that a packet of tickets awaited my arrival. But when, after a headlong rush over the Alps and far away into the Midlands, I reached the Town Hall, insufferable indignities were put upon me. The stewards on the floor declared that my seat was in the gallery; the stewards in the gallery insisted that it was on the floor; and finally, when it became plain that no seat at all had been reserved, I was thrust ignominiously into a corner in company with a couple of draughts and an echo, and left to brood vengefully over the performance. On the Passion Music day I escaped the corner, and shared a knifeboard at the back of the gallery with a steward who kept Bach off by reading the Birmingham Daily Post, and breathed so hard when he came to the bankruptcy list that it was plain that every firm mentioned in it was heavily in his debt.

Under these circumstances, no right-minded person will grudge me a certain vindictive satisfaction in recording that the performance of the St Matthew Passion, which was what I came from Venice to hear, was not, on the whole, a success. No doubt it was something to have brought the chorus to the point of singing such difficult music accurately and steadily. But a note-perfect performance is only the raw material of an artistic performance; and what the Birmingham Festival achieved was very little more than such raw material. In the opening chorus, the plaintive, poignant melody in triple time got trampled to pieces by the stolid trudging of the choir from beat to beat. The violins in the orchestra shewed the singers how it ought to be done; but the lesson was thrown away; the trudging continued; and Richter, whom we have so often seen beating twelve-eight time for his orchestra with a dozen sensitive beats in every bar, made no attempt to cope with the British chorister, and simply marked one, two, three, four, like a drill-sergeant. The rest of the performance did nothing to shew any special sympathy with Bach's religious music on Richter's part.

It is, of course, to be considered that the necessity for having the Passion sung from Sterndale Bennett's edition, no other being available with the English words, may have compelled him to be content with the best performance, according to that edition, attainable in the time at his disposal; so that he, whilst wishing to give the work "à la Wagner," as the Dresdeners used to say, may have had to put up with it "à la Mendelssohn" in despair of getting anything better. But, then, why did he let those piteous questions from the second chorus to the first come out with a shout like the *sforzandos* in the roughest and most vigorous pages of Beethoven? And why did he allow the remonstrances of the disciples about the pot of ointment to be sung by the same mass of voices, and with the same savage turbulence, as the outbursts of wrath and mockery from the crowd at Pilate's house and Golgotha? Such matters as these might have been quite easily set right. Perhaps the safest conclusion is that half the shortcoming was due to Richter not having taken Bach's Passion Music to heart, and the other half to Sterndale Bennett, to lack of time for rehearsal, and to the impregnable density of that most terrific of human institutions, the British chorus.

For no one who knows Bach intimately will need to be told that our plan of compensating for the absence of some ten or eleven skilful and sympathetic singers by substituting ten or eleven hundred stolid and maladroit ones will not answer with his music, however strong-lunged the ten or eleven hundred may be. One comparatively easy thing the Birmingham chorus could do well, and that was to sing the chorales. These, accordingly, were excellently given. The rest was leather and prunella. Even the thunder and lightning chorus had no electricity in it.

Rather unexpectedly, where Richter failed to make any mark, Mr Stockley, the local conductor, had a brilliant success. The performance of The Messiah which he conducted was the triumph of the festival. Not that Mr Stockley is a greater conductor than Richter; but he knows The Messiah as Richter apparently does not know the St Matthew Passion; and he has the courage of that knowledge, and of his familiarity with the choir. I have rarely been more agreeably surprised than when I began incredulously to realize that Mr Stockley was in the secret which in London is strictly kept between Handel and myself. I need not now repeat what I said on the occasion of the Handel Festival as to the proper execution of the florid traits in Handel's choruses, and as to the vivacious *tempo* which is necessary to bring out their brightness and vigor. Suffice it to say that if Mr Manns or Mr Barnby, or any of our London conductors, had been present (perhaps they were) to hear For he shall purify taken in *my* manner—which is also Mr Stockley's, which is also Handel's—they must have wondered whether this impetuously confident music could indeed be read from the same notes as the dull, lumbering, heavy-footed, choral monster they have so often goaded along at the Albert Hall and the Crystal Palace.

No doubt the younger members of the band and the soloists were a little taken aback by the absolute refusal of the conductor to drag the *tempo* in order to shew off their tone. But if any complaints or deridings reach the committee, let it fortify itself behind the undeniable fact that the performance had a hearty success and a freedom from tedium quite unknown on Messiah nights in London. If ever, during Mr Stockley's time, the committee entrusts a work of Handel's to any strange conductor, however eminent, it will shew itself incapable of understanding when it is well served.

It is not easy to fit Villiers Stanford's Eden with a critical formula which will satisfy all parties. If I call it brilliant balderdash, I shall not only be convicted of having used an "ungenteel" expression, but I shall grievously offend those friends of his whose motto is *Floreat Stanford: ruat caelum!* If, on the other hand, I call it a masterpiece of scholarship and

272

genius, and expatiate on its erudite modal harmonies and its
brilliant instrumentation, I shall hardly feel that I have expressed my own inmost mind. Not that I am prejudiced
against modal harmonies. I can harmonize themes in keys
other than that of C, and leave out all the sharps and flats
against any man alive; and though for the life of me I never
can remember which of the scales produced in this manner
is the mixophrygian mode, and which the hypoionian, or
Dorian, or what not, yet I am content to be able to perpetrate
the harmonies and to leave more learned men to fit them
with their proper names. But what I cannot do is to persuade
myself that if I write in this fashion my music will sound
angelic, and that if I use the ordinary major and minor scales
the result will be comparatively diabolic. I find it works out
rather the other way.

I know, of course, that several modern composers, from
Handel to Beethoven, and from Beethoven to Bourgault-
Ducoudray, have done very pretty things in the modal man-
ner. But when Professor Stanford asks me to admit that his
choristers are angels merely because they persistently sing
B flat instead of B natural in the key of C major (as the
Siamese band used to do when they played our national
anthem, to our great alarm, on stone dulcimers), I feel that
he is becoming exorbitant. I see no reason why heaven should
be behind earth in the use of the leading note in the scale.
Perhaps this is not serious criticism; but I really cannot take
Eden seriously. From the mixolydian motet at the beginning
to the striking up of Three Blind Mice to the words Sleep,
Adam, Sleep by the Archangel Michael at the end, I caught
not a single definite purpose or idea at all commensurate
with the huge pretension of the musical design. That pretension is the ruin of Eden. There is one interlude which I
should applaud if it were a piece of hurdy-gurdy music for a
new setting of Linda di Chamounix; and there are plenty of
other passages which would be acceptable on similar terms.

But in a work which stands or falls as a great musical
epic, they only made me wonder what Mr Stanford would

think of me if I took advantage of my literary craftsmanship
to write inane imitations of Milton's Paradise Lost with all
the latest graces of style, and got my friends to go into raptures over its grammar and its correct scansion. However,
who am I that I should be believed, to the disparagement of
eminent musicians? If you doubt that Eden is a masterpiece
ask Dr Parry and Dr Mackenzie, and they will applaud it to
the skies. Surely Dr Mackenzie's opinion is conclusive; for
is he not the composer of Veni Creator, guaranteed as excellent music by Professor Stanford and Dr Parry? You
want to know who Dr Parry is? Why, the composer of Blest
Pair of Sirens, as to the merits of which you have only to
consult Dr Mackenzie and Professor Stanford. Nevertheless, I remain unshaken in my opinion that these gentlemen
are wasting their talent and industry. The sham classics
which they are producing are worth no more than the forgotten pictures of Hilton and epics of Hoole.

Dvořák's Requiem bored Birmingham so desperately
that it was unanimously voted a work of extraordinary depth
and impressiveness, which verdict I record with a hollow
laugh, and allow the subject to drop by its own portentous
weight. Besides, I do not wish to belie that steward who introduced me to his colleague on Thursday morning (when I
was looking for a seat) as "one of these complimentary
people."

Considering the mass of work to be prepared, the execution was, on the whole, highly creditable, though I doubt
if Dvořák thought so, as most of the fatigue, the bad intonation, and the blunders of band, chorus, and principals fell to
his lot on the Requiem day. All the English music was well
done. The band achieved a splendid performance of Brahms's
Symphony in F (No. 3); of Beethoven's Seventh Symphony,
especially the last three movements; of the Walkürenritt,
concerning which our gifted Hans must be slightly mad,
considering the outrageous position he gave it in the program; and of the accompaniments to the last act of Tannhäuser, and to the concertos played by Joachim. Of the solo

singers, only Lloyd and Santley did their work with any great
distinction. Miss Anna Williams, in The Messiah, took
But Thou didst not leave out of the mouth of the tenor—a
proceeding which I can gasp and stare at, but not criticize.

Of the Crystal Palace Concerts, which began last Saturday, more anon. Popper duly made his appearance, and
proved quite as fine a violoncellist as his great reputation
had led us all to expect.

21 October 1891

THE reaction after the feverish musical activity of
last year seems to continue. Last week London had
to live until Saturday on the expectations raised by
Signor Lago's prospectus, and on the rival enterprise of Sir
Augustus Harris. The most interesting point about the
Lago enterprise is the transfer of Italian opera to a theatre of
reasonable size—one in which such a work as Donizetti's
Elisire d'Amore might possibly come to life again if any
sort of serious trouble were taken with it. The spread of
musical knowledge and cheap pianos must sooner or later
produce a crop of cheap editions of the non-copyright operas
of the old repertory; and that in turn must lead to a revival
of that repertory, not at Covent Garden, but on stages like
those of the Lyric and Prince of Wales Theatres. The
notion that the march of modern music has left Rossini,
Donizetti, and Bellini hopelessly behind, because their
palmy days at the Royal Italian Opera are gone by, is like
the illusion that prevails in literary circles to the effect that
nobody now reads the novels of Grant, James, Fenimore
Cooper, or Alexandre Dumas père, because they have
ceased to be reviewed or discussed by literary experts.

When the day comes—and it is surely coming—when
opera-singers at ten pounds a week or less will be more
competent in every way than those who now demand from
thirty to a hundred, plenty of small theatrical capitalists,
who now would as soon think of running an empire as an
opera-house, will try the effect of the enchanting old tunes

and the inspiriting old rum-tum on the social strata which are being lifted into the region of dramatic music by the great social upheaval of the School Board. Depend upon it, Signor Lago, in moving from Covent Garden to the Shaftesbury, is marching in the track of evolution, and is leaving Sir Augustus, as far as so-called cheap opera is concerned, behind him. If he fulfils his promise of producing Wagner's Flying Dutchman there, he will have the advantage of working on the same scale as Carl Rosa at the Lyceum in 1876. And the Flying Dutchman had a success on that occasion, both artistic and financial, which it has never attained elsewhere in London.

The subject of cheapness in musical and other literature was forced upon me yesterday by the spectacle, in Ricordi's shop window, of the vocal score of Mascagni's Cavalleria Rusticana, published by Sonzogno of Milan, price ten shillings net. Having already seen this score at Milan offered for the Italian equivalent of ten shillings, and refused to pay any such monstrous price for a one-act opera, I passed on, musing on the enormous stupidity of Italian shopkeeping from the English point of view. In Venice the other day a friend of mine went into a shop and asked the price of a certain article. Twenty-five francs was the answer. My friend bid three, an offer which was waved off as a pleasantry on the part of the English gentleman. He, however, made no move until the shopkeeper came down to four, when he bid three-and-a-half, at which figure the transaction was closed to the satisfaction of both parties. Now, far be it from me to pretend that if that child of the South had been an Englishman, with an establishment in Oxford Street, he would have been one whit honester. But he would have found, first, that my friend's time, being worth so many guineas an hour, was too valuable to admit of his patronizing shops where it took longer than two minutes to make a purchase; and, second, that the shopkeeper who makes money in London is he who sells twenty articles at a profit of a half-penny each, instead of selling one at a profit of sixpence.

Hence, though we can hold our own in commercial dishonesty with any foreigner ever born, we have *unico prezzo* in all our shops, and we can buy Professor Stanford's Eden in vocal score, mixolydian motets and all, for half the price of Cavalleria Rusticana, though the latter does not contain one-third as much new copyright music as the former. I do not profess to be a man of business (though musical criticism includes business, as the whole includes the part), but I respectfully submit to Ricordi, Sonzogno, and continental music publishers generally, that vocal scores are not in any country the luxuries of the rich, and that the way to make money by them is through low prices and large sales. Such prices as sixteen shillings and twenty shillings for scores of Boito's Mefistofele and the last seven works of Wagner are not remunerative; they are simply prohibitive. The astonishing thing is that Novello, or some other London and American firm, does not purchase these copyrights from the present holders, and make a large haul by reversing the greedy and shortsighted policy at present in force.

Although I have not, at the moment of writing this, seen Cavalleria Rusticana, my refusal to buy the score has not left me in total ignorance of the work. Do not be alarmed, I am not going to perpetrate an "analysis." Those vivid emotions which the public derive from descriptions of "postludes brought to a close on the pedal of A, the cadence being retarded by four chords forming an arpeggio of a diminished seventh, each grade serving as tonic for a perfect chord," must be sought elsewhere than in these columns. It is perhaps natural that gentlemen who are incapable of criticism should fall back on parsing; but, for my own part, I find it better to hold my tongue when I have nothing to say. Yet I cannot help chuckling at the tricks they play on their innocent editors. An editor never does know anything about music, though his professions to that effect invariably belie his secret mind.

I have before me a journal in which the muscial critic has induced the editor to allow him to launch into music type in

277

order to give a suggestion of a certain "fanciful and suggestive orchestral design" in Cavalleria Rusticana. The quota-
tion consists of a simple figuration of the common chord of
G sharp minor, with "etc." after it. If a literary critic had
offered this editor such a sample of the style of Shakespear as

"Now is the," etc.

he would probably have remonstrated. But he is perfectly
happy with his chord of G sharp minor, which is ten times
more absurd. And yet that editor devotes a column of his
paper to criticizing me in the most disrespectful manner.
Can he wonder that my sense of public duty does not permit me to remain silent on the subject of his utter incapacity
within my special province?

The fact is, I have heard the music of Cavalleria Rusticana, and can certify that it is a youthfully vigorous piece of
work, with abundant snatches of melody broken obstreperously off on one dramatic pretext or another. But, lively and
promising as it is, it is not a whit more so than the freshest
achievements of Mr Hamish MacCunn and Mr Cliffe. The
people who say, on the strength of it, that Verdi has found a
successor and Boito a competitor, would really say anything.
Mascagni has shewn nothing of the originality or distinction which would entitle him to such a comparison. If he
had, I am afraid I should now be defending him against a
chorus of disparagement, instead of deprecating a repetition
of the laudatory extravagances which so often compel me to
take the ungracious attitude of demurring to the excesses of
the criticism instead of the cordial one of pointing out what
is good in the composition. Already I have read things about
Cavalleria Rusticana which would require considerable
qualification if they were applied to Die Meistersinger or
Don Giovanni.

Max Bruch's new violin concerto, No. 3, in D minor,
was played for the first time in public in England by Mr
Hans Wessely on the 11th, at the South Place Sunday
Popular Concerts. Sarasate had the second turn at it on

Saturday last, with the advantage of an orchestra. I did not
hear either performance. I take the opportunity, however,
of mentioning the admirable way in which things are kept
going at South Place, where a concert of the best chamber
music, on the lines of the Monday and Saturday Popular
Concerts, is open every Sunday evening at seven to anyone
who chooses to walk in and listen. The programs are in no
way less severe than those at St James's Hall; but the Finsbury working man comes in, sits it out, and puts what he
can into the plate to help to keep the concerts going. If one
of our prosperous west-enders would go down some Sunday and put into the plate the same percentage of his week's
income as that contributed by his Finsbury neighbor, he
would make the committee's mind easy for the rest of the
season.

In mentioning Herr Popper's performance at the
Crystal Palace I forbore to deal specially with his concerto,
because, to tell the truth, I was puzzled by its abruptly ending after what I had supposed to be only the first movement.
I now find that I was right. Popper, through no fault of his
own, did not succeed in getting to the Palace in time for
rehearsal; and it was thought better not to venture on the
last two movements at first sight. Mr Manns was anxious
to explain to the audience; but Popper has an objection—
rather unusual in the profession—to have a fuss made about
him. At last Saturday's concert Hans Sitt conducted an
overture of his own, composed for a play Don Juan d'Austria,
a play by Leschivo, of whose fame I confess myself wholly
ignorant. The overture is clever and interesting, steering,
somewhat in the manner of Berlioz, between the Wagnerian-
tone picture and the formal "absolute music" overture. On
the purely musical side, and especially in its rhythmic
structure, it shews that Mendelssohn's influence is not dead
yet. Mr Barton McGuckin sang Lend me your aid very
well, and afterwards gave us a couple of songs by Mr Bemberg, the composer of Elaine, the forthcoming novelty
at Mr D'Oyly Carte's opera-house. Mr Bemberg, like

Mr Goring Thomas, follows the French school, even to the
extreme of calling his Hindoo chant a "Chant Hindoo." It is
much in the style of Massenet, and throws no more light on
Elaine than that the composer can utter with sufficient taste
and address any inspiration that may come to him. Miss
Adeline de Lara played Rubinstein's concerto in D minor.
Considering that Miss de Lara's frame is not of the most
powerful build, and that her technique is rather that of
Henselt than of Rubinstein, her performance may fairly be
described as extraordinary. On her last appearance at the
Palace her fingers were startlingly rapid and accurate; but
the hardness of her touch, and the nervous tension at which
she played, shewed that the effort demanded by the manual
execution left her little energy to spare for artistic treatment.
She was able to play the piano, but not to play with it. On
Saturday her finger-work was as brilliant as before; but it
seemed to be much further within her utmost resources,
and to leave her comparatively at ease. Her class as a pianist
cannot, however, be determined until she lets us hear her
play the concertos of greater masters than Rubinstein.

28 October 1891

IF experience had not convinced me these many years
that theatre managers of all kinds, and operatic im-
presarii in particular, retain to the end the madness
which first led them to their profession, I should be tempted
to remonstrate with Signor Lago for getting a good thing
like Cavalleria Rusticana, and tying Crispino e la Comare
round its neck. As a member of a Northern race, I refuse to
have patience with Crispino. Any grasshopper with a mod-
erately good ear could write reams of such stuff after spending three months in Italy. Offenbach's lightest operetta
looms in intellectual majesty above this brainless lilting,
with its colorless orchestration and its exasperatingly light-
hearted and empty-headed recitatives, accompanied by
sickly chords on the violoncello with the third always in the
bass. Perhaps Coquelin might make the farcical adventures

of the shoemaker amusing; but Ciampi is not Coquelin: he
is not even Ciampi in his prime. The simple-minded Italians
of Soho, if they could obtain a *biglietto d' ingresso* for a shilling,
would no doubt bless Signor Lago for restoring to them, in
a foreign land, a sort of entertainment which gratifies their
love of strumming and singing without for a moment dis-
turbing that sunny stagnation of mind, the least disturbance
of which they hate worse than cold baths. But in England
the climate, the national character, and the prices of admission, are against such entertainments. When I spoke, last
week, of the possibilities of a revival of the old repertory, I
was thinking, as far as comic opera is concerned, of such
works as Il Barbière, Don Pasquale, Les Deux Journées,
Fra Diavolo, or La Grande Duchesse, and by no means of
the second-hand wares of Cimarosa or Ricci. The operas
which did not cross the Italian frontier when they were
young, will not do so now that they are old. I also stipulated
that they should be fairly well done; and, to be more particular, I may say that one of the conditions of their well-
doing is that the buffo, however comic, shall sing instead of
quacking, and that the tenor who revives Come gentil for us
shall not have a shattering tremolo. This last remark is not,
I assure you, a side-thrust at Crispino, which consists of two
hours of Ciampi's buffooneries with no tenor at all, and is,
indeed, so childish an affair that I really think that any party
of musical boys and girls could improvise something just as
clever and funny, just as one improvises a charade or a game
of dumb crambo. In a very comfortable country-house (if
such a thing exists), or out picnicking in the woods on a
summer day, the Crispino style of entertainment would not
come amiss; but in a crowded theatre, with one's mind made
up to have some value for money paid at the doors, it is not
good enough. In all friendliness to Signor Lago's enterprise, I recommend him to get rid of Crispino with all possible expedition, and either to give Cavalleria Rusticana by
itself, without any padding, or else have it followed by a
single act of one of Wagner's operas, played without cuts.

Why not, for instance, the second act of Parsifal?

Of the music of Cavalleria (with the stress on the pen-
ultimate vowel, if you please: it is a mistake to suppose that
the Italians call it Cavvlearea) I have already intimated that
it is only what might reasonably be expected from a clever
and spirited member of a generation which has Wagner,
Gounod, and Verdi at its fingers' ends, and which can demand, and obtain, larger instrumental resources for a ballet
than Mozart had at his disposal for his greatest operas and
symphonies. Far more important than that, it has a public
trained to endure, and even expect, continuous and passionate melody, instead of the lively little allegros of the old
school, which were no more than classically titivated jigs and
hornpipes; and to relish the most poignant discords—tonic
ninths, elevenths, and thirteenths, taken unprepared in all
sorts of inversions (you see, I can be as erudite as anybody
else when I choose)—without making a wry face, as their
fathers, coddled on the chromatic confectionery of Spohr
and his contemporaries, used to do when even a dominant
seventh visited their ears too harshly.

Even today you may still see here and there a big, strong,
elderly man whimpering when they play the Tannhäuser
overture at him, and declaring that there is no "tune" in it,
and that the harmony is all discord, and the instrumentation all noise. Our young lions no longer have this infantile
squeamishness and petulance to contend with, even in Italy.
They may lay about them, harmonically and instrumentally,
as hard as they please without rebuke: even the pedants
have given up calling on them to observe "those laws of form
to which the greatest masters have not disdained to submit"
—which means, in effect, to keep Pop Goes thé Weasel continually before them as a model of structure and modulation. Consequently, opera now offers to clever men with a
turn for music and the drama an unprecedented opportunity for picturesque, brilliant, apt, novel, and yet safely
familiar and popular combinations and permutations of the
immense store of musical "effects" garnered up in the

scores of the great modern composers, from Mozart to Wagner and Berlioz. This is the age of second-hand music. There is even growing up a school of composers who are poets and thinkers rather than musicians, but who have selected music as their means of expression out of the love of it inspired in them by the works of really original masters. It is useless to pretend that Schumann was a creative musician as Mendelssohn was one, or Boito as Verdi, or Berlioz as Gounod. Yet Schumann's setting of certain scenes from Goethe's Faust is enormously more valuable than Mendelssohn's St Paul; we could spare La Traviata better than Mefistofele; whilst Berlioz actually towers above Gounod as a French composer.

And this because, on the non-musical side of their complex art, Mendelssohn and Gounod were often trivial, genteel, or sentimental, and Verdi obvious and melodramatic, whilst Schumann was deeply serious, Berlioz extraordinarily acute in his plans and heroic in his aims, and Boito refined, subtle, and imaginative. The great composer is he who, by the rarest of chances, is at once a great musician and a great poet—who has Brahms's wonderful ear without his commonplace mind, and Molière's insight and imagination without his musical sterility. Thus it is that you get your Mozart or your Wagner—only here we must leave Molière out, as Wagner, on the extra-musical side, is comparable to nobody but himself. The honor of the second place in the hierarchy I shall not attempt to settle. Schumann, Berlioz, Boito, and Raff, borrowing music to express their ideas, have, it must be admitted, sometimes touched an even higher level of originality than Schubert, Mendelssohn, and Goetz, who had to borrow ideas for their music to express, and were unquestionably superior only in the domain of absolute music.

But nobody except the directors of the Philharmonic Society will claim any higher than fourth place for those who have borrowed both their ideas and their music, and vulgarized both in the process—your Bruchs, Rubinsteins,

Moszkowskis, Benoits, Ponchiellis, and other gentlemen rather more likely to see this article and get their feelings hurt if I mentioned their names. Brahms, as a unique example of excess in one department and entire deficiency in the other, may take his place where he pleases, provided I am out of earshot of his Requiem.

I offer these illustrations to explain the difference between my critical method and that of the gentlemen who keep only one quality of margarine, which they spread impartially over all composers of established reputation; so that you shall not detect one hair's breadth of difference in their estimates of Beethoven and Meyerbeer, Wagner and Sir Arthur Sullivan, John Sebastian Bach and the President of the Royal Academy of Music. As they speak today of Mascagni, and will speak of Mozart at the forthcoming centenary celebration, they spoke yesterday of Dvořák and Villiers Stanford, four months ago of Handel, and a year ago of Moszkowski and Benoit.

The worst of it is, that the public judgment has become so pauperized by this butter bounty, that although I habitually stretch good-nature to the verge of weakness in extenuating and hushing up all manner of avoidable deficiencies in the performances I criticize, yet I find myself held up as a ruthless and malignant savage because, in spite of all my efforts to be agreeable, a little perspective will occasionally creep into my column, and will betray, for instance, the fact that I consider Ivanhoe as hardly equal in all respects to Lohengrin, and am a little loth to declare offhand that Dr Parry's oratorios are an improvement on Handel's. Some day I think I will go further, and let out the whole truth; for since I get no credit for my forbearance, it often comes into my mind that I may as well be hung for a sheep as a lamb.

All this is a mere preamble to the remark that Mascagni has set Cavalleria Rusticana to expressive and vigorous music, which music he has adapted to the business of the stage with remarkable judgment and good sense. That is the exact truth about it; and so, Mascagni being disposed of with this very considerable eulogy (implying that he is a man in a thousand, though not in a million), I go on to say that Vignas, the tenor, is completely satisfactory, both as singer and actor, in the part of Turiddu; that there is no fault to be found with Mlle Bremn and Miss Damian in the mezzo-soprano and contralto parts; that Signorina Musiani, who is not a bit older or stouter than Miss Eames, has some genuine pathos and a voice of fine natural quality to offer as a set-off to a rather serious tremolo; and that Signor Brombara is so afflicted with the same complaint that he would be better advised to resort to dumb show, since he acts with much conviction.

The conclusion of the duet Vendetta avro, which consists of several melodramatic exclamations delivered simultaneously, fortissimo, by Miss Musiani and Signor Brombara, was the most trying moment in the opera, as neither of the voices was steady enough for any pitch to be discernible. Brombara is, I fear, incurable, and must look for fame to countries where the tremolo is popular. Miss Musiani might possibly get the better of hers, though I am not very sanguine as to her losing her taste for it. However, all five principal artists do their work in the most artistic spirit, and succeed in justifying the credible side of the reputation of the opera—which is saying a good deal, considering how loudly the trumpet has been blown. If the body of tone from the ladies of the chorus were a trifle richer and stronger, and the harmonium in the church less remote in pitch from the band, there would be nothing but the tremolos to complain of. Would it be an impertinence on my part, by the bye, to remark that tremolo and vibrato are not synonymous terms? There is not even the most distant relationship or resemblance between them. One is a defect of the gravest kind: the other is one of the most precious graces a dramatic singer can acquire—if it can be acquired at all. There is no difficulty in acquiring the tremolo. No doubt these facts are well known: still, on looking over the papers lately I thought I would just mention them.

I hear that a few operatic performances are given every week at Covent Garden; but I presume they are of no particular importance, as my attention has not been specially called to them.

4 November 1891

I MUST say that I think Signor Lago has gone just a little past bearing in his mounting of The Flying Dutchman. I know very well that it is not within the power of any scenic artist, however lavishly supplied with capital, to put upon the stage the picture of the ocean which Wagner has conjured up with the orchestra. The tossing seas of the stage are but sorry makeshifts, whether they are revolutions of huge green canvas corkscrews, as at Covent Garden; or flat painter boards swinging to and fro from frankly visible ropes, as in the William Tell tempest at the same home of stage realism; or small boys industriously jumping up and down under a billowy carpet, as in the Halliday version of David Copperfield. The wind can never roar at the wing with the mighty volume and infinite compass which makes even Margate sublime in a storm; and though the advance of civilization has made the more expensive qualities of stage lightning as smokeless as the newest gunpowder, and may some day even evolve an Italian chorus capable of turning up smartly on the deck of a tempest-tossed ship and hauling and hoisting with something approaching a hearty "Yo heave Ho," yet no stage sea will ever bear that ship along, or rush seething past into her white wake as it rushes past Daland's ship in the orchestra at the end of the first act of the Dutchman.

Therefore, I can imagine Lago pleading that, since adequate staging of the work is impossible, and since a miss is as bad as a mile, matters would have been no better if he had spent ten times as much money and taken a hundred times as much pains. And, indeed, had he on this ground frankly abandoned all pretence, and reverted to the Elizabethan method of placarding the stage in the first and last acts, I should have heartily applauded his courage, and watched the result with interest. But the moment he committed himself to doing anything whatsoever, he committed himself to doing it as well as it could be done with the resources at his command; and the smaller the resources, the greater the occasion for making the most of them. Now, I do not think that any person can pretend that as much is done at the Shaftesbury as might be done without the expenditure of one extra penny. All the energy of the management seems to have been exhausted by the effort of procuring a small copy of the Victory at the Naval Exhibition, and rooting it so monumentally in the Shaftesbury stage that even I could ride out the storm in her without a qualm. This desirable vessel is allotted to Daland. The Dutchman is provided with the butt-end of a very poor imitation of a fishing lugger with impracticable ropes. The Victory also is furnished with unpatent immovable rigging. Besides these craft, there is one prima donna's spinning-wheel (practicable) out of Faust, for Miss Damian, and three broken and incomplete ones (desperately impracticable) for the chorus.

Signor Lago has virtually gone to Miss Macintyre, and said: "If I place these properties at your disposal, and undertake to abstain from repeated rehearsals and to scrupulously violate all Wagner's stage directions, do you think you can make The Flying Dutchman a success for me? It says much for Miss Macintyre's courage and devotion that she appears to have answered in the affirmative. If so, Signor Lago has certainly kept his agreement to the letter. I could not pledge myself to train a choir of St Bernard dogs in three rehearsals to sing the sailors' choruses as accurately and intelligently as Signor Lago's choristers sang them on the first night; but nobody who has ever enjoyed the friendship of an intelligent dog would have been quite incredulous if Mr Heinrich Mehrmann had made some such offer. The simple rollicking chorus at the beginning of the last act, and the Ho-yoho-yoho, as easily picked up as a street cry: not a bit of either could they sing decently. They did not even rise to the

287

dance, perhaps because the timbers of the Victory were too frail to stand the stamping; but it might easily have been stage-managed so as to take place on the quay if there had been any capable person in command. As to the miserable travesty which accompanied such mutilated fragments of the scene between the two crews and the girls on shore as were attempted, it would be waste of time to pretend to take it seriously. And yet, properly done, that episode would draw all London.

Everything in the last act was of a piece with the initial absurdity of making the scene identical with that of the first act. Even when the principal singers came on to rescue us from the chorus, the tenor got an attack of goat-bleat which nearly incapacitated him; and the curtain came down amid roars of laughter at the apotheosis of Senta, who had no sooner plunged into the deep in the person of Miss Macintyre than she rose resplendent from her dip in the person of a soft, plump, smiling, golden-haired lassie, whose extravagantly remote resemblance to Miss Macintyre took in nobody but the ghost of Vanderdecken, which hugged her with enthusiasm.

If the members of the orchestra had not known their business better than the stage-manager and the chorus, the performance would have been impossible; but for all that, they did not greatly distinguish themselves. It was evident that there had been little rehearsal—probably the instruments were only used at one repetition, at which there was, of course, no time to pay any special attention to the band. All the men simply got through anyhow they could, and went away thankful at having earned their salaries without an actual breakdown.

As to Arditi, his position was only appreciable by experts. There he sat for three mortal hours, incessantly active, desperately anxious, bothered by discrepancies between the score and the band parts which eventually drove him to conduct from the pianoforte copy, feeling his way after a careless singer here, pulling the band together for a dash out of a difficulty there, rescuing somebody from destruction every two minutes or so, expecting every bar to be the last, and yet keeping a clear beat to meet every glance at his baton. If he had been thirty-six, instead of sixty-six, and if he had felt sure of the sympathy of the whole house, instead of having too much reason to believe that he was more likely to get the blame of all the shortcoming, the ordeal would still have been a cruel one.

As it was, I think Arditi should at once receive a pension from the Civil List so as to relieve him from the necessity of wasting his skill in saving scratch performances from the fate they deserve. I wonder what would happen if Signor Lago had a conductor like Costa, whom I once saw dealing with a hitch in the ball scene in Don Giovanni by putting down his stick with ineffable contempt, freezing the whole stage and orchestra by refusing even to look at them, and then quietly resuming after an awful pause. But I doubt whether, if that were done at the Shaftesbury, any human power could set the frozen works going again.

Fortunately for Signor Lago, the second act of The Flying Dutchman requires no staging worth mentioning, and lies almost altogether in the hands of the two principal artists. Blanchard, who played Vanderdecken, has the music at his fingers' ends. He was thoroughly in earnest, and did his best all through. He has a sufficiently powerful voice, remarkably equal from top to bottom (an immense advantage for this particular part); and though its steadiness and purity of tone have been much impaired by his continental training, still, as he did what he could to minimize his defects, it carried him through with a very respectable measure of success. His acting was too sentimental: he was rather the piously afflicted widower than the obstinate and short-tempered skipper who declared, in profane terms, that he would get round the Cape in spite of Providence if he had to keep trying until the Day of Judgment. But this fault, again, was relieved a little by his substantial stage presence and effective make-up.

289

Artistically, I think he had more to do with such effect as
the work was able to make under the circumstances than
Miss Macintyre, who was, nevertheless, the favorite of the
evening. She is undoubtedly an interesting young lady; and
the pit, captivated by her auburn hair and her Scottish
beauty, resolved, to a man, to see her triumphantly through.
And they did. Whenever she threw herself at the footlights
in the heroic elation of youth, and sent a vigorous B natural
tearing over them, the applause could hardly be restrained
until the fall of the curtain. But whether it is that I have seen
so many stage generations of brave and bonnie lassies doing
this very thing (and too many of them have since lost the
power of doing that without ever having acquired the power
of doing anything better), or whether because my own hair
is more or less auburn, the waves of enthusiasm broke over
me as over a rock, damping me without moving or warming
me. I can see that Miss Macintyre is a true Scot in her
susceptibility to a good story, especially a legend. Tell her
all about Gretchen, Senta, or Rebecca, and you find her
intelligence and imagination on the alert at once, whereas
many an Italian prima donna, under the same circumstances,
would barely tolerate the information as an irksome and not
very important guide to her stage business.

So far, so good. But the story-teller's instinct may be
keen enough in a young lady to make her vividly imagine
incidents and emotions, without raising her an inch above
the commonplace in her power of imagining and realizing
beauty of musical tone, eloquence and variety of musical
diction, or grace and dignity of movement and gesture. And
here it is that Miss Macintyre breaks down. Her notion of
dramatic singing at present hardly goes beyond intensely
imagining herself to be the person in the drama, and then
using the music to relieve her pent-up excitement. This is
better than no notion at all; but, all the same, it is the notion
of a schoolgirl, and not of an experienced artist. In un-
strained situations it leaves her without ideas; in strenuous
ones it results in her simply singing excitably, or standing

with every muscle, from her jaw down to her wrists, in a state of tension as utterly subversive of grace as the attitude of a terrified horse, which is a perfect example of sincerity of conception without artistic grace of expression.

I would ask Miss Macintyre to go and see Miss Ada Rehan in the latest variety show devised by Mr Daly for the squandering of that lady's exquisite talent, and to ask herself whether it is possible to imagine Miss Rehan standing for an instant on the stage—or indeed anywhere else—as Senta stood the other night for several minutes on the entry of Vanderdecken. I shall not do her the injustice of asking her whether she is satisfied to rely on the fact that her person, apart from what she does with it, has a pleasant appearance, just as her voice, apart from her artistic use of it, has a pleasant sound; for beyond a doubt she would indignantly answer, No. But where, then, are the original acquirements which she should by this time have added to the laborious work of her teacher? Are they only those vigorous high notes with which, in the strength of her youth, she exhilarates the gallery, and that conventional *piano* which, being produced with a rigid chin, inevitably ends flat? Surely these are a small store of graces for a singer who claims the most ambitious parts in grand opera. They did not avail with Handel at the Crystal Palace, or with Bach at Birmingham. No: Senta may be a popular success; but I shake my head, and shall continue shaking it, auburn locks and all, until Miss Macintyre plays the part better—much better—than that.

I have only space for a word as to Paderewski, who seems to have kept his head and stuck to his work in spite of lionizing; for his playing is positively better, technically, than when he last played in London. It is quite true that he has cut his hair, but only a little. After his farewell recital I shall have something more particular to say concerning his performance of the Waldstein sonata. Mr Henschel gave the first of his London Symphony Concerts on Thursday. I was unable to be present; but from what my deputy reports of the fullness of the room and the impression produced, the prospects of the enterprise seem satisfactory. The remaining concerts are fixed for the 12th and 26th of November, the 14th of January, and the 11th and 25th of February.

18 November 1891

ISEE that an association of pianoforte manufacturers in New York, the headquarters of the Steinway pitch, which is the highest standard pitch in the world, has decided to adopt French pitch for its instruments in future. Now here, at last, is a move worth all the platonic discussions that have ever been held at the Society of Arts and in St James's Hall, as far as immediate practical results are concerned. Whether this step has been taken by the New York reformers in pursuit of an ideal, or whether it is simply a market operation of the usual American kind, need not be too curiously considered. It is sufficient that the pitch question is again being talked about; that the more it is talked about, the better; and that most of my readers depend on me to put them in a position to talk intelligently about it.

Let me explain, then, for the benefit of the bewildered outsider, what French pitch means. If, in composing a piece of music, I write down the note A, meaning the A in the middle of the pianoforte, nobody knows the exact pitch of the musical sound I want to have played. All that can be said is that I mean it to be a third higher than the note I write down as F, and a fourth lower than the note I write down as D; but this is like saying that an omer is the tenth part of an ephah, which, however explicit, does not get rid of the question of how much an ephah is (further than that it is obviously ten omers). Now, in 1858, the French Government appointed a commission, of which Rossini, Berlioz, Meyerbeer, Auber, Halévy, and Ambroise Thomas were members, to settle what this A should indicate. They fixed on the note produced by 435 vibrations per second; and that pitch $(A = 435)$ is what is called French pitch to this day. Costa, however, did not agree with the French commission, and ordained that, whatever the French might choose to mean by A, the London Philharmonic Society should mean by it a note produced by 452 vibrations per second—about two-thirds of a semitone higher than the 435-vibration A.

The utterances of the Philharmonic Society being deeply respected throughout Great Britain by all responsible citizens who are entirely ignorant of music, it was thereupon set forth in the Queen's regulations that the Philharmonic pitch should be adopted by our military bands. Therefore A = 452 is the regulation pitch at Kneller Hall, where our military bandsmen are trained; and from that centre it has spread over India and the Colonies. But the American eagle treated the British lion as the British lion had treated the French commission. It soared six vibrations higher. Steinway, the king of pianoforte makers, tuned up to A = 458; and the Theodore Thomas orchestra used very nearly this pitch, that is to say A = 456. The complete liberty of the individual to choose his own pitch being thus triumphantly established, we have every organ builder setting up a fancy "concert pitch" and a fancy "church pitch," and calling both of them "standards" (all other makers' pitches being spurious); so that a church organ will have any pitch from about 441 up to the St Paul's pitch of 445, whilst concert organs are made a little sharp or flat to Philharmonic pitch, the makers seeming not to care whether they tune to 453 or 451 so long as it is not 452, which is what it ought to be on Philharmonic principles.

Now try to conceive in your mind's ear a grand international concert in the Albert Hall, with the St Paul's organ lent for the occasion to reinforce the permanent one, and the band assisted by contingents of players, civil and military, from American and the Continent. Imagine the process of tuning—the Albert Hall organ leading off with an A at concert pitch, the church organ responding, horribly flat, with an A at church pitch, the French and German oboists following a good ten vibrations flatter, the Philharmonic men asserting the dignity of England two-thirds of a semitone sharp, and the Americans and the military coming in with a crash, sharp even to the Philharmonic. Let us now suppose that, after sufficient wrangling, Philharmonic pitch carries the day, and the instruments which cannot reach it are silenced.

The Ninth Symphony of Beethoven is put in rehearsal. The sopranos complain bitterly of the strain of the repeated high notes in the choral section. Up jumps the ghost of Beethoven to declare that his music is perfectly singable, but that his symphony has been transposed up from the key of D to that of E flat, and is nearly a quarter of a tone sharp even at that. He then returns to the shades, execrating the folly of a generation which tries to give his works and those of Handel and Mozart the vulgarest sort of cavalry-band shrillness. So Beethoven is abandoned; and the closing scene from Götterdämmerung is put into rehearsal, only to half-kill the unfortunate prima donna. Whereupon the ghost of Wagner explains that, though he did not contemplate so low a pitch as Beethoven's, he certainly did mean his music to be sung at French pitch, and not at Philharmonic. Consequently the arrangements have to be altered, and the pitch changed to French.

This is no sooner done than Dr Mackenzie and Professor Villiers Stanford declare that they cannot now permit either the Dream of Jubal or Eden to be played at the concert, as the low pitch would destroy all the brilliancy of their instrumentation. It being felt that no really great musical festival would be complete without these works, the whole scheme falls through; and the agitation for a uniform pitch proceeds with renewed vigor.

The opponents of reform lay great stress on the commercial difficulties of any change. These difficulties arise from the fact that the various pitches come into play not only in performances, but in the manufacture of instruments. Every instrument which produces notes of definite pitch at all is constructed to be at its best at a certain pitch; and though it may be lengthened or shortened, or screwed up or let down within narrow limits to some other pitch, yet the change will be for the worse both as to quality of tone and (in keyed wind-instruments) accuracy of intonation also. A Stradivarius violin cannot be safely screwed up to concert pitch in England and America without certain structural fortifications which can hardly leave the tone unaffected; and old hands declare that the effect of the violoncellos in the orchestra is quite altered by the substitution of the modern thin strings for the thick ones formerly used at the old low pitch. Still, with stringed instruments, the change is at least possible: a new pitch does not mean a new fiddle.

With keyed wind-instruments it is often said that a change so great as that from Philharmonic to French is impossible; and as first-rate instruments of this class are quite as dear as the best cottage pianofortes, the opposition of the players to any change involving the purchase of new instruments might be expected to be very strong, and to be counterbalanced by a corresponding anxiety on the part of the manufacturers to promote the change. Both players and manufacturers seem, however, to be so little concerned about the matter that I am emboldened to relate my earliest experience of the alleged impossibility of French pitch for the wood wind. When I was a small boy I had a sort of family interest in a casual operatic performance, at which the singers and the conductor very much wanted French pitch. The band, though extremely sympathetic and obliging, pointed out that this could not be. The strings would have been only too happy; the brass could have managed at a pinch; there was no question about the alacrity of the drum in sinking; and the flute, oboe, and bassoon did not deny that they could do something to meet the conductor's views.

But the clarinet was the difficulty. It was, they all said, a universally admitted fact, familiar alike to the musician and the physicist, that the pitch of a clarinet is an unalterable and eternal natural phenomenon. And the more the poor conductor struck his "diapason normal" tuning-fork at the beginning of the first rehearsal, the more the clarinettist (there was but one) blew a melancholy response nearly a half a tone sharp to it. So the conductor sighed; and the rehearsal went forward at Philharmonic pitch. That evening the conductor privately interviewed the clarinettist. He suggested that if the instrument could be altered (for the occasion only) at a cost of, say, a guinea, he would willingly place that sum in the artist's hands for the purpose. A pause ensued, during which the clarinettist steadfastly and solemnly contemplated the conductor, and the conductor, with equal gravity, contemplated the clarinettist back again. Then the guinea changed hands; and the twain parted.

At the second rehearsal the conductor took out his fork as before, and, disregarding an impatient groan from the band, sweetly said, "Do you think, Mr Blank, that if you were to insert a washer in that clarinet, you could get down to my fork?" At this apparently naïve suggestion the band could hardly refrain from open derision. Laughter, and cries of "Yes, Joe: try the washer," lasted until Mr Blank, after a brief manipulation of his instrument, responded to the fork by an A dead in unison with it. With the fury of the betrayed band, and the quantity of spirits Mr Blank probably had to buy for them out of his guinea before recovering their trust, I need not here occupy myself. Suffice it to say that I never read the declarations of impossibility which recur regularly as often as the pitch controversy is renewed, without thinking of Mr Blank and his simple device of the washer which cost a guinea. I do not suggest that Mr Blank is typical of the London orchestral player of today. A large proportion of Mr B.'s colleagues were either illiterate persons, or tipplers, or both. Today they would be self-respecting members of the community, classed as artists and gentlemen, not to mention that they would be also more skilful and refined, if not steadier or more accurate, in their playing.

But I see no reason to believe that orchestras have at all got the better of their old reluctance to take any avoidable extra trouble, or of their readiness to allege impossibility to any conductor or singer who can be put off with such a plea.

Consequently it is not surprising to find that when the conductor wants the high pitch for the sake of orchestral "brilliancy"; when basses and contraltos want it to ease their low notes; when high baritones of the Count di Luna school, and "dramatic" sopranos with just four notes at the tip-top of their voices and all the rest of their compass a wreck, want it so as to have as much screaming and as little singing as possible, it is no wonder that French pitch is found "impossible." But will someone kindly explain—for, like Rosa Dartle, I only want to know—why when Patti at Covent Garden and Nilsson at Her Majesty's declined to sing at the Costa pitch, the impossible was achieved and the pitch came down? Also why, at a festival, when the low-pitched church organ commands the situation one day, and the high-pitched concert organ usurps its place on the morrow, the band manages to be equal to both occasions? Why, again, is it that members of the Philharmonic band are also members of the Queen's private band, where French pitch is the rule. Why, in short, the alleged impossibilities are so often got over when it becomes apparent that they *must* be got over? I really do not know the right answer to these questions.

It may be that the impossibilities are in fact not got over, except by elderly players whose instruments were originally made for the low pitch—that the results are never quite satisfactory—that the younger players keep a second set of instruments for the opera—that they raise their pitch a little and transpose their parts half a tone down instead of attempting to flatten their instruments—that some wood wind players, in correcting their upper octaves in the blowing, are less put out by a strange pitch than others. A hundred considerations beyond my ken may be patent to men with a more detailed knowledge of the subject than I possess. But of one thing I am certain; and that is, that "can't," when delivered *sans phrase*, always means, in this connection, "wont."

My own opinion is that of six hundred out of the seven hundred musicians consulted by the Society of Arts. In all the respects as to which one pitch can be said to be better or worse than another, I believe—in fact I know—that there is every possible objection to Philharmonic pitch, and no objection to French, except that it is a trifle too high for seventeenth and eighteenth century music, including the works of Handel, Bach, Haydn, Mozart, and Beethoven. Both pitches, I understand, are obnoxious to calculators as presenting fractional vibration numbers; but as I find that the results of my own attempts at calculation are equally inaccurate whether I deal with whole numbers or fractional ones, I have left that consideration entirely out of account.

25 November 1891

LAST Wednesday, whilst Eden was in progress at the Albert Hall, I resisted the fascination of Professor Stanford's mixolydian minstrelsy like another Odysseus, and was about to devote the evening to my neglected private affairs, when I happened to pass through Bow Street on my way home. To my surprise, I found Covent Garden all alight and alive, as if in the middle of the season. So I stopped to read the bills; and there, sure enough, was the announcement that Gounod's Philémon et Baucis was at that moment just going to begin, and that Bruneau's Le Rêve would be given the next night.

Conceive the situation. When the summer season begins I shall be invited on the opening night to witness Gounod's Faust, with A. as Faust, B. as Mephistopheles, C. as Valentine, and Z. (first time) as Margaret. My next invitation will be to see Faust with B. as Valentine and C. as Mephistopheles, but cast otherwise as before. Third invitation, Gounod's Faust, as before except for the début of Miss Y. as Siebel. Fourth invitation, Gounod's Faust, cast as before, except first appearance for the season of the champion tenor as Faust, a part I have heard him play fifty times. On arriving at the theatre I shall find a printed slip on my stall to say that the champion tenor is indisposed, and that Signor A. has kindly consented to oblige the management by taking
298

the part of Faust at very short notice, my indulgence being therefore requested for him. After that, to prevent Faust growing on me like brandy, I shall positively refuse to go any more. The management will then put me through a precisely similar course of Les Huguenots, with an occasional Carmen (Miss Zélie de Lussan and the useful A. again) by way of variety. All this I must suffer because my criticisms help Sir Augustus Harris to stand up against the tyranny of his "princely tenors" and their all-powerful guarantor-patrons. But now that he is master of the situation, with something new and interesting to shew, he leaves me to find it out from placards, musical criticisms, and other forms of advertisement. Such is managerial gratitude.

However, I must confess it was a luxury to find my old stall obtainable for five shillings, and when I went in, I found them, to my intense astonishment—I suppose that there is no place in the world but Covent Garden where such a thing would be done—actually eking out the prelude to Philémon et Baucis with the overture to Tannhäuser, which was being conducted with immense spirit by a French gentleman who did not understand one bar of it, but who "worked-up" the finish with a truly Gallic glitter and grandiosity. Only, shallow and mundane as M. Jehin's conception of the work was—and it was both to the verge of downright desecration—he did not at all fail to get his conception executed, and that, too, with much more refinement and precision than Signori Mancinelli, Bevignani, and Randegger obtain from the same players in the season. With Gounod, being no longer out of his depth in German waters, he was quite successful; and I should have nothing but praise for him but for that unlucky and ridiculous notion of making a *lever du rideau*—and what a malapropos one!—of the Tannhäuser overture.

Philémon et Baucis is a charming work, all pure play from beginning to end, but play of the most exquisite kind —a tranquilly happy recreation for really hard-worked and fine-strung men and women. I say "hard-worked" with

intent; for I know well the sort of objection that is always
made to these quiet little art luxuries. It is an age, we are told,
of stress and strain, of fierce struggle for existence, in which
men come to the theatre exhausted by work, and requiring
something stimulating, exciting, amusing, and easily intelligible. If you search for a typical apostle of this view, you
will generally find him to be a gentleman some six stone over
his proper weight, who, not being permitted by his wife and
housemaids to lounge about the house after breakfast, goes
down in a first-class carriage to the City, where he receives
a number of illiterate letters, and dictates equally illiterate
answers to his clerks; goes out and eats confectionery enough
to make a schoolboy blush; writes one private letter (an ap-
pointment with his doctor about his liver); meets his fellow-
citizens, and tries to get the better of them in the dull sort of
whist without cards which he calls "business"; takes a snack
and two glasses of sherry to sustain him while he loafs at a
bar and brags in whatever his particular line of brag may be;
tries a little more whist; takes a heavy meal called lunch;
orders something new to wear; goes to his club for afternoon
tea and the evening papers until it is time to pay visits or go
home to dinner; and finally turns up at the theatre, under
compulsion of his fashionable wife and daughters, in the
character of a victim of brain-pressure, as aforesaid. That
man does not do as much real work in ten years as I have to
put into every five lines I write; yet, whilst his clerks swelter
willingly in an uncomfortable crow's-nest for half-a-crown
during four and a half hours of Die Meistersinger, he yawns
in his box for an hour or so, secretly wishing that the opera
were a dog-fight, and only imperfectly consoled by the advertisement of his money afforded to polite society by his
wife's diamonds. Real work cultivates a man instead of brutalizing him; and what we want at present is more recreation for cultivated men, and less sacrifice of all our artistic
resources to the stimulation of underworked or wholly
idle persons, with all their higher appreciatory organs in an
advanced stage of fatty degeneration. Who ever heard a

capable and active individual in sound health complain of a good play or opera as overstraining his or her faculties?

Philémon pleased me so well that I went to see Le Rêve on the following night. With Gounod to shew how to write angelic music, Zola to provide a poem exactly suited to the exploitation of Gounod's discovery, and Wagner to shew how to weave the heavenly strains into a continuous tissue from end to end of each act, Bruneau has been able to compile an opera which would have ranked as a miracle fifty years ago. Verily, our young composers are entering into a magnificent inheritance—though do not forget that it requires a large natural endowment to enter into that inheritance as fully as Bruneau has done. The score is full of the most delicate melody; and the harmonies and orchestral coloring are appropriately tender and imaginative.

Like all Frenchmen, Bruneau vindicates his originality by a few *hardiesses*, as, for instance, the introduction of the washerwoman's dance at the close of the first act in blood-curdling defiance of the harmony, the senseless drum business at the words "Le voilà! mon rêve de bonheur" at the end of the procession scene, and the clever and wonderfully successful imitation of the effect of a peal of bells by the wind instruments earlier in the same scene. Only a French audience could thoroughly relish the sentimentality of the bishop, which reaches a climax in the melancholy tootlings of the wood wind when he says,

> Laisse-moi te parler, mon fils, avec douceur,
> Au nom de ta mère adorée,
> Toujours présente, tant pleurée, etc.

Indeed, the whole affair is frightfully sentimental; but the bishop is the only character who goes a little too far for British patience in this direction.

As to the performance, it was so good that I forgot that I was in Covent Garden until, at the end of the last scene but one, the band got up and went home, leaving the opera unfinished and the audience sitting wondering whether the entertainment was really over, and, if so, whether they would get back as they went out an eighth of the money they had paid for admission. But nobody gave me back a farthing; and Sir Augustus Harris consequently owes me sevenpence-halfpenny, which, as far as I can see, he has not the remotest intention of paying. Except for this sufficiently flagrant omission, there was nothing to complain of. Mlle Simonnet's soprano voice, well produced as it is, would completely conquer any English audience if she would only aim, in forming her upper notes, at the round tone which we—rightly, as I think—prefer to the shriller, thinner quality which the French like. The lady is otherwise well graced, and is an excellent artist in all respects. Engel imitates Jean de Reszke too obviously, and in energetic moments his voice trembles; but in the quieter and tenderer passages of Felicien and Philémon he sang unexceptionably. As to Bouvet and Lorrain, the tremolo often made it impossible to distinguish the pitch of their notes. In the parts of Jupiter and Vulcan they wobbled so inveterately that the only perceptible difference between their shakes and their ordinary notes lay in the fact that in the first case they shook on purpose, and in the second they did it because they could not help themselves. But the tremolo is not so much a vice in them as a mistaken point of honor; and I found myself ready to forgive almost any defect of style in my delight at the artistic spirit in which the whole company worked together. Certainly, nothing could have been less like the inorganic proceeding of the summer companies.

2 December 1891

ALTHOUGH, like my fellow-critics, I have been wallowing in virtuosity for weeks past, I have fallen so behindhand with the mere chronicle of the season that I hardly know where to pick it up again. It is clearly too late to hark back to Paderewski, who has had time to make what they call a colossal success in New York since he played here. I am reminded of him chiefly by the fact that, after an interval during which nobody ventured to play the pianoforte, Stavenhagen has come and measured himself against his supplanter, challenging comparison in every line of his programs, which are full of Beethoven, Chopin, Liszt, and so on. This was only to be expected; for Stavenhagen is not deficient in perseverance; and he was first-favorite among the young lions until Paderewski came. He had the advantage of coming from the school of Liszt, a much nobler, if a less muscle-hardening, one than that of Paderewski's master Leschetitzky, some of whose superficialities and vulgarities cling to his most famous pupil to this day, as you may hear in his reading, for instance, of the Appassionata sonata. However, when Paderewski's pupilage came to an end, and Liszt died, the more Paderewski forgot his master the better player he became, whilst the more Stavenhagen forgot his the worse player he became. When Stavenhagen came over last year he was positively silly. Instead of his old Titanic victories over Liszt's sonatas, Todtentänzes, and the like, he was shewing off fatuous little crispnesses and neatnesses of execution with childish exultation, poor Beethoven's earlier concertos serving as hobby-horses for the occasion. It was amazing to see a young man's musical soul shrunk that much in so short a time. But we put up with him smilingly—pretended that he was as wonderful as ever—and why? Simply because the case was made romantically delightful by the fact that he brought a bride with him, and that any other condition than one of abject infatuation would have been unpardonable in him. Did he not give an orchestral concert, and make her sing to us huge scenas of his own composition, vast in conception, instrumented with tone colors of oceanic depth, sounding like veiled echoes of the last act of Götterdämmerung? Not for all the solar system would I have hinted then that Beethoven's early concertos were never meant to be rapped out, *staccatissimo*, like a succession of postman's knocks. As to the musical public, need I say that it was charmed—that Stavenhagen and his wife threatened for a moment to eclipse the popularity of Mrs Kendal and her husband? For in England there is nothing so popular in a public performer as perfect domesticity, except perhaps the extreme reverse. But this could not last always: it was plain that Stavenhagen must presently get back to the serious business of his profession.

The question was whether he would be able to do so— whether he had in himself the inspiration that never failed him whilst Liszt was at his elbow. That was what was in my mind when I went to the Crystal Palace last Saturday week to hear him play Beethoven's fourth concerto. Would it be again a series of variations on the postman's knock, or would it be Beethoven? As usual, the facts turned out to be neither snow-white nor jet-black, but grey, and sometimes rather a dark grey. It was, to begin with, an advance on last year that the concerto chosen was the fourth, and not the third. But there was too much—a great deal too much—of the postman still; and I should almost have lost patience, and given up Stavenhagen as hopelessly lapsed and lost, but for his recital on the following Tuesday, when, though he partly failed, he failed more heroically.

His long selection from Chopin brought him fairly into the lists against Paderewski; and his onslaught on the A flat polonaise (an encore) was terrific. He went at it like a thousand blacksmiths; and if he could only have combined his tremendous ebullition of nervous excitement with the sangfroid needed to hold and control it, he might have brought his fine Lisztian reading off successfully. As it was, he maintained the combat to the end with such smashing energy that he was encored a second time, and returned to the piano to play a nocturne, and to find the instrument worth about thirty pounds less than before the polonaise began. Later on, he shewed us the fruits of his Weimar "studies in transcendent execution" by playing a prodigious series of pianoforte presentments of Suoni la tromba, which were announced as "for the first time," but which, if I mistake not, he had played once before in St James's Hall. He may take my word for it, however, that no amount of transcendent execution alone will regain for him the position he has nearly let slip through his fingers.

What is the matter at present is that he has taken serious and beautiful works of Beethoven, and played them frivolously and boyishly because they are technically easy to him; whereas Paderewski has played us a few of Mendelssohn's Songs without Words, still easier from the technical point of view, and brought back all their almost forgotten delicacy and poetic beauty. After that, it is vain to point out that Paderewski once came to smash in Liszt's Erl King transcription after Stavenhagen had played it without missing a note, or that he was beaten by a certain passage in Chopin's funeral march sonata which Stavenhagen could possibly have mastered. These are mere accidents, as indeed we have seen by the fact that the last time we had the Erl King from Paderewski it was faultless; whilst Stavenhagen's last attempt at it was nearly as unlucky as the earlier one of Paderewski.

So long as Paderewski can take a simple piece of music in which any schoolgirl could be made finger-perfect by her teacher, and can play it for all that it is worth as tone poetry, whilst Stavenhagen trips over it only to shew how much easier it is to him than to the schoolgirl, so long can Stavenhagen never be mentioned in the same breath with Paderewski as a player. But surely a young man of such capacity as Stavenhagen has shewn can retrieve a position so simple as that is. Let him abandon the postman's knock at once and for ever, and cap Paderewski's Mendelssohn by a Mozart sonata—say that noble one in A minor, which certainly requires something more than a thrashing left hand and a flying right one, but which, with much less than half Stavenhagen's manipulative skill, and ten fingers with feeling and song in them, could be restored to its rightful place high up among the highest pianoforte classics.

I had almost forgotten Madame Stavenhagen, who sang us several songs at the recital. She has a very good voice and a very good ear: what she lacks in sensibility of vocal touch. If she would only cultivate that quality, and then communicate it magnetically to her husband's left hand, the future would be a golden one for both of them.

By ill luck, I have been unable so far to get to a single Popular Concert this season, and consequently only know by hearsay of the revolution there—the substitution of Howell and Popper for the veteran Piatti, and of Isaÿe for Madame Neruda. I will not deny that, when changes of this kind are made, I am glad to see them made too soon rather than too late. Of all the duties of a critic, there is none harder than giving a hint to the veteran who lags superfluous. To have to say, "My dear Sir, or Madam: when you play or sing I can hear the old tone, the old style, the old expression, just as well as you can; but, if you dont mind my saying so, I am afraid the young people are beginning to disagree with us on the subject"—that is far worse than to have to perform a surgical operation, because you dont get thanked for it, and chloroform is out of the question. Suppose, for instance, that some day down at the Crystal Palace I were to detect, with a sudden heartstroke (even critics get such things), some ominous sign that would send me to Grove's Dictionary to see how long ago Mr Manns was born, what would I be expected to do then? Well, I am afraid I should either hold my tongue or prevaricate like a police witness on the subject. Meanwhile, let me congratulate Mr Manns on being still far better than the next best man, and on having, among many other recent feats which I have not had space to chronicle, conducted only ten days ago a most brilliant performance of the last three movements of Beethoven's Seventh Symphony (the band slept through the first *allegro*), and on Saturday last an equally fine performance of Mendelssohn's Scotch symphony, in which, however, I contend for a more sympathetic transition from the middle section of the first movement to the recapitulation. In passing, by the bye, I would like to ask the advocates of the high pitch how they like it in the *allegretto* of the Seventh

Symphony. I know no more flagrant instance of a beautiful piece of music spoiled to propitiate the ghost of Sir Michael Costa.

The third London Symphony Concert was given on Thursday last; but the only one of the series I have heard has been the second, at which I found a great improvement in the orchestra in point of finish and delicacy of detail. The mass of tone from the full band is brighter and purer than before; and Henschel conducts better, although he still retains enough of the habits of the player and singer to make him occasionally flurry himself and prevent the band from looking at him by cutting at every crotchet in the bar with his stick, instead of simply keeping his hand on the *tempo* with as few beats as possible. At this concert Isaÿe played Mendelssohn's concerto magnificently: Sarasate and Joachim rolled into one could have done no more. Popper gave a concert on Wednesday last, at which he performed a good deal of his own music, which is elegant and fanciful in its lighter phases, and elegiac on its sentimental side. He is as unlike his rival Hollman in appearance and temperament as his violoncello is unlike an ophicleide, so that there is no lack of novelty about his style to Londoners; and he is, on his own plane, the best player in the world, as far as we know here. Gerardy, hugely petted by the public, needs a good deal of indulgence both for himself and his instrument after Popper. Another prodigy, young Max Hambourg, gave a pianoforte recital at Steinway Hall, and once more played Bach better than ony other composer on his program. With such a training as Eugene Holliday has had from Rubinstein, this Russian lad might astonish the world some day; but he does not seem to be exactly in the way of getting it at present.

9 December 1891

THE Mozart Centenary has made a good deal of literary and musical business this week. Part of this is easy enough, especially for the illustrated papers. Likenesses of Mozart at all ages; view of Salzburg; portrait

of Marie Antoinette (described in the text as "the ill-fated"),
to whom he proposed marriage at an early age; picture of
the young composer, two and a half feet high, crushing the
Pompadour with his "Who is this woman that refuses to
kiss me? The Queen kissed me! (Sensation)"; facsimile of
the original MS. of the first four bars of La ci darem, and the
like. These, with copious paraphrases of the English translation of Otto Jahn's great biography, will pull the journal-
ists proper through the Centenary with credit. The critic's
task is not quite so easy.

The word is, of course, Admire, admire, admire; but unless you frankly trade on the ignorance of the public, and
cite as illustrations of his unique genius feats that come easily
to dozens of organists and choir-boys who never wrote, and
never will write, a bar of original music in their lives; or pay
his symphonies and operas empty compliments that might
be transferred word for word, without the least incongruity,
to the symphonies of Spohr and the operas of Offenbach; or
represent him as composing as spontaneously as a bird sings,
on the strength of his habit of perfecting his greater compositions in his mind before he wrote them down—unless
you try these well-worn dodges, you will find nothing to
admire that is peculiar to Mozart: the fact being that he,
like Praxiteles, Raphael, Molière, or Shakespear, was no
leader of a new departure or founder of a school.

He came at the end of a development, not at the beginning of one; and although there are operas and symphonies, and even pianoforte sonatas and pages of instrumental scoring of his, on which you can put your finger and
say, "Here is final perfection in this manner; and nobody,
whatever his genius may be, will ever get a step further on
these lines," you cannot say, "Here is an entirely new vein
of musical art, of which nobody ever dreamt before Mozart."
Haydn, who made the mould for Mozart's symphonies, was
proud of Mozart's genius because he felt his own part in it:
he would have written the E flat symphony if he could, and,
though he could not, was at least able to feel that the man

who had reached that pre-eminence was standing on his old shoulders. Now, Haydn would have recoiled from the idea of composing—or perpetrating, as he would have put it— the first movement of Beethoven's Eroica, and would have repudiated all part in leading music to such a pass.

The more far-sighted Gluck not only carried Mozart in his arms to within sight of the goal of his career as an opera composer, but even cleared a little of the new path into which Mozart's finality drove all those successors of his who were too gifted to waste their lives in making weak dilutions of Mozart's scores, and serving them up as "classics." Many Mozart worshippers cannot bear to be told that their hero was not the founder of a dynasty. But in art the highest success is to be the last of your race, not the first. Anybody, almost, can make a beginning: the difficulty is to make an end—to do what cannot be bettered.

For instance, if the beginner were to be ranked above the consummator, we should, in literary fiction, have to place Captain Mayne Reid, who certainly struck a new vein, above Dickens, who simply took the novel as he found it, and achieved the feat of compelling his successor (whoever he may be), either to create quite another sort of novel, or else to fall behind his predecessor as at best a superfluous imitator. Surely, if so great a composer as Haydn could say, out of his greatness as a man, "I am not the best of my school, though I was the first," Mozart's worshippers can afford to acknowledge, with equal gladness of spirit, that their hero was not the first, though he was the best. It is always like that. Praxiteles, Raphael and Co., have great men for their pioneers, and only fools for their followers.

So far everybody will agree with me. This proves either that I am hopelessly wrong or that the world has had at least half a century to think the matter over in. And, sure enough, a hundred years ago Mozart was considered a desperate innovator: it was his reputation in this respect that set so many composers—Meyerbeer, for example—cultivating innovation for its own sake. Let us, therefore, jump a hundred years forward, right up to date, and see whether there is any phenomenon of the same nature in view today. We have not to look far. Here, under our very noses, is Wagner held up on all hands as the founder of a school and the arch-musical innovator of our age. He himself knew better; but since his death I appear to be the only person who shares his view of the matter. I assert with the utmost confidence that in 1991 it will be seen quite clearly that Wagner was the end of the nineteenth-century, or Beethoven school, instead of the beginning of the twentieth-century school; just as Mozart's most perfect music is the last word of the eighteenth century, and not the first of the nineteenth. It is none the less plain because everyone knows that Il Seraglio was the beginning of the school of nineteenth-century German operas of Mozart, Beethoven, Weber, and Wagner; that Das Veilchen is the beginning of the nineteenth-century German song of Schubert, Mendelssohn, and Schumann; and that Die Zauberflöte is the ancestor, not only of the Ninth Symphony, but of the Wagnerian allegorical music-drama, with personified abstractions instead of individualized characters as *dramatis personæ*. But Il Seraglio and Die Zauberflöte do not belong to the group of works which constitute Mozart's consummate achievement—Don Juan, Le Nozze di Figaro, and his three or four perfect symphonies. They are nineteenth-century music heard advancing in the distance, as his Masses are seventeenth-century music retreating in the distance. And, similarly, though the future fossiliferous critics of 1991, after having done their utmost, without success, to crush twentieth-century music, will be able to shew that Wagner (their chief classic) made one or two experiments in that direction, yet the world will rightly persist in thinking of him as a characteristically nineteenth-century composer of the school of Beethoven, greater than Beethoven by as much as Mozart was greater than Haydn. And now I hope I have saved my reputation by saying something at which everybody will exclaim, "Bless me! what nonsense!" Nevertheless, it is true; and our would-be Wagners had better look to it; for all their efforts to exploit the apparently inexhaustible wealth of musical material opened up at Bayreuth only prove that Wagner used it up to the last ounce, and that secondhand Wagner is more insufferable, because usually more pretentious, than even secondhand Mozart used to be.

For my own part, if I do not care to rhapsodize much about Mozart, it is because I am so violently prepossessed in his favor that I am capable of supplying any possible deficiency in his work by my imagination. Gounod has devoutly declared that Don Giovanni has been to him all his life a revelation of perfection, a miracle, a work without fault. I smile indulgently at Gounod, since I cannot afford to give myself away so generously (there being, no doubt, less of me); but I am afraid my fundamental attitude towards Mozart is the same as his. In my small-boyhood I by good luck had an opportunity of learning the Don thoroughly; and if it were only for the sense of the value of fine workmanship which I gained from it, I should still esteem that lesson the most important part of my education. Indeed, it educated me artistically in all sorts of ways, and disqualified me only in one—that of criticizing Mozart fairly. Everyone appears a sentimental, hysterical bungler in comparison when anything brings his finest work vividly back to me. Let me take warning by the follies of Oublicheff, and hold my tongue.

The people most to be pitied at this moment are the unfortunate singers, players, and conductors who are suddenly called upon to make the public *hear* the wonders which the newspapers are describing so lavishly. At ordinary times they simply refuse to do this. It is quite a mistake to suppose that Mozart's music is not in demand. I know of more than one concert-giver who asks every singer he engages for some song by Mozart, and is invariably met with the plea of excessive difficulty. You cannot "make an effect" with Mozart, or work your audience up by playing on their hysterical susceptibilities.

Nothing but the finest execution—beautiful, expressive,

311

and intelligent—will serve; and the worst of it is, that the
phrases are so perfectly clear and straightforward, that you
are found out the moment you swerve by a hair's breadth
from perfection, whilst, at the same time, your work is so
obvious, that everyone thinks it must be easy, and puts you
down remorselessly as a duffer for botching it. Naturally,
then, we do not hear much of Mozart; and what we do hear
goes far to destroy his reputation. But there was no getting
out of the centenary: something had to be done. Accordingly, the Crystal Palace committed itself to the Jupiter
Symphony and the Requiem; and the Albert Hall, by way
of varying the entertainment, announced the Requiem and
the Jupiter Symphony.

The Requiem satisfied that spirit of pious melancholy in
which we celebrate great occasions; but I think the public
ought to be made rather more sharply aware of the fact that
Mozart died before the Requiem was half finished, and that
his widow, in order to secure the stipulated price, got one of
her husband's pupils, whose handwriting resembled his, to
forge enough music to complete it. Undoubtedly Mozart
gave a good start to most of the movements; but, suggestive
as these are, very few of them are artistically so satisfactory
as the pretty Benedictus, in which the forger escaped from
the taskwork of cobbling up his master's hints to the free
work of original composition. There are only about four
numbers in the score which have any right to be included in
a centenary program. As to the two performances, I cannot
compare them, as I was late for the one at the Albert Hall.

The Jupiter Symphony was conducted by Mr Manns in
the true heroic spirit; and he was well seconded by the wind
band; but the strings disgraced themselves. In the first movement even what I may call the common decencies of execution were lacking: Mr Manns should have sent every fiddler
of them straight back to school to learn how to play scales
cleanly, steadily, and finely. At the Albert Hall, there was
no lack of precision and neatness; but Mr Henschel's reading was, on the whole, the old dapper, empty, *petit-maître*

one of which I, at least, have had quite enough. Happily, Mr Henschel immediately redeemed his failure—for such it was—by a really fine interpretation of the chorus of priests from the Zauberflöte. This, with Mr Lloyd's delivery of one of the finest of Mozart's concert arias, Mr Norman Salmond's singing of a capital English version of Non più andrai, and the Crystal Palace Band's performance of the Masonic Dirge, were the successes of the celebration. I should add that Mr Joseph Bennett, fresh from throwing his last stone at Wagner, modestly wrote a poem for recitation between the Requiem and the Symphony. He appeals to Mozart, with evidently sincere emotion, to accept his lines, in spite of any little shortcomings,

> Since 'tis from the heart they flow,
> Bright with pure affection's glow.

Perhaps Dr Mackenzie or Dr Parry, in view of a well-known observation of Beaumarchais, may set Mr Bennett's ode to music some of these days. Mr Herkomer, too, has helped by drawing a fancy portrait of Mozart. I have compared it carefully with all the accredited portraits, and can confidently pronounce it to be almost supernaturally unlike the original.

16 December 1891

THE thirty-three years that have elapsed since Cornelius composed his Barber of Bagdad, which the Royal College students introduced to England last Wednesday at the Savoy Theatre, have taken all the point out of its defiant Wagnerisms. The younger generation simply do not recognize them, so commonplace have they become. Older hands will have noted one or two progressions, which were copied, with controversial intention, out of Wagner's scores at a time when they were to be found nowhere else. But nowadays it is hardly conceivable that there should ever have been such a fuss about the work as that which ended in Liszt's withdrawal from the Weimar Theatre. In listening to it one catches a reminiscence of Meyerbeer here, or an anticipation of Götz there; but Wagner is the last composer suggested, although, on reflection, it is easy to see that in 1858 there was nobody else from whom a man with so little musical originality as Cornelius could have learned how to compose an opera which was at that period so unconventional.

Its late arrival here is due, not to any peculiarity in the work itself, but to the poverty of our operatic resources, which has limited us for so many years to grand opera on the one hand, and opera bouffe on the other, with no intermediate theatre for the higher artistic forms of light and comic opera. I need not now repeat all that I said on this point when La Basoche was produced. Suffice it that The Barber of Bagdad—very different from our threadbare old acquaintance, once so prosperous, the Barber of Seville—is an excellent specimen of comic opera taken seriously in an artistic sense. The concerted music is remarkably good, especially a quintet, Oh, Mustapha! in the second act, which is, besides, highly comic. The weakest parts are the patter solos of the barber, which are too ponderous in their movement and heavy in their style for any country on earth except Germany. Such doggerel as Lore academical, physical, chemical; Learning grammatical; Facts mathematical; Rules arithmetical, trigonometrical, etc., etc., etc., if they *must* be set to music for the hundredth time, had better still be set in the time-honored lilt which Sir Arthur Sullivan, following the example of Mozart and Rossini, chose for the lists of accomplishments of the Major-General in The Pirates or the Colonel in Patience.

The performance at the Savoy was of the usual Royal College sort, carefully prepared as a task by the principals, and enjoyed as a rare bit of fun by the chorus and band, but uninspired and amateurish. The tenor, Mr William Green, had to struggle not only against the irrational but uncontrollable nervousness of a novice, but against the rational nervousness caused by his having neither been taught how to produce his voice nor succeeded in finding out a safe method for himself. He was anything but happy during the first act, singing mostly flat; but in the second, when the worst was over and he was beginning to feel more at ease, he rallied, and came off with glory. I still hold to my opinion that in none of these large music-teaching institutions is there, as yet, any instruction to be had in the physical act of singing. When I see a set of pupils among whom there is a certain clearly evident agreement as to aiming at certain graces and avoiding certain blemishes of style, I conclude that they have had some common teaching on these points.

But when I find, at the same time, that one of them will produce his voice as if he were trying to crack a walnut between his vocal cords, whilst his neighbor depends on spasms of the diaphragm for vocal execution, and yet another regards the judicious use of the nose as the true secret of tone-coloring, then I naturally conclude that the motto of the professorial staff is, "Make yourself a singer as best you can; and we will then give you excellent precepts as to what a singer should and should not do." Fortunately, most of the cast of The Barber of Bagdad were clever enough to have come to no serious harm under this system. Mr Sandbrook and Mr Magrath are comparatively old hands: the first much improved, the second not so much so. Mr Magrath has the misfortune to be an Irishman, with all that musical facility and native genius which have prevented so many of his countrymen from going on to acquire a seriously cultivated artistic sensibility.

Let no Englishman regret what in Ireland is called his stupidity—meaning his congenital incapacity to talk brilliantly about subjects and practise adroitly arts of which he knows next to nothing. This observation might perhaps, from Mr Magrath's point of view, have been more appropriately made in the course of an essay on national characteristics than in a notice of his performance as Aboul Hassan Ali Eben Bekar; but it explains why I decline to give him as much credit for his accomplishments as I should had he been born on a soil where they do not, like Mr Scadder's public buildings, "grow spontaneous." Miss Bruckshaw, as Morgiana, was perhaps the most completely satisfactory member of the cast, though Mr William White, who played the Cadi, might, by his freedom from the awkwardness which all the rest shewed, more or less, have borne off that distinction but for his rather thin voice, which was certainly outclassed by Miss Bruckshaw's.

Miss Pattie Hughes made a bouncing old woman, full of youth; and the orchestra was good in a pleasant, juvenile way, and would have been better had Mr Stanford conducted them with a broader, freer hand, instead of checking their every attempt to get fairly into their own stride. The austerities of the mixolydian mode are out of place when romping through a comic opera overture with a young orchestra.

I have nothing to offer as to the host of concerts last Thursday except my apologies. I should explain that whereas other men have fixed hours of work and Sundays off, I am compelled to adopt the simpler plan of going on until I drop; so that I have sometimes been tempted to petition the House of Commons to pass a special Factory Act to deal with my case. On Thursday, having worked without intermission since the 4th of October, I surveyed the awful weather, and determined that I had rather die than do another stroke of work. I longed to sit in a very easy chair and do absolutely nothing but lazily watch another person working hard in some interesting way entirely unconnected with music. After a moment's reflection I went to my dentist's. There is nothing that soothes me more after a long and maddening course of pianoforte recitals than to sit and have my teeth drilled by a finely skilled hand. But my dentist's complexion was yellower, and his eyes wearier than my own as he informed me that not for any human patient would he do a stroke of work that afternoon. So I went home disappointed. This, observe, is the literal truth, and not an extravaganza invented for the occasion. I add this assurance because, though I can always make my extravaganzas appear credible, I cannot make the truth appear so.

316